UNIVERSITY CASEBOOK SERIES®

2026 STATUTORY APPENDIX AND CASE SUPPLEMENT TO

COX, BOK & GORMAN'S

LABOR LAW

CASES AND MATERIALS

EIGHTEENTH EDITION

MATTHEW W. FINKIN
Research Professor of Law
University of Illinois

TIMOTHY P. GLYNN
Andrea J. Catania Endowed Professor of Law
Seton Hall University School of Law

FOUNDATION PRESS

860 Blue Gentian Road, Suite 350
Eagan, MN 55121
1-877-888-1330

Published in the United States of America

ISBN: 979-8-31770-390-5

TABLE OF CONTENTS

TABLE OF CASES

The principal cases are in bold type.

UNIVERSITY CASEBOOK SERIES®

2026 STATUTORY APPENDIX AND CASE SUPPLEMENT TO

COX, BOK & GORMAN'S

LABOR LAW

CASES AND MATERIALS

EIGHTEENTH EDITION

SHERMAN ACT

26 Stat. 209 (1890), as amended, 15 U.S.C. §§ 1 et seq. (1988).

Sec. 1. Every contract, combination in the form of a trust or otherwise, or conspiracy, in restraint of trade or commerce among the several States, or with foreign nations, is hereby declared to be illegal. Every person who shall make any such contract or engage in any such combination or conspiracy, shall be deemed guilty of a misdemeanor, and, on conviction thereof, shall be punished by fine not exceeding five thousand dollars, or by imprisonment not exceeding one year, or by both said punishments, in the discretion of the court.

Sec. 2. Every person who shall monopolize, or attempt to monopolize, or combine or conspire with any other person or persons, to monopolize any part of the trade or commerce among the several States, or with foreign nations, shall be deemed guilty of a misdemeanor, and, on conviction thereof, shall be punished by fine not exceeding five thousand dollars, or by imprisonment not exceeding one year, or by both said punishments, in the discretion of the court.

Sec. 3. Every contract, combination in form of trust or otherwise, or conspiracy, in restraint of trade or commerce in any territory of the United States or of the District of Columbia, or in restraint of trade or commerce between any such territory and another, or between any such territory or territories and any State or States or the District of Columbia, or with foreign nations, or between the District of Columbia and any State or States or foreign nations, is hereby declared illegal. Every person who shall make any such contract or engage in any such combination or conspiracy, shall be deemed guilty of a misdemeanor, and, on conviction thereof, shall be punished by fine not exceeding five thousand dollars, or by imprisonment not exceeding one year, or by both said punishments, in the discretion of the court.

Sec. 4. The several circuit courts of the United States are hereby invested with jurisdiction to prevent and restrain violations of this act; and it shall be the duty of the several district attorneys of the United States, in their respective districts, under the direction of the Attorney General, to institute proceedings in equity to prevent and restrain such violations. Such proceedings may be by way of petition setting forth the case and praying that such violation shall be enjoined or otherwise prohibited. When the parties complained of shall have been duly notified of such petition the court shall proceed, as soon as may be, to the hearing and determination of the case; and pending such petition and before final decree, the court may at any time make such temporary restraining order or prohibition as shall be deemed just in the premises.

Sec. 5. Whenever it shall appear to the court before which any proceeding under section 4 of this act may be pending, that the ends of justice require that other parties should be brought before the court, the court may cause them to be summoned, whether they reside in the district in which the court is held or not; and subpoenas to that end may be served in any district by the marshal thereof.

Sec. 6. Any property owned under any contract or by any combination, or pursuant to any conspiracy (and being the subject thereof) mentioned in section 1 of this act, and being in the course of transportation from one State to another, or to a foreign country, shall be forfeited to the United States, and may be seized and condemned by like proceedings as those provided by law for the forfeiture, seizure, and condemnation of property imported into the United States contrary to law.

Sec. 7. Any person who shall be injured in his business or property by any other person or corporation by reason of anything forbidden or declared to be unlawful by this act, may sue therefor in any Circuit Court of the United States in the district in which the defendant resides or is found, without respect to the amount in controversy, and shall recover three-fold the damages sustained, and the costs of suit, including a reasonable attorney's fee.

Sec. 8. That the word "person," or "persons" wherever used in this act shall be deemed to include corporations and associations existing under or authorized by the laws of either the United States, the laws of any State or the laws of any foreign country.

CLAYTON ACT

38 Stat. 730 (1914), as amended, 15 U.S.C. §§ 12 et seq. (1988).

Be it enacted by the Senate and House of Representatives of the United States of America in Congress assembled, That "anti-trust laws," as used herein, includes the Act entitled "An Act to protect trade and commerce against unlawful restraints and monopolies", approved July second, eighteen hundred and ninety [Sherman Act, supra.] * * *

* * *

Sec. 6. That the labor of a human being is not a commodity or article of commerce. Nothing contained in the anti-trust laws shall be construed to forbid the existence and operation of labor, agricultural, or horticultural organizations, instituted for the purposes of mutual help, and not having capital stock or conducted for profit, or to forbid or restrain individual members of such organizations from lawfully carrying out the legitimate objects thereof; nor shall such organizations, or the members thereof, be held or construed to be illegal combinations or conspiracies in restraint of trade, under the anti-trust laws.

* * *

Sec. 16. That any person, firm, corporation, or association shall be entitled to sue for and have injunctive relief, in any court of the United States having jurisdiction over the parties, against threatened loss or damage by a violation of the anti-trust laws, including sections two, three, seven and eight of this Act, when and under the same conditions and principles as injunctive relief against threatened conduct that will cause loss or damage is granted by courts of equity, under the rules governing such proceedings, and upon the execution of proper bond against damages for an injunction improvidently granted and a showing that the danger of irreparable loss or damage is immediate, a preliminary injunction may issue: *Provided,* That nothing herein contained shall be construed to entitle any person, firm, corporation, or association, except the United States, to bring suit in equity for injunctive relief against any common carrier subject to the provisions of the Act to regulate commerce, approved February fourth, eighteen hundred and eighty-seven, in respect of any matter subject to the regulation, supervision, or other jurisdiction of the Interstate Commerce Commission.

* * *

Sec. 20. That no restraining order or injunction shall be granted by any court of the United States, or a judge or the judges thereof, in any case between an employer and employees, or between employers and employees, or between employees, or between persons employed and persons seeking employment, involving, or growing out of, a dispute concerning terms or conditions of employment, unless necessary to prevent irreparable injury to property, or to a property right, of the party making the application, for which injury there is no adequate remedy at law, and such property or property right must be described with particularity in the application, which must be in writing and sworn to by the applicant or by his agent or attorney.

And no such restraining order or injunction shall prohibit any person or persons, whether singly or in concert, from terminating any relation of employment, or from ceasing to perform any work or labor, or from recommending, advising, or persuading others by peaceful means so to do; or from attending at any place where any such person or persons may lawfully be, for the purpose of peacefully obtaining or communicating information, or from peacefully persuading any person to work or to abstain from working; or from ceasing to patronize or to employ any party to such dispute, or from recommending, advising, or persuading others by peaceful and lawful means so to do; or from paying or giving to, or withholding from, any person engaged in such dispute, any strike benefits or other moneys or things of value; or from peaceably assembling in a lawful manner, and for lawful purposes; or from doing any act or thing which might lawfully be done in the absence of such dispute by any party thereto; nor shall any of the acts specified in this paragraph be considered or held to be violations of any law of the United States.

* * *

NORRIS-LAGUARDIA ACT

47 Stat. 70 (1932), 29 U.S.C. §§ 101–15 (1988).

Sec. 1. No court of the United States, as herein defined, shall have jurisdiction to issue any restraining order or temporary or permanent injunction in a case involving or growing out of a labor dispute, except in a strict conformity with the provisions of this Act; nor shall any such restraining order or temporary or permanent injunction be issued contrary to the public policy declared in this Act.

Sec. 2. In the interpretation of this Act and in determining the jurisdiction and authority of the courts of the United States, as such jurisdiction and authority are herein defined and limited, the public policy of the United States is hereby declared as follows:

Whereas under prevailing economic conditions, developed with the aid of governmental authority for owners of property to organize in the corporate and other forms of ownership association, the individual unorganized worker is commonly helpless to exercise actual liberty of contract and to protect his freedom of labor, and thereby to obtain acceptable terms and conditions of employment, wherefore, though he should be free to decline to associate with his fellows, it is necessary that he have full freedom of association, self-organization, and designation of representatives of his own choosing, to negotiate the terms and conditions of his employment, and that he shall be free from the interference, restraint, or coercion of employers of labor, or their agents, in the designation of such representatives or in self-organization or in other concerted activities for the purpose of collective bargaining or other mutual aid or protection; therefore, the following definitions of, and limitations upon, the jurisdiction and authority of the courts of the United States are hereby enacted.

Sec. 3. Any undertaking or promise, such as is described in this section, or any other undertaking or promise in conflict with the public policy declared in section 2 of this Act, is hereby declared to be contrary to the public policy of the United States, shall not be enforceable in any court of the United States and shall not afford any basis for the granting of legal or equitable relief by any such court, including specifically the following:

Every undertaking or promise hereafter made, whether written or oral, express or implied, constituting or contained in any contract or agreement of hiring or employment between any individual, firm, company, association, or corporation, and any employee or prospective employee of the same whereby

(a) Either party to such contract or agreement undertakes or promises not to join, become, or remain a member of any labor organization or of any employer organization; or

(b) Either party to such contract or agreement undertakes or promises that he will withdraw from an employment relation in the event that he joins, becomes, or remains a member of any labor organization or of any employer organization.

Sec. 4. No court of the United States shall have jurisdiction to issue any restraining order or temporary or permanent injunction in any case involving or growing out of any labor dispute to prohibit any person or persons participating or interested in such dispute (as these terms are herein defined) from doing, whether singly or in concert, any of the following acts:

(a) Ceasing or refusing to perform any work or to remain in any relation of employment;

(b) Becoming or remaining a member of any labor organization or of any employer organization, regardless of any such undertaking or promise as is described in section 3 of this Act;

(c) Paying or giving to, or withholding from, any person participating or interested in such labor dispute, any strike or unemployment benefits or insurance, or other moneys or things of value;

(d) By all lawful means aiding any person participating or interested in any labor dispute who is being proceeded against in, or is prosecuting, any action or suit in any court of the United States or of any State;

(e) Giving publicity to the existence of, or the facts involved in, any labor dispute, whether by advertising, speaking, patrolling, or by any other method not involving fraud or violence;

(f) Assembling peaceably to act or to organize to act in promotion of their interests in a labor dispute;

(g) Advising or notifying any person of an intention to do any of the Acts heretofore specified;

(h) Agreeing with other persons to do or not to do any of the acts heretofore specified; and

(i) Advising, urging, or otherwise causing or inducing without fraud or violence the acts heretofore specified, regardless of any such undertaking or promise as is described in section 3 of this Act.

Sec. 5. No court of the United States shall have jurisdiction to issue a restraining order or temporary or permanent injunction upon the ground that any of the persons participating or interested in a labor dispute constitute or are engaged in an unlawful combination or conspiracy because of the doing in concert of the acts enumerated in section 4 of this Act.

Sec. 6. No officer or member of any association or organization, and no association or organization participating or interested in a labor dispute, shall be held responsible or liable in any court of the United

States for the unlawful acts of individual officers, members, or agents, except upon clear proof of actual participation in, or actual authorization of, such acts, or of ratification of such acts after actual knowledge thereof.

Sec. 7. No court of the United States shall have jurisdiction to issue a temporary or permanent injunction in any case involving or growing out of a labor dispute, as herein defined, except after hearing the testimony of witnesses in open court (with opportunity for cross-examination) in support of the allegations of a complaint made under oath, and testimony in opposition thereto, if offered, and except after findings of fact by the court, to the effect—

(a) That unlawful acts have been threatened and will be committed unless restrained or have been committed and will be continued unless restrained, but no injunction or temporary restraining order shall be issued on account of any threat or unlawful act excepting against the person or persons, association, or organization making the threat or committing the unlawful act or actually authorizing or ratifying the same after actual knowledge thereof;

(b) That substantial and irreparable injury to complainant's property will follow:

(c) That as to each item of relief granted greater injury will be inflicted upon complainant by the denial of relief than will be inflicted upon defendants by the granting of relief;

(d) That complainant has no adequate remedy at law; and

(e) That the public officers charged with the duty to protect complainant's property are unable or unwilling to furnish adequate protection.

Such hearing shall be held after due and personal notice thereof has been given, in such manner as the court shall direct, to all known persons against whom relief is sought, and also to the chief of those public officials of the county and city within which the unlawful acts have been threatened or committed charged with the duty to protect complainant's property: *Provided, however,* That if a complainant shall also allege that, unless a temporary restraining order shall be issued without notice, a substantial and irreparable injury to complainant's property will be unavoidable, such a temporary restraining order may be issued upon testimony under oath, sufficient, if sustained, to justify the court in issuing a temporary injunction upon a hearing after notice. Such a temporary restraining order shall be effective for no longer than five days and shall become void at the expiration of said five days. No temporary restraining order or temporary injunction shall be issued except on condition that complainant shall first file an undertaking with adequate security in an amount to be fixed by the court sufficient to recompense those enjoined for any loss, expense, or damage caused by the improvident or erroneous issuance of such order or injunction, including all reasonable costs (together with a reasonable attorney's fee) and expense of defense against the order or against the granting of any injunctive relief sought in the same proceeding and subsequently denied by the court.

The undertaking herein mentioned shall be understood to signify an agreement entered into by the complainant and the surety upon which a decree may be rendered in the same suit or proceeding against said complainant and surety, upon a hearing to assess damages of which hearing complainant and surety shall have reasonable notice, the said complainant and surety submitting themselves to the jurisdiction of the court for that purpose. But nothing herein contained shall deprive any party having a claim or cause of action under or upon such undertaking from electing to pursue his ordinary remedy by suit at law or in equity.

Sec. 8. No restraining order or injunctive relief shall be granted to any complainant who has failed to comply with any obligation imposed by law which is involved in the labor dispute in question, or who has failed to make every reasonable effort to settle such dispute either by negotiation or with the aid of any available governmental machinery of mediation or voluntary arbitration.

Sec. 9. No restraining order or temporary or permanent injunction shall be granted in a case involving or growing out of a labor dispute, except on the basis of findings of fact made and filed by the court in the record of the case prior to the issuance of such restraining order or injunction; and every restraining order or injunction granted in a case involving or growing out of a labor dispute shall include only a prohibition of such specific act or acts as may be expressly complained of in the bill of complaint or petition filed in such case and as shall be expressly included in said findings of fact made and filed by the court as provided herein.

Sec. 10. Whenever any court of the United States shall issue or deny any temporary injunction in a case involving or growing out of a labor dispute, the court shall, upon the request of any party to the proceedings and on his filing the usual bond for costs, forthwith certify as in ordinary cases the record of the case to the circuit court of appeals for its review. Upon the filing of such record in the circuit court of appeals, the appeal shall be heard and the temporary injunctive order affirmed, modified, or set aside with the greatest possible expedition, giving the proceedings precedence over all other matters except older matters of the same character.

Sec. 11.* In all cases arising under this Act in which a person shall be charged with contempt in a court of the United States (as herein defined), the accused shall enjoy the right to a speedy and public trial by an impartial jury of the State and district wherein the contempt shall

* Sections 11 and 12 were repealed in 1948, 62 Stat. 862. The text of Section 11 is now in 18 U.S.C. § 3692 (1982); Rule 42 of the Federal Rules of Criminal Procedure now governs the matters formerly treated in Section 12.

have been committed: *Provided,* That this right shall not apply to contempts committed in the presence of the court or so near thereto as to interfere directly with the administration of justice or to apply to the misbehavior, misconduct, or disobedience of any officer of the court in respect to the writs, orders, or process of the court.

Sec. 12.* The defendant in any proceeding for contempt of court may file with the court a demand for the retirement of the judge sitting in the proceeding, if the contempt arises from an attack upon the character or conduct of such judge and if the attack occurred elsewhere than in the presence of the court or so near thereto as to interfere directly with the administration of justice. Upon the filing of any such demand the judge shall thereupon proceed no further, but another judge shall be designated in the same manner as is provided by law. The demand shall be filed prior to the hearing in the contempt proceeding.

Sec. 13. When used in this Act, and for the purposes of this Act—

(a) A case shall be held to involve or to grow out of a labor dispute when the case involves persons who are engaged in the same industry, trade, craft, or occupation; or have direct or indirect interests therein; or who are employees of the same employer; or who are members of the same or an affiliated organization of employers or employees; whether such dispute is (1) between one or more employers or associations of employers and one or more employees or associations of employees; (2) between one or more employers or associations of employers and one or more employers or associations of employers; or (3) between one or more employees or associations of employees and one or more employees or associations of employees; or when the case involves any conflicting or competing interests in a "labor dispute" (as hereinafter defined) of "persons participating or interested" therein (as hereinafter defined).

(b) A person or association shall be held to be a person participating or interested in a labor dispute if relief is sought against him or it, and if he or it is engaged in the same industry, trade, craft, or occupation in which such dispute occurs, or has a direct or indirect interest therein, or is a member, officer, or agent of any association composed in whole or in part of employers or employees engaged in such industry, trade, craft, or occupation.

(c) The term "labor dispute" includes any controversy concerning terms or conditions of employment, or concerning the association or representation of persons in negotiating, fixing, maintaining, changing, or seeking to arrange terms or conditions of employment, regardless of whether or not the disputants stand in the proximate relation of employer and employee.

(d) The term "court of the United States" means any court of the United States whose jurisdiction has been or may be conferred or defined or limited by Act of Congress, including the courts of the District of Columbia.

Sec. 14. If any provision of this Act or the application thereof to any person or circumstance is held unconstitutional or otherwise invalid, the remaining provisions of the Act and the application of such provisions to other persons or circumstances shall not be affected thereby.

Sec. 15. All Acts and parts of Acts in conflict with the provisions of this Act are hereby repealed.

RAILWAY LABOR ACT

44 Stat., Part II, 577 (1926), as amended;
45 U.S.C. §§ 151–88 (1988).

TITLE I

Sec. 1. When used in this Act and for the purposes of this Act—

First. The term "carrier" includes any express company, sleeping-car company, carrier by railroad, subject to the Interstate Commerce Act, and any company which is directly or indirectly owned or controlled by or under common control with any carrier by railroad and which operates any equipment or facilities or performs any service (other than trucking service) in connection with the transportation, receipt, delivery, elevation, transfer in transit, refrigeration or icing, storage, and handling of property transported by railroad, and any receiver, trustee, or other individual or body, judicial or otherwise, when in the possession of the business of any such "carrier": *Provided, however,* That the term "carrier" shall not include any street, interurban, or suburban electric railway, unless such railway is operating as a part of a general steam-railroad system of transportation, but shall not exclude any part of the general steam-railroad system of transportation now or hereafter operated by any other motive power. The Interstate Commerce Commission is authorized and directed upon request of the Mediation Board or upon complaint of any party interested to determine after hearing whether any line operated by electric power falls within the terms of this proviso. The term "carrier" shall not include any company by reason of its being engaged in the mining of coal, the supplying of coal to a carrier where delivery is not beyond the mine tipple, and the operation of equipment or facilities therefor, or in any of such activities.

Second. The term "Adjustment Board" means the National Railroad Adjustment Board created by this Act.

Third. The term "Mediation Board" means the National Mediation Board created by this Act.

Fourth. The term "commerce" means commerce among the several States or between any State, Territory, or the District of Columbia and any foreign nation, or between any Territory or the District of Columbia and any State, or between any Territory and any other Territory, or between any Territory and the District of Columbia, or within any Territory or the District of Columbia, or between points in the same State but through any other State or any Territory or the District of Columbia or any foreign nation.

Fifth. The term "employee" as used herein includes every person in the service of a carrier (subject to its continuing authority to supervise and direct the manner of rendition of his service) who performs any work defined as that of an employee or subordinate official in the orders of the

Interstate Commerce Commission now in effect, and as the same may be amended or interpreted by orders hereafter entered by the Commission pursuant to the authority which is conferred upon it to enter orders amending or interpreting such existing orders: *Provided, however*, That no occupational classification made by order of the Interstate Commerce Commission shall be construed to define the crafts according to which railway employees may be organized by their voluntary action, nor shall the jurisdiction or powers of such employee organizations be regarded as in any way limited or defined by the provisions of this Act or by the orders of the Commission. The term "employee" shall not include any individual while such individual is engaged in the physical operations consisting of the mining of coal, the preparation of coal, the handling (other than movement by rail with standard railroad locomotives) of coal not beyond the mine tipple, or the loading of coal at the tipple.

Sixth. The term "representative" means any person or persons, labor union, organization, or corporation designated either by a carrier or group of carriers or by its or their employees, to act for it or them.

Seventh. The term "district court" includes the United States District Court for the District of Columbia; and the term "circuit court of appeals" includes the United States Court of Appeals for the District of Columbia.

This Act may be cited as the "Railway Labor Act."

Sec. 2. The purposes of the Act are:

(1) To avoid any interruption to commerce or to the operation of any carrier engaged therein; (2) to forbid any limitation upon freedom of association among employees or any denial, as a condition of employment or otherwise, of the right of employees to join a labor organization; (3) to provide for the complete independence of carriers and of employees in the matter of self-organization; (4) to provide for the prompt and orderly settlement of all disputes concerning rates of pay, rules, or working conditions; (5) to provide for the prompt and orderly settlement of all disputes growing out of grievances or out of the interpretation or application of agreements covering rates of pay, rules, or working conditions.

First. It shall be the duty of all carriers, their officers, agents, and employees to exert every reasonable effort to make and maintain agreements concerning rates of pay, rules, and working conditions, and to settle all disputes, whether arising out of the application of such agreements or otherwise, in order to avoid any interruption to commerce or to the operation of any carrier growing out of any dispute between the carrier and the employees thereof.

Second. All disputes between a carrier or carriers and its or their employees shall be considered, and, if possible, decided, with all expedition, in conference between representatives designated and authorized so to confer, respectively, by the carrier or carriers and by the employees thereof interested in the dispute.

Third. Representatives, for the purposes of this Act, shall be designated by the respective parties without interference, influence, or coercion by either party over the designation of representatives by the other; and neither party shall in any way interfere with, influence, or coerce the other in its choice of representatives. Representatives of employees for the purposes of this Act need not be persons in the employ of the carrier, and no carrier shall, by interference, influence, or coercion seek in any manner to prevent the designation by its employees as their representatives of those who or which are not employees of the carrier.

Fourth. Employees shall have the right to organize and bargain collectively through representatives of their own choosing. The majority of any craft or class of employees shall have the right to determine who shall be the representative of the craft or class for the purposes of this Act. No carrier, its officers or agents, shall deny or in any way question the right of its employees to join, organize, or assist in organizing the labor organization of their choice, and it shall be unlawful for any carrier to interfere in any way with the organization of its employees, or to use the funds of the carrier in maintaining or assisting or contributing to any labor organization, labor representative, or other agency of collective bargaining, or in performing any work therefor, or to influence or coerce employees in an effort to induce them to join or remain or not to join or remain members of any labor organization or to deduct from the wages of employees any dues, fees, assessments, or other contributions payable to labor organizations, or to collect or to assist in the collection of any such dues, fees, assessments, or other contributions: *Provided*, That nothing in this Act shall be construed to prohibit a carrier from permitting an employee, individually, or local representatives of employees from conferring with management during working hours without loss of time, or to prohibit a carrier from furnishing free transportation to its employees while engaged in the business of a labor organization.

Fifth. No carrier, its officers, or agents shall require any person seeking employment to sign any contract or agreement promising to join or not to join a labor organization; and if any such contract has been enforced prior to the effective date of this Act, then such carrier shall notify the employees by an appropriate order that such contract has been discarded and is no longer binding on them in any way.

Sixth. In case of a dispute between a carrier or carriers and its or their employees, arising out of grievances or out of the interpretation or application of agreements concerning rates of pay, rules, or working conditions, it shall be the duty of the designated representative or representatives of such carrier or carriers and of such employees, within ten days after the receipt of notice of a desire on the part of either party to confer in respect to such dispute, to specify a time and place at which such conference shall be held: *Provided*, (1) That the place so specified shall be situated upon the line of the carrier involved or as otherwise mutually agreed upon; and (2) that the time so specified shall allow the designated conferees reasonable opportunity to reach such place of conference, but shall not exceed twenty days from the receipt of such notice: *And provided further*, That nothing in this Act shall be construed to supersede the provisions of any agreement (as to conferences) then in effect between the parties.

Seventh. No carrier, its officers, or agents shall change the rates of pay, rules, or working conditions of its employees, as a class as embodied in agreements except in the manner prescribed in such agreements or in section 6 of this Act.

Eighth. Every carrier shall notify its employees by printed notices in such form and posted at such times and places as shall be specified by the Mediation Board that all disputes between the carrier and its employees will be handled in accordance with the requirements of this Act, and in such notices there shall be printed verbatim, in large type, the third, fourth, and fifth paragraphs of this section. The provisions of said paragraphs are hereby made a part of the contract of employment between the carrier and each employee, and shall be held binding upon the parties, regardless of any other express or implied agreements between them.

Ninth. If any dispute shall arise among a carrier's employees as to who are the representatives of such employees designated and authorized in accordance with the requirements of this Act, it shall be the duty of the Mediation Board, upon request of either party to the dispute, to investigate such dispute and to certify to both parties, in writing, within thirty days after the receipt of the invocation of its services, the name or names of the individuals or organizations that have been designated and authorized to represent the employees involved in the dispute, and certify the same to the carrier. Upon receipt of such certification the carrier shall treat with the representative so certified as the representative of the craft or class for the purposes of this Act. In such an investigation, the Mediation Board shall be authorized to take a secret ballot of the employees involved, or to utilize any other appropriate method of ascertaining the names of their duly designated and authorized representatives in such manner as shall insure the choice of representatives by the employees without interference, influence, or coercion exercised by the carrier. In the conduct of any election for the purposes herein indicated the Board shall designate who may participate in the election and establish the rules to govern the election, or may appoint a committee of three neutral persons who after hearing shall within ten days designate the employees who may participate in the election. The Board shall have access to and have power to make copies of the books and records of the carriers to obtain and utilize such information as may be deemed necessary by it to carry out the purposes and provisions of this paragraph.

Tenth. The willful failure or refusal of any carrier, its officers, or agents to comply with the terms of the third, fourth, fifth, seventh, or eighth paragraph of this section shall be a misdemeanor, and upon conviction thereof the carrier, officer, or agent offending shall be subject to a fine of not less than $1,000 nor more than $20,000 or imprisonment for not more than six months, or both fine and imprisonment, for each offense, and each day during which such carrier, officer, or agent shall willfully fail or refuse to comply with the terms of the said paragraphs of this section shall constitute a separate offense. It shall be the duty of any United States attorney to whom any duly designated representative of a carrier's employees may apply to institute in the proper court and to prosecute under the direction of the Attorney General of the United States, all necessary proceedings for the enforcement of the provisions of this section, and for the punishment of all violations thereof and the costs and expenses of such prosecution shall be paid out of the appropriation for the expenses of the courts of the United States: *Provided,* That nothing in this Act shall be construed to require an individual employee to render labor or service without his consent, nor shall anything in this Act be construed to make the quitting of his labor by an individual employee an illegal act; nor shall any court issue any process to compel the performance by an individual employee of such labor or service, without his consent.

Eleventh. Notwithstanding any other provisions of this chapter, or of any other statute or law of the United States, or Territory thereof, or of any State, any carrier or carriers as defined in this chapter and a labor organization or labor organizations duly designated and authorized to represent employees in accordance with the requirements of this chapter shall be permitted—

(a) to make agreements, requiring, as a condition of continued employment, that within sixty days following the beginning of such employment, or the effective date of such agreements, whichever is the later, all employees shall become members of the labor organization representing their craft or class: *Provided,* That no such agreement shall require such condition of employment with respect to employees to whom membership is not available upon the same terms and conditions as are generally applicable to any other member or with respect to employees to whom membership was denied or terminated for any reason other than the failure of the employee to tender the periodic dues, initiation fees, and assessments (not including fines and penalties) uniformly required as a condition of acquiring or retaining membership.

(b) to make agreements providing for the deduction by such carrier or carriers from the wages of its or their employees in a craft or class and payment to the labor organization representing the craft or class of such employees, of any periodic dues, initiation fees, and assessments (not including fines and penalties) uniformly required as a condition of acquiring or retaining membership: *Provided*, That no such agreement shall be effective with respect to any individual employee until he shall have furnished the employer with a written assignment to the labor organization of such membership dues, initiation fees, and assessments, which shall be revocable in writing after the expiration of one year or upon the termination date of the applicable collective agreement, whichever occurs sooner.

* * *

Sec. 3. First. There is hereby established a Board, to be known as the "National Railroad Adjustment Board", the members of which shall be selected within thirty days after June 21, 1934, and it is hereby provided—

(a) That the said Adjustment Board shall consist of thirty-four members, seventeen of whom shall be selected by the carriers and seventeen by such labor organizations of the employees, national in scope, as have been or may be organized in accordance with the provisions of section 2 of this Act.

(b) The carriers, acting each through its board of directors or its receiver or receivers, trustee or trustees, or through an officer or officers designated for that purpose by such board, trustee or trustees, or receiver or receivers, shall prescribe the rules under which its representatives shall be selected and shall select the representatives of the carriers on the Adjustment Board and designate the division on which each such representative shall serve, but no carrier or system of carriers shall have more than one voting representative on any division of the Board.

(c) Except as provided in the second paragraph of subsection (h) of this section, the national labor organizations as defined in paragraph (a) of this section, acting each through the chief executive or other medium designated by the organization or association thereof, shall prescribe the rules under which the labor members of the Adjustment Board shall be selected and shall select such members and designate the division on which each member shall serve; but no labor organization shall have more than one voting representative on any division of the Board.

* * *

(h) The said Adjustment Board shall be composed of four divisions, whose proceedings shall be independent of one another, and the said divisions as well as the number of their members shall be as follows:

First division: To have jurisdiction over disputes involving train- and yard-service employees of carriers; that is, engineers, firemen, hostlers, and outside hostler helpers, conductors, trainmen, and yard-service employees. This division shall consist of eight members, four of whom shall be selected and designated by the carriers and four of whom shall be selected and designated by the labor organizations * * *.

Second division: To have jurisdiction over disputes involving machinists, boilermakers, blacksmiths, sheet-metal workers, electrical workers, car men, the helpers and apprentices of all the foregoing, coach cleaners, power-house employees, and railroad-shop laborers. This division shall consist of ten members, five of whom shall be selected by the carriers and five by the national labor organizations of the employees.

Third division: To have jurisdiction over disputes involving station, tower, and telegraph employees, train dispatchers, maintenance-of-way men, clerical employees, freight handlers, express, station, and store employees, signal men, sleeping-car conductors, sleeping-car porters, and maids and dining-car employees. This division shall consist of ten members, five of whom shall be selected by the carriers and five by the national labor organizations of employees.

Fourth division: To have jurisdiction over disputes involving employees of carriers directly or indirectly engaged in transportation of passengers or property by water, and all other employees of carriers over which jurisdiction is not given to the first, second, and third divisions. This division shall consist of six members, three of whom shall be selected by the carriers and three by the national labor organizations of the employees.

(i) The disputes between an employee or group of employees and a carrier or carriers growing out of grievances or out of the interpretation or application of agreements concerning rates of pay, rules, or working conditions, including cases pending and unadjusted on the date of approval of this Act, shall be handled in the usual manner up to and including the chief operating officer of the carrier designated to handle such disputes; but, failing to reach an adjustment in this manner, the disputes may be referred by petition of the parties or by either party to the appropriate division of the Adjustment Board with a full statement of the facts and all supporting data bearing upon the disputes.

(j) Parties may be heard either in person, by counsel, or by other representatives, as they may respectively elect, and the several divisions of the Adjustment Board shall give due notice of all hearings to the employee or employees and the carrier or carriers involved in any disputes submitted to them.

(k) Any division of the Adjustment Board shall have authority to empower two or more of its members to conduct hearings and make findings upon disputes, when properly submitted, at any place designated by the division: *Provided, however*, That except as provided in paragraph (h) of this section, final awards as to any such dispute must be made by the entire division as hereinafter provided.

* * *

(m) The awards of the several divisions of the Adjustment Board shall be stated in writing. A copy of the awards shall be furnished to the respective parties to the controversy, and the awards shall be final and binding upon both parties to the dispute. In case a dispute arises involving an interpretation of the award the division of the Board upon request of either party shall interpret the award in the light of the dispute.

(n) A majority vote of all members of the division of the Adjustment Board eligible to vote shall be competent to make an award with respect to any dispute submitted to it.

(*o*) In case of an award by any division of the Adjustment Board in favor of petitioner, the division of the Board shall make an order, directed to the carrier, to make the award effective and, if the award includes a requirement for the payment of money, to pay the employee the sum to which he is entitled under the award on or before a day named. In the event any division determines that an award favorable to the petitioner should not be made in any dispute referred to it, the division shall make an order to the petitioner stating such determination.

(p) If a carrier does not comply with an order of a division of the Adjustment Board within the time limit in such order, the petitioner, or any person for whose benefit such order was made, may file in the District Court of the United States for the district in which he resides or in which is located the principal operating office of the carrier, or through which the carrier operates, a petition setting forth briefly the causes for which he claims relief, and the order of the division of the Adjustment Board in the premises. Such suit in the District Court of the United States shall proceed in all respects as other civil suits, except that on the trial of such suit the findings and order of the division of the Adjustment Board shall be conclusive on the parties, and except that the petitioner shall not be liable for costs in the district court nor for costs at any subsequent stage of the proceedings, unless they accrue upon his appeal, and such costs shall be paid out of the appropriation for the expenses of the courts of the United States. If the petitioner shall finally prevail he shall be allowed a reasonable attorney's fee, to be taxed and collected as a part of the costs of the suit. The district courts are empowered, under the rules of the court governing actions at law, to make such order and enter such judgment, by writ of mandamus or otherwise, as may be appropriate to enforce or set aside the order of the division of the Adjustment Board: *Provided, however*, That such order may not be set aside except for failure of the division to comply with the requirements of this chapter, for failure of the order to conform, or confine itself, to matters within the scope of the division's jurisdiction, or for fraud or corruption by a member of the division making the order.

(q) If any employee or group of employees, or any carrier, is aggrieved by the failure of any division of the Adjustment Board to make an award in a dispute referred to it, or is aggrieved by any of the terms of an award or by the failure of the division to include certain terms in such award, then such employee or group of employees or carrier may file in any United States district court in which a petition under paragraph

(p) could be filed, a petition for review of the division's order. A copy of the petition shall be forthwith transmitted by the clerk of the court to the Adjustment Board. The Adjustment Board shall file in the court the record of the proceedings on which it based its action. The court shall have jurisdiction to affirm the order of the division, or to set it aside, in whole or in part, or it may remand the proceeding to the division for such further action as it may direct. On such review, the findings and order of the division shall be conclusive on the parties, except that the order of the division may be set aside, in whole or in part, or remanded to the division, for failure of the division to comply with the requirements of this chapter, for failure of the order to conform, or confine itself, to matters within the scope of the division's jurisdiction, or for fraud or corruption by a member of the division making the order. The judgment of the court shall be subject to review as provided in sections 1291 and 1254 of title 28, United States Code.

(r) All actions at law based upon the provisions of this section shall be begun within two years from the time the cause of action accrues under the award of the division of the Adjustment Board, and not after.

* * *

Second. Nothing in this section shall be construed to prevent any individual carrier, system, or group of carriers and any class or classes of its or their employees, all acting through their representatives, selected in accordance with the provisions of this Act, from mutually agreeing to the establishment of system, group, or regional boards of adjustment for the purpose of adjusting and deciding disputes of the character specified in this section. In the event that either party to such a system, group, or regional board of adjustment is dissatisfied with such arrangement, it may upon ninety days' notice to the other party elect to come under the jurisdiction of the Adjustment Board.

* * *

Sec. 4. First. * * * There is hereby established, as an independent agency in the executive branch of the Government, a board to be known as the "National Mediation Board," to be composed of three members appointed by the President, by and with the advice and consent of the Senate, not more than two of whom shall be of the same political party. Each member of the Mediation Board in office on January 1, 1965, shall be deemed to have been appointed for a term of office which shall expire on July 1 of the year his term would have otherwise expired. The terms of office of all successors shall expire three years after the expiration of the terms for which their predecessors were appointed; but any member appointed to fill a vacancy occurring prior to the expiration of the term of which his predecessor was appointed shall be appointed only for the unexpired term of his predecessor. * * *

A member of the Board may be removed by the President for inefficiency, neglect of duty, malfeasance in office, or ineligibility, but for no other cause.

* * *

Sec. 5. First. The parties, or either party, to a dispute between an employee or group of employees and a carrier may invoke the services of the Mediation Board in any of the following cases:

(a) A dispute concerning changes in rates of pay, rules, or working conditions not adjusted by the parties in conference.

(b) Any other dispute not referable to the National Railroad Adjustment Board and not adjusted in conference between the parties or where conferences are refused.

The Mediation Board may proffer its services in case any labor emergency is found by it to exist at any time.

In either event the said Board shall promptly put itself in communication with the parties to such controversy, and shall use its best efforts, by mediation, to bring them to agreement. If such efforts to bring about an amicable settlement through mediation shall be unsuccessful, the said Board shall at once endeavor as its final required action (except as provided in paragraph third of this section and in section 10 of this Act) to induce the parties to submit their controversy to arbitration, in accordance with the provisions of this Act.

If arbitration at the request of the Board shall be refused by one or both parties, the Board shall at once notify both parties in writing that its mediatory efforts have failed and for thirty days thereafter, unless in the intervening period the parties agree to arbitration, or an emergency board shall be created under section 10 of this Act, no change shall be made in the rates of pay, rules, or working conditions or establish practices in effect prior to the time the dispute arose.

* * *

Sec. 6. Carriers and representatives of the employees shall give at least thirty days' written notice of an intended change in agreements affecting rates of pay, rules, or working conditions, and the time and place for the beginning of conference between the representatives of the parties interested in such intended changes shall be agreed upon within ten days after the receipt of said notice, and said time shall be within the thirty days provided in the notice. In every case where such notice of intended change has been given, or conferences are being held with reference thereto, or the services of the Mediation Board have been requested by either party, or said Board has proffered its services, rates of pay, rules, or working conditions shall not be altered by the carrier until the controversy has been finally acted upon as required by section 5 of this Act, by the Mediation Board, unless a period of ten days has elapsed after termination of conferences without request for or proffer of the services of the Mediation Board.

Sec. 7. First. Whenever a controversy shall arise between a carrier or carriers and its or their employees which is not settled either in conference between representatives of the parties or by the appropriate adjustment board or through mediation, in the manner provided in the preceding sections, such controversy may, by agreement of the parties to such controversy, be submitted to the arbitration of a board of three (or, if the parties to the controversy so stipulate, of six) persons: *Provided, however,* That the failure or refusal of either party to submit a controversy to arbitration shall not be construed as a violation of any legal obligation imposed upon such party by the terms of this Act or otherwise.

Second. Such board of arbitration shall be chosen in the following manner:

(a) In the case of a board of three, the carrier or carriers and the representatives of the employees, parties respectively to the agreement to arbitrate, shall each name one arbitrator; the two arbitrators thus chosen shall select a third arbitrator. If the arbitrators chosen by the parties shall fail to name the third arbitrator within five days after their first meeting, such third arbitrator shall be named by the Mediation Board.

(b) In the case of a board of six, the carrier or carriers and the representatives of the employees, parties respectively to the agreement to arbitrate, shall each name two arbitrators; the four arbitrators thus chosen shall, by a majority vote, select the remaining two arbitrators. If the arbitrators chosen by the parties shall fail to name the two arbitrators within fifteen days after their first meeting, the said two arbitrators, or as many of them as have not been named, shall be named by the Mediation Board.

Third. (a) When the arbitrators selected by the respective parties have agreed upon the remaining arbitrator or arbitrators, they shall notify the Mediation Board, and, in the event of their failure to agree upon any or upon all of the necessary arbitrators within the period fixed by this Act, they shall, at the expiration of such period, notify the Mediation Board of the arbitrators selected, if any, or of their failure to make or complete such selection.

(b) The board of arbitration shall organize and select its own chairman and make all necessary rules for conducting its hearings: *Provided, however,* That the board of arbitration shall be bound to give the parties to the controversy a full and fair hearing, which shall include an opportunity to present evidence in support of their claims, and an opportunity to present their case in person, by counsel, or by other representative as they may respectively elect.

* * *

Sec. 9. First. The award of a board of arbitration, having been acknowledged as herein provided, shall be filed in the clerk's office of the district court designated in the agreement to arbitrate.

Second. An award acknowledged and filed as herein provided shall be conclusive on the parties as to the merits and facts of the controversy submitted to arbitration, and unless, within ten days after the filing of the award, a petition to impeach the award, on the grounds hereinafter set forth, shall be filed in the clerk's office of the court in which the award has been filed, the court shall enter judgment on the award, which judgment shall be final and conclusive on the parties.

Third. Such petition for the impeachment or contesting of any award so filed shall be entertained by the court only on one or more of the following grounds:

(a) That the award plainly does not conform to the substantive requirements laid down by this Act for such awards, or that the proceedings were not substantially in conformity with this Act;

(b) That the award does not conform, nor confine itself, to the stipulations of the agreement to arbitrate; or

(c) That a member of the board of arbitration rendering the award was guilty of fraud or corruption; or that a party to the arbitration practiced fraud or corruption which fraud or corruption affected the result of the arbitration. *Provided, however*, That no court shall entertain any such petition on the ground that an award is invalid for uncertainty; in such case the proper remedy shall be a submission of such award to a reconvened board, or subcommittee thereof, for interpretation, as provided by this Act: *Provided further*, That an award contested as herein provided shall be construed liberally by the court, with a view to favoring its validity, and that no award shall be set aside for trivial irregularity or clerical error, going only to form and not to substance.

* * *

Sec. 10. If a dispute between a carrier and its employees be not adjusted under the foregoing provisions of this Act and should, in the judgment of the Mediation Board, threaten substantially to interrupt interstate commerce to a degree such as to deprive any section of the country of essential transportation service, the Mediation Board shall notify the President, who may thereupon, in his discretion, create a board to investigate and report respecting such dispute. Such board shall be composed of such number of persons as to the President may seem desirable: *Provided, however*, That no member appointed shall be pecuniarily or otherwise interested in any organization of employees or any carrier. The compensation of the members of any such board shall be fixed by the President. Such board shall be created separately in each instance and it shall investigate promptly the facts as to the dispute and make a report thereon to the President within thirty days from the date of its creation.

* * *

After the creation of such board, and for thirty days after such board has made its report to the President, no change, except by agreement, shall be made by the parties to the controversy in the conditions out of which the dispute arose.

* * *

TITLE II

Sec. 201. All of the provisions of title I of this Act, except the provisions of section 3 thereof, are extended to and shall cover every common carrier by air engaged in interstate or foreign commerce, and every carrier by air transporting mail for or under contract with the United States Government, and every air pilot or other person who performs any work as an employee or subordinate official of such carrier or carriers, subject to its or their continuing authority to supervise and direct the manner of rendition of his service.

Sec. 202. The duties, requirements, penalties, benefits, and privileges prescribed and established by the provisions of title I of this Act, except section 3 thereof, shall apply to said carriers by air and their employees in the same manner and to the same extent as though such carriers and their employees were specifically included within the definition of "carrier" and "employee", respectively, in section 1 thereof.

Sec. 203. The parties or either party to a dispute between an employee or a group of employees and a carrier or carriers by air may invoke the services of the National Mediation Board and the jurisdiction of said Mediation Board is extended to any of the following cases:

(a) A dispute concerning changes in rates of pay, rules, or working conditions not adjusted by the parties in conference.

(b) Any other dispute not referable to an adjustment board, as hereinafter provided, and not adjusted in conference between the parties, or where conferences are refused.

The National Mediation Board may proffer its services in case any labor emergency is found by it to exist at any time.

The services of the Mediation Board may be invoked in a case under this title in the same manner and to the same extent as are the disputes covered by section 5 of title I of this Act.

Sec. 204. The disputes between an employee or group of employees and a carrier or carriers by air growing out of grievances, or out of interpretation or application of agreements concerning rates of pay, rules, or working conditions, including cases pending and unadjusted on the date of approval of this Act before the National Labor Relations Board, shall be handled in the usual manner up to and including the chief operating officer of the carrier designated to handle such disputes; but, failing to reach an adjustment in this manner, the disputes may be referred by petition of the parties or by either party to an appropriate adjustment board, as hereinafter provided, with a full statement of the facts and supporting data bearing upon the disputes.

It shall be the duty of every carrier and of its employees, acting through their representatives, selected in accordance with the provisions of this title, to establish a board of adjustment of jurisdiction not exceeding the jurisdiction which may be lawfully exercised by system, group, or regional boards of adjustment, under the authority of section 3, Title I, of this Act.

Such boards of adjustment may be established by agreement between employees and carriers either on any individual carrier, or system, or group of carriers by air and any class or classes of its or their employees; or pending the establishment of a permanent National Board of Adjustment as hereinafter provided. Nothing in this Act shall prevent said carriers by air, or any class or classes of their employees, both acting through their representatives selected in accordance with provisions of this title, from mutually agreeing to the establishment of a National Board of Adjustment of temporary duration and of similarly limited jurisdiction.

* * *

NATIONAL LABOR RELATIONS ACT*

49 Stat. 449 (1935), as amended; 29 U.S.C. §§ 151–69 (1988).

FINDINGS AND POLICIES

Sec. 1. The denial by **some** employers of the right of employees to organize and the refusal by **some** employers to accept the procedure of collective bargaining lead to strikes and other forms of industrial strife or unrest, which have the intent or the necessary effect of burdening or obstructing commerce by (a) impairing the efficiency, safety, or operation of the instrumentalities of commerce; (b) occurring in the current of commerce; (c) materially affecting, restraining, or controlling the flow of raw materials or manufactured or processed goods from or into the channels of commerce, or the prices of such materials or goods in commerce; or (d) causing diminution of employment and wages in such volume as substantially to impair or disrupt the market for goods flowing from or into the channels of commerce.

The inequality of bargaining power between employees who do not possess full freedom of association or actual liberty of contract, and employers who are organized in the corporate or other forms of ownership association substantially burdens and affects the flow of commerce, and tends to aggravate recurrent business depressions, by depressing wage rates and the purchasing power of wage earners in industry and by preventing the stabilization of competitive wage rates and working conditions within and between industries.

Experience has proved that protection by law of the right of employees to organize and bargain collectively safeguards commerce from injury, impairment, or interruption, and promotes the flow of commerce by removing certain recognized sources of industrial strife and unrest, by encouraging practices fundamental to the friendly adjustment of industrial disputes arising out of differences as to wages, hours, or other working conditions, and by restoring equality of bargaining power between employers and employees.

Experience has further demonstrated that certain practices by some labor organizations, their officers, and members have the intent or the necessary effect of burdening or obstructing commerce by preventing the free flow of goods in such commerce through strikes and other forms of industrial unrest or through concerted activities which impair the interest of the public in the free flow of such commerce. The elimination of such practices is

* The text of the original Wagner Act of 1935 is printed in roman type; the Taft-Hartley amendments of 1947 are in boldface type; the Landrum-Griffin amendments of 1959 are in italics; the 1974 amendments are underscored. Deleted matter is in brackets; bracketed matter in regular roman type was deleted in 1947, and bracketed matter in boldface type was deleted in 1959. Other amendments and deletions are specifically noted.

a necessary condition to the assurance of the rights herein guaranteed.

It is hereby declared to be the policy of the United States to eliminate the causes of certain substantial obstructions to the free flow of commerce and to mitigate and eliminate these obstructions when they have occurred by encouraging the practice and procedure of collective bargaining and by protecting the exercise by workers of full freedom of association, self-organization, and designation of representatives of their own choosing, for the purpose of negotiating the terms and conditions of their employment or other mutual aid or protection.

DEFINITIONS

Sec. 2. When used in this Act—

(1) The term "person" includes one or more individuals, labor organizations, partnerships, associations, corporations, legal representatives, trustees, trustees in bankruptcy, or receivers.

(2) The term "employer" includes any person acting [in the interest of] **as an agent** of an employer, directly or indirectly, but shall not include the United States **or any wholly owned Government corporation, or any Federal Reserve Bank,** or any State or political subdivision thereof, **[or any corporation or association operating a hospital, if no part of the net earnings inures to the benefit of any private shareholder or individual,]*** or any person subject to the Railway Labor Act, as amended from time to time, or any labor organization (other than when acting as an employer), or anyone acting in the capacity of officer or agent of such labor organization.

(3) The term "employee" shall include any employee, and shall not be limited to the employees of a particular employer, unless the Act explicitly states otherwise, and shall include any individual whose work has ceased as a consequence of, or in connection with, any current labor dispute or because of any unfair labor practice, and who has not obtained any other regular and substantially equivalent employment, but shall not include any individual employed as an agricultural laborer, or in the domestic service of any family or person at his home, or any individual employed by his parent or spouse, **or any individual having the status of an independent contractor, or any individual employed as a supervisor, or any individual employed by an employer subject to the Railway Labor Act, as amended from time to time, or by any other person who is not an employer as herein defined.**

(4) The term "representatives" includes any individual or labor organization.

(5) The term "labor organization" means any organization of any kind, or any agency or employee representation committee or plan, in which employees participate and which exists for the purpose, in whole

---

* The bracketed matter was deleted in 1974, by 88 Stat. 395 (1974).

or in part, of dealing with employers concerning grievances, labor disputes, wages, rates of pay, hours of employment, or conditions of work.

(6) The term "commerce" means trade, traffic, commerce, transportation, or communication among the several States, or between the District of Columbia or any Territory of the United States and any State or other Territory, or between any foreign country and any State, Territory, or the District of Columbia, or within the District of Columbia or any Territory, or between points in the same State but through any other State or any Territory or the District of Columbia or any foreign country.

(7) The term "affecting commerce" means in commerce, or burdening or obstructing commerce or the free flow of commerce, or having led or tending to lead to a labor dispute burdening or obstructing commerce or the free flow of commerce.

(8) The term "unfair labor practice" means any unfair labor practice listed in section 8.

(9) The term "labor dispute" includes any controversy concerning terms, tenure or conditions of employment, or concerning the association or representation of persons in negotiating, fixing, maintaining, changing, or seeking to arrange terms or conditions of employment, regardless of whether the disputants stand in the proximate relation of employer and employee.

(10) The term "National Labor Relations Board" means the National Labor Relations Board provided for in section 3 of this Act.

(11) The term "supervisor" means any individual having authority, in the interest of the employer, to hire, transfer, suspend, lay off, recall, promote, discharge, assign, reward, or discipline other employees, or responsibly to direct them, or to adjust their grievances, or effectively to recommend such action, if in connection with the foregoing the exercise of such authority is not of a merely routine or clerical nature, but requires the use of independent judgment.

(12) The term "professional employee" means—

(a) any employee engaged in work (i) predominantly intellectual and varied in character as opposed to routine mental, manual, mechanical, or physical work; (ii) involving the consistent exercise of discretion and judgment in its performance; (iii) of such a character that the output produced or the result accomplished cannot be standardized in relation to a given period of time; (iv) requiring knowledge of an advanced type in a field of science or learning customarily acquired by a prolonged course of specialized intellectual instruction and study in an institution of higher learning or a hospital, as distinguished from a general academic education or from an apprenticeship or from

training in the performance of routine mental, manual, or physical processes; or

(b) any employee, who (i) has completed the courses of specialized intellectual instruction and study described in clause (iv) of paragraph (a), and (ii) is performing related work under the supervision of a professional person to qualify himself to become a professional employee as defined in paragraph (a).

(13) In determining whether any person is acting as an "agent" of another person so as to make such other person responsible for his acts, the question of whether the specific acts performed were actually authorized or subsequently ratified shall not be controlling.

(14) The term "health care institution" shall include any hospital, convalescent hospital, health maintenance organization, health clinic, nursing home, extended care facility, or other institution devoted to the care of sick, infirm, or aged person.

NATIONAL LABOR RELATIONS BOARD

Sec. 3.* (a) The National Labor Relations Board (hereinafter called the "Board") created by this Act prior to its amendment by the Labor Management Relations Act, 1947, is continued as an agency of the United States, except that the Board shall consist of five instead of three members, appointed by the President by and with the advice and consent of the Senate. Of the two additional members so provided for, one shall be appointed for a term of five years and the other for a term of two years. Their successors, and the successors of the other members, shall be appointed for terms of five years each, excepting that any individual chosen to fill a vacancy shall be appointed only for the unexpired term of the member whom he shall succeed. The President shall designate one member to serve as Chairman of the Board. Any member of the Board may be removed by the President, upon notice and hearing, for neglect of duty or malfeasance in office, but for no other cause.

(b) **The Board is authorized to delegate to any group of three or more members any or all of the powers which it may itself exercise.** *The Board is also authorized to delegate to its regional directors its powers under section 9 to determine the unit appropriate for the purpose of collective bargaining, to investigate and provide for hearings, and determine whether a question of representation exists, and to direct an election or take a secret ballot under subsection (c) or (e) of section 9 and certify the results thereof, except that upon the filing of a request*

* The changes made in Sections 3 and 4 by the Taft-Hartley amendments were so extensive, that the typeface designations for these two sections show only the 1947 and 1959 amendments.

therefor with the Board by any interested person, the Board may review any action of a regional director delegated to him under this paragraph, but such a review shall not, unless specifically ordered by the Board, operate as a stay of any action taken by the regional director. **A vacancy in the Board shall not impair the right of the remaining members to exercise all of the powers of the Board, and three members of the Board shall, at all times, constitute a quorum of the Board, except that two members shall constitute a quorum of any group designated pursuant to the first sentence hereof. The Board shall have an official seal which shall be judicially noticed.**

(c) The Board shall at the close of each fiscal year make a report in writing to Congress and to the President [stating in detail the cases it has heard, the decisions it has rendered, the names, salaries, and duties of all employees and officers in the employ or under the supervision of the Board, and an account of all moneys it has disbursed.]* summarizing significant case activities and operations for that fiscal year.

(d) There shall be a General Counsel of the Board who shall be appointed by the President, by and with the advice and consent of the Senate, for a term of four years. The General Counsel of the Board shall exercise general supervision over all attorneys employed by the Board (other than administrative law judges and legal assistants to Board members) and over the officers and employees in the regional offices. He shall have final authority, on behalf of the Board, in respect of the investigation of charges and issuance of complaints under section 10, and in respect of the prosecution of such complaints before the Board, and shall have such other duties as the Board may prescribe or as may be provided by law.** *In case of a vacancy in the office of the General Counsel the President is authorized to designate the officer or employee who shall act as General Counsel during such vacancy, but no person or persons so designated shall so act (1) for more than forty days when the Congress is in session unless a nomination to fill such vacancy shall have been submitted to the Senate, or (2) after the adjournment sine die of the session of the Senate in which such nomination was submitted.*

Sec. 4. (a) Each member of the Board and the General Counsel of the Board [shall receive a salary of $12,000 per annum,] shall be eligible for reappointment, and shall not engage in any other business, vocation, or employment. The Board shall appoint an executive secretary, and such attorneys, examiners, and regional directors, and such other employees as it may from time to time find necessary for the proper performance of its duties. The Board may not employ any attorneys for the purpose of reviewing transcripts of hearings or preparing drafts of

---

* The bracketed matter was deleted in part in 1975 and in part in 1982, and the matter following was added in 1982.

** The title "administrative law judge" was adopted in 5 U.S.C. § 3105, in 1972.

opinions except that any attorney employed for assignment as a legal assistant to any Board member may for such Board member review such transcripts and prepare such drafts. No administrative law judge's report shall be reviewed, either before or after its publication, by any person other than a member of the Board or his legal assistant, and no administrative law judge shall advise or consult with the Board with respect to exceptions taken to his findings, rulings, or recommendations. The Board may establish or utilize such regional, local, or other agencies, and utilize such voluntary and uncompensated services, as may from time to time be needed. Attorneys appointed under this section may, at the direction of the Board, appear for and represent the Board in any case in court. Nothing in this Act shall be construed to authorize the Board to appoint individuals for the purpose of conciliation or mediation, or for economic analysis.

(b) All of the expenses of the Board, including all necessary traveling and subsistence expenses outside the District of Columbia incurred by the members or employees of the Board under its orders, shall be allowed and paid on the presentation of itemized vouchers therefor approved by the Board or by any individual it designates for that purpose.

Sec. 5. The principal office of the Board shall be in the District of Columbia, but it may meet and exercise any or all of its powers at any other place. The Board may, by one or more of its members or by such agents or agencies as it may designate, prosecute any inquiry necessary to its functions in any part of the United States. A member who participates in such an inquiry shall not be disqualified from subsequently participating in a decision of the Board in the same case.

Sec. 6. The Board shall have authority from time to time to make, amend, and rescind, **in the manner prescribed by the Administrative Procedure Act,** such rules and regulations as may be necessary to carry out the provisions of this Act. [Such rules and regulations shall be effective upon publication in the manner which the Board shall prescribe.]

RIGHTS OF EMPLOYEES

Sec. 7. Employees shall have the right to self-organization, to form, join, or assist labor organizations, to bargain collectively through representatives of their own choosing, and to engage in other concerted activities for the purpose of collective bargaining or other mutual aid or protection, **and shall also have the right to refrain from any or all of such activities except to the extent that such right may be affected by an agreement requiring membership in a labor organization as a condition of employment as authorized in section 8(a)(3).**

UNFAIR LABOR PRACTICES

Sec. 8. (a) It shall be an unfair labor practice for an employer—

(1) to interfere with, restrain, or coerce employees in the exercise of the rights guaranteed in section 7;

(2) to dominate or interfere with the formation or administration of any labor organization or contribute financial or other support to it: *Provided*, That subject to rules and regulations made and published by the Board pursuant to section 6, an employer shall not be prohibited from permitting employees to confer with him during working hours without loss of time or pay;

(3) by discrimination in regard to hire or tenure of employment or any term or condition of employment to encourage or discourage membership in any labor organization: *Provided*, That nothing in this Act, or in any other statute of the United States, shall preclude an employer from making an agreement with a labor organization (not established, maintained, or assisted by any action defined in **section 8(a) of** this Act as an unfair labor practice) to require as a condition of employment membership therein **on or after the thirtieth day following the beginning of such employment or the effective date of such agreement, whichever is the later, (i)** if such labor organization is the representative of the employees as provided in section 9(a), in the appropriate collective-bargaining unit covered by such agreement when made, **[and has at the time the agreement was made or within the preceding twelve months received from the Board a notice of compliance with Section 9(f), (g), (h)], and (ii) unless following an election held as provided in section 9(e) within one year preceding the effective date of such agreement, the Board shall have certified that at least a majority of the employees eligible to vote in such election have voted to rescind the authority of such labor organization to make such an agreement:*** ***Provided further*, That no employer shall justify any discrimination against an employee for nonmembership in a labor organization (A) if he has reasonable grounds for believing that such membership was not available to the employee on the same terms and conditions generally applicable to other members, or (B) if he has reasonable grounds for believing that membership was denied or terminated for reasons other than the failure of the employee to tender the periodic dues and the initiation fees uniformly required as a condition of acquiring or retaining membership;**

(4) to discharge or otherwise discriminate against an employee because he has filed charges or given testimony under this Act;

* The (ii) provision was added in 1951 by 65 Stat. 601.

(5) to refuse to bargain collectively with the representatives of his employees, subject to the provisions of section 9(a).

(b) It shall be an unfair labor practice for a labor organization or its agents—

(1) to restrain or coerce (A) employees in the exercise of the rights guaranteed in section 7: *Provided*, That this paragraph shall not impair the right of a labor organization to prescribe its own rules with respect to the acquisition or retention of membership therein; or (B) an employer in the selection of his representatives for the purposes of collective bargaining or the adjustment of grievances;

(2) to cause or attempt to cause an employer to discriminate against an employee in violation of subsection (a)(3) or to discriminate against an employee with respect to whom membership in such organization has been denied or terminated on some ground other than his failure to tender the periodic dues and the initiation fees uniformly required as a condition of acquiring or retaining membership;

(3) to refuse to bargain collectively with an employer, provided it is the representative of his employees subject to the provisions of section 9(a);

(4)*(i)* **to engage in, or to induce or encourage [the employees of any employer]** *any individual employed by any person engaged in commerce or in an industry affecting commerce* **to engage in, a strike or a [concerted] refusal in the course of [their]** *his* **employment to use, manufacture, process, transport, or otherwise handle or work on any goods, articles, materials, or commodities or to perform any services[,]**; *or (ii) to threaten, coerce, or restrain any person engaged in commerce or in an industry affecting commerce,* **where** *in either case* **an object thereof is—**

(A) forcing or requiring any employer or self-employed person to join any labor or employer organization [or any employer or other person to cease using, selling, handling, transporting, or otherwise dealing in the products of any other producer, processor, or manufacturer, or to cease doing business with any other person;] *or to enter into any agreement which is prohibited by section 8(e);*

(B) forcing or requiring any **[any employer or other]** *person to cease using, selling, handling, transporting, or otherwise dealing in the products of any other producer, processor, or manufacturer, or to cease doing business with any other person, or* **forcing or requiring any other employer to recognize or bargain with a labor organization as the**

representative of his employees unless such labor organization has been certified as the representative of such employees under the provisions of section 9[;]; *Provided, That nothing contained in this clause (B) shall be construed to make unlawful, where not otherwise unlawful, any primary strike or primary picketing;*

(C) forcing or requiring any employer to recognize or bargain with a particular labor organization as the representative of his employees if another labor organization has been certified as the representative of such employees under the provisions of section 9;

(D) forcing or requiring any employer to assign particular work to employees in a particular labor organization or in a particular trade, craft, or class rather than to employees in another labor organization or in another trade, craft, or class, unless such employer is failing to conform to an order or certification of the Board determining the bargaining representative for employees performing such work:

***Provided*, That nothing contained in this subsection (b) shall be construed to make unlawful a refusal by any person to enter upon the premises of any employer (other than his own employer), if the employees of such employer are engaged in a strike ratified or approved by a representative of such employees whom such employer is required to recognize under this Act:** *Provided further, That for the purposes of this paragraph (4) only, nothing contained in such paragraph shall be construed to prohibit publicity, other than picketing, for the purpose of truthfully advising the public, including consumers and members of a labor organization, that a product or products are produced by an employer with whom the labor organization has a primary dispute and are distributed by another employer, as long as such publicity does not have an effect of inducing any individual employed by any person other than the primary employer in the course of his employment to refuse to pick up, deliver, or transport any goods, or not to perform any services, at the establishment of the employer engaged in such distribution:*

(5) to require of employees covered by an agreement authorized under subsection (a)(3) the payment, as a condition precedent to becoming a member of such organization, of a fee in an amount which the Board finds excessive or discriminatory under all the circumstances. In making such a finding, the Board shall consider, among other relevant factors, the practices and customs of labor organizations in the particular industry, and the wages currently paid to the employees affected; [and]

(6) to cause or attempt to cause an employer to pay or deliver or agree to pay or deliver any money or other thing of value, in the nature of an exaction, for services which are not performed or not to be performed[.]; *and*

(7) to picket or cause to be picketed, or threaten to picket or cause to be picketed, any employer where an object thereof is forcing or requiring an employer to recognize or bargain with a labor organization as the representatives of his employees, or forcing or requiring the employees of an employer to accept or select such labor organization as their collective bargaining representative, unless such labor organization is currently certified as the representative of such employees:

(A) where the employer has lawfully recognized in accordance with this Act any other labor organization and a question concerning representation may not appropriately be raised under section 9(c) of this Act.

(B) where within the preceding twelve months a valid election under section 9(c) of this Act has been conducted, or

(C) where such picketing has been conducted without a petition under section 9(c) being filed within a reasonable period of time not to exceed thirty days from the commencement of such picketing: Provided, That when such a petition has been filed the Board shall forthwith, without regard to the provisions of section 9(c)(1) or the absence of a showing of a substantial interest on the part of the labor organization, direct an election in such unit as the Board finds to be appropriate and shall certify the results thereof: Provided further, That nothing in this subparagraph (C) shall be construed to prohibit any picketing or other publicity for the purpose of truthfully advising the public (including consumers) that an employer does not employ members of, or have a contract with, a labor organization, unless an effect of such picketing is to induce any individual employed by any other person in the course of his employment, not to pick up, deliver or transport any goods or not to perform any services.

Nothing in this paragraph (7) shall be construed to permit any act which would otherwise be an unfair labor practice under this section 8(b).

(c) The expressing of any views, argument, or opinion, or the dissemination thereof, whether in written, printed, graphic, or visual form, shall not constitute or be evidence of an unfair labor practice under any of the provisions of this Act, if such expression contains no threat of reprisal or force or promise of benefit.

(d) For the purposes of this section, to bargain collectively is the performance of the mutual obligation of the employer and

the representative of the employees to meet at reasonable times and confer in good faith with respect to wages, hours, and other terms and conditions of employment, or the negotiation of an agreement, or any question arising thereunder, and the execution of a written contract incorporating any agreement reached if requested by either party, but such obligation does not compel either party to agree to a proposal or require the making of a concession: *Provided*, That where there is in effect a collective-bargaining contract covering employees in an industry affecting commerce, the duty to bargain collectively shall also mean that no party to such contract shall terminate or modify such contract, unless the party desiring such termination or modification—

(1) serves a written notice upon the other party to the contract of the proposed termination or modification sixty days prior to the expiration date thereof, or in the event such contract contains no expiration date, sixty days prior to the time it is proposed to make such termination or modification;

(2) offers to meet and confer with the other party for the purpose of negotiating a new contract or a contract containing the proposed modifications;

(3) notifies the Federal Mediation and Conciliation Service within thirty days after such notice of the existence of a dispute, and simultaneously therewith notifies any State or Territorial agency established to mediate and conciliate disputes within the State or Territory where the dispute occurred, provided no agreement has been reached by that time; and

(4) continues in full force and effect, without resorting to strike or lock-out, all the terms and conditions of the existing contract for a period of sixty days after such notice is given or until the expiration date of such contract, whichever occurs later:

The duties imposed upon employers, employees, and labor organizations by paragraphs (2), (3), and (4) shall become inapplicable upon an intervening certification of the Board, under which the labor organization or individual, which is a party to the contract, has been superseded as or ceased to be the representative of the employees subject to the provisions of section 9(a), and the duties so imposed shall not be construed as requiring either party to discuss or agree to any modification of the terms and conditions contained in a contract for a fixed period, if such modification is to become effective before such terms and conditions can be reopened under the provisions of the contract. Any employee who engages in a strike within [the sixty-day] any notice period specified in this subsection, or who engages in any strike within the appropriate period specified in subsection (g) of this section, **shall lose his status as an employee of the employer engaged in the particular labor dispute, for the purposes of sections 8, 9, and 10 of this Act, but such loss of status for such employee shall terminate if and when he is reemployed by such employer.** Whenever the collective bargaining involves employees of a health care institution, the provisions of this section 8(d) shall be modified as follows:

(A) The notice of section 8(d)(1) shall be ninety days; the notice of section 8(d)(3) shall be sixty days; and the contract period of section 8(d)(4) shall be ninety days.

(B) Where the bargaining is for an initial agreement following certification or recognition, at least thirty days' notice of the existence of a dispute shall be given by the labor organization to the agencies set forth in section 8(d)(3).

(C) After notice is given to the Federal Mediation and Conciliation Service under either clause (A) or (B) of this sentence, the Service shall promptly communicate with the parties and use its best efforts, by mediation and conciliation, to bring them to agreement. The parties shall participate fully and promptly in such meetings as may be undertaken by the Service for the purpose of aiding in a settlement of the dispute.

(e) It shall be an unfair labor practice for any labor organization and any employer to enter into any contract or agreement, express or implied, whereby such employer ceases or refrains or agrees to cease or refrain from handling, using, selling, transporting or otherwise dealing in any of the products of any other employer, or to cease doing business with any other person, and any contract or agreement entered into heretofore or hereafter containing such an agreement shall be to such extent unenforceable and void: Provided, That nothing in this subsection (e) shall apply to an agreement between a labor organization and an employer in the construction industry relating to the contracting or subcontracting of work to be done at the site of the construction, alteration, painting, or repair of a building, structure, or other work: Provided further, That for the purposes of this subsection (e) and section 8(b)(4)(B) the terms "any employer", "any person engaged in commerce or an industry affecting commerce", and "any person" when used in relation to the terms "any other producer, processor, or manufacturer", "any other employer", or "any other person" shall not include persons in the relation of a jobber, manufacturer, contractor, or subcontractor working on the goods or premises of the jobber or manufacturer or performing parts of an integrated process of production in the apparel and clothing industry: Provided further, That nothing in this Act shall prohibit the enforcement of any agreement which is within the foregoing exception.

(f) It shall not be an unfair labor practice under subsections (a) and (b) of this section for an employer engaged primarily in the building and construction industry to make an agreement covering employees engaged (or who, upon their employment, will be engaged) in the building and construction industry with a labor organization of which building and construction employees are members (not established, maintained, or assisted by any action defined in section 8(a) of this Act as an unfair practice) because (1) the majority status of such labor organization has not been established under the provisions of section 9 of this Act lab prior to the making of such agreement, or (2) such agreement requires as a condition of employment, membership in such labor organization after the seventh day following the beginning of such employment or the effective date of the agreement, whichever is later, or (3) such agreement requires the employer to notify such labor organization of opportunities for employment with such employer, or gives such labor organization an opportunity to refer qualified applicants for such employment, or (4) such agreement specifies minimum training or experience qualifications for employment or provides for priority in opportunities for employment based upon length of service with such employer, in the industry or in the particular geographical area: Provided, That nothing in this subsection shall set aside the final proviso to section 8(a)(3) of this Act: Provided further, That any agreement which would be invalid, but for clause (1) of this subsection, shall not be a bar to a petition filed pursuant to section 9(c) or 9(e).*

(g) A labor organization before engaging in any strike, picketing, or other concerted refusal to work at any health care institution shall, not less than ten days prior to such action, notify the institution in writing and the Federal Mediation and Conciliation Service of that intention, except that in the case of bargaining for an initial agreement following certification or recognition the notice required by this subsection shall not be given until the expiration of the period specified in clause (B) of the last sentence of section 8(d) of this Act. The notice shall state the date and time that such action will commence. The notice, once given, may be extended by the written agreement of both parties.

REPRESENTATIVES AND ELECTIONS

Sec. 9. (a) Representatives designated or selected for the purposes of collective bargaining by the majority of the employees in a unit appropriate for such purposes, shall be the exclusive representatives of all the employees in such unit for the purposes of collective bargaining in respect to rates of pay, wages, hours of employment, or other conditions of employment: *Provided*, That any individual employee or a

* Sec. 8(f) was inserted in the Act by subsec. (a) of Sec. 705 of Public Law 86–257. Sec. 705(b) provides:

Nothing contained in the amendment made by subsection (a) shall be construed as authorizing the execution or application of agreements requiring membership in a labor organization as a condition of employment in any State or Territory in which such execution or application is prohibited by State or Territorial law.

group of employees shall have the right at any time to present grievances to their employer **and to have such grievances adjusted, without the intervention of the bargaining representative, as long as the adjustment is not inconsistent with the terms of a collective-bargaining contract or agreement then in effect: *Provided further*, That the bargaining representative has been given opportunity to be present at such adjustment.**

(b) The Board shall decide in each case whether, in order to assure to employees the fullest freedom in exercising the rights guaranteed by this Act, the unit appropriate for the purposes of collective bargaining shall be the employer unit, craft unit, plant unit, or subdivision thereof: ***Provided*, That the Board shall not (1) decide that any unit is appropriate for such purposes if such unit includes both professional employees and employees who are not professional employees unless a majority of such professional employees vote for inclusion in such unit; or (2) decide that any craft unit is inappropriate for such purposes on the ground that a different unit has been established by a prior Board determination, unless a majority of the employees in the proposed craft unit vote against separate representation or (3) decide that any unit is appropriate for such purposes if it includes, together with other employees, any individual employed as a guard to enforce against employees and other persons rules to protect property of the employer or to protect the safety of persons on the employer's premises; but no labor organization shall be certified as the representative of employees in a bargaining unit of guards if such organization admits to membership, or is affiliated directly or indirectly with an organization which admits to membership, employees other than guards.**

[(c) Whenever a question affecting commerce arises concerning the representation of employees, the Board may investigate such controversy and certify to the parties, in writing, the name or names of the representatives that have been designated or selected. In any such investigation, the Board shall provide for an appropriate hearing upon due notice, either in conjunction with a proceeding under section 10 or otherwise, and may take a secret ballot of employees, or utilize any other suitable method to ascertain such representatives.]

(c)(1) Whenever a petition shall have been filed, in accordance with such regulations as may be prescribed by the Board—

(A) by an employee or group of employees or any individual or labor organization acting in their behalf alleging that a substantial number of employees (i) wish to be represented for collective bargaining and that their employer declines to recognize their representative as the representative defined in section 9(a), or (ii) assert that the

individual or labor organization, which has been certified or is being currently recognized by their employer as the bargaining representative, is no longer a representative as defined in section 9(a); or

(B) by an employer, alleging that one or more individuals or labor organizations have presented to him a claim to be recognized as the representative defined in section 9(a);

the Board shall investigate such petition and if it has reasonable cause to believe that a question of representation affecting commerce exists shall provide for an appropriate hearing upon due notice. Such hearing may be conducted by an officer or employee of the regional office, who shall not make any recommendations with respect thereto. If the Board finds upon the record of such hearing that such a question of representation exists, it shall direct an election by secret ballot and shall certify the results thereof.

(2) In determining whether or not a question of representation affecting commerce exists, the same regulations and rules of decision shall apply irrespective of the identity of the persons filing the petition or the kind of relief sought and in no case shall the Board deny a labor organization a place on the ballot by reason of an order with respect to such labor organization or its predecessor not issued in conformity with section 10(c).

(3) No election shall be directed in any bargaining unit or any subdivision within which, in the preceding twelve-month period, a valid election shall have been held. Employees [on strike] *engaged in an economic strike* **who are not entitled to reinstatement shall [not] be eligible to vote** *under such regulations as the Board shall find are consistent with the purposes and provisions of this Act in any election conducted within twelve months after the commencement of the strike.* **In any election where none of the choices on the ballot receives a majority, a run-off shall be conducted, the ballot providing for a selection between the two choices receiving the largest and second largest number of valid votes cast in the election.**

(4) Nothing in this section shall be construed to prohibit the waiving of hearings by stipulation for the purpose of a consent election in conformity with regulations and rules of decision of the Board.

(5) In determining whether a unit is appropriate for the purposes specified in subsection (b) the extent to which the employees have organized shall not be controlling.

(d) Whenever an order of the Board made pursuant to section 10(c) is based in whole or in part upon facts certified following an investigation pursuant to subsection (c) of this section and there is a petition for the enforcement or review of such order, such certification and the record of such investigation shall be included in the transcript of the entire record required to be filed under section 10(e) or 10(f), and thereupon the decree of the court enforcing, modifying, or setting aside in whole or in part the order of the Board shall be made and entered upon the pleadings, testimony, and proceedings set forth in such transcript.

(e)*(1) Upon the filing with the Board, by 30 per centum or more of the employees in a bargaining unit covered by an agreement between their employer and a labor organization made pursuant to section 8(a)(3), of a petition alleging they desire that such authority be rescinded, the Board shall take a secret ballot of the employees in such unit, and shall certify the results thereof to such labor organization and to the employer.

(2) No election shall be conducted pursuant to this subsection in any bargaining unit or any subdivision within which, in the preceding twelve-month period, a valid election shall have been held.

[Subsections (f), (g) and (h) were deleted by the Labor-Management Reporting and Disclosure Act.]

PREVENTION OF UNFAIR LABOR PRACTICES

Sec. 10. (a) The Board is empowered, as hereinafter provided, to prevent any person from engaging in any unfair labor practice (listed in section 8) affecting commerce. This power shall not be affected by any other means of adjustment or prevention that has been or may be established by agreement, law, or otherwise: ***Provided*, That the Board is empowered by agreement with any agency of any State or Territory to cede to such agency jurisdiction over any cases in any industry (other than mining, manufacturing, communications, and transportation except where predominantly local in character) even though such cases may involve labor disputes affecting commerce, unless the provision of the State of Territorial statute applicable to the determination of such cases by such agency is inconsistent with the corresponding provision of this Act or has received a construction inconsistent therewith.**

(b) Whenever it is charged that any person has engaged in or is engaging in any such unfair labor practice, the Board, or any agent or agency designated by the Board for such purposes, shall have power to

* As enacted in 1947, Section 9(e) had three subsections. In 1951, the first subsection was deleted and the two remaining subsections were renumbered (1) and (2). 65 Stat. 601. The deleted subsection required, as a condition to the inclusion of a union-shop provision in a collective agreement, that a majority of employees authorize such inclusion in a Board-conducted election.

issue and cause to be served upon such person a complaint stating the charges in that respect, and containing a notice of hearing before the Board or a member thereof, or before a designated agent or agency, at a place therein fixed, not less than five days after the serving of said complaint: ***Provided*, That no complaint shall issue based upon any unfair labor practice occurring more than six months prior to the filing of the charge with the Board and the service of a copy thereof upon the person against whom such charge is made, unless the person aggrieved thereby was prevented from filing such charge by reason of service in the armed forces, in which event the six-month period shall be computed from the day of his discharge.** Any such complaint may be amended by the member, agent, or agency conducting the hearing or the Board in its discretion at any time prior to the issuance of an order based thereon. The person so complained of shall have the right to file an answer to the original or amended complaint and to appear in person or otherwise and give testimony at the place and time fixed in the complaint. In the discretion of the member, agent, or agency conducting the hearing or the Board, any other person may be allowed to intervene in the said proceeding and to present testimony. [In any such proceeding the rules of evidence prevailing in courts of law or equity shall not be controlling.] **Any such proceeding shall, so far as practicable, be conducted in accordance with the rules of evidence applicable in the district courts of the United States under the rules of civil procedure for the district courts of the United States, adopted by the Supreme Court of the United States pursuant to section 2072 of Title 28.**

(c) The testimony taken by such member, agent, or agency or the Board shall be reduced to writing and filed with the Board. Thereafter, in its discretion, the Board upon notice may take further testimony or hear argument. If upon [all] **the preponderance of** the testimony taken the Board shall be of the opinion that any person named in the complaint has engaged in or is engaging in any such unfair labor practice, then the Board shall state its findings of fact and shall issue and cause to be served on such person an order requiring such person to cease and desist from such unfair labor practice, and to take such affirmative action including reinstatement of employees with or without back pay, as will effectuate the policies of this Act: ***Provided*, That where an order directs reinstatement of an employee, back pay may be required of the employer or labor organization, as the case may be, responsible for the discrimination suffered by him: *And provided further*, That in determining whether a complaint shall issue alleging a violation of section 8(a)(1) or section 8(a)(2), and in deciding such cases, the same regulations and rules of decision shall apply irrespective of whether or not the labor organization affected is affiliated with a labor organization national or international in scope.** Such order may further require such person to make reports from time to time showing the extent to which it has complied with the order.

If upon [all] **the preponderance of** the testimony taken the Board shall not be of the opinion that the person named in the complaint has engaged in or is engaging in any such unfair labor practice, then the Board shall state its findings of fact and shall issue an order dismissing the said complaint. **No order of the Board shall require the reinstatement of any individual as an employee who has been suspended or discharged, or the payment to him of any back pay, if such individual was suspended or discharged for cause. In case the evidence is presented before a member of the Board, or before an administrative law judge or judges* thereof, such member, or such judge or judges, as the case may be, shall issue and cause to be served on the parties to the proceeding a proposed report, together with a recommended order, which shall be filed with the Board, and if no exceptions are filed within twenty days after service thereof upon such parties, or within such further period as the Board may authorize, such recommended order shall become the order of the Board and become effective as therein prescribed.**

(d) Until [**a transcript of**] the record in a case shall have been filed in a court, as hereinafter provided, the Board may at any time, upon reasonable notice and in such manner as it shall deem proper, modify or set aside, in whole or in part, any finding or order made or issued by it.

(e) The Board shall have power to petition any [United States] court of appeals of the United States [(including the United States court of appeals for the District of Columbia)] or if all the courts of appeals to which application may be made are in vacation, any [United States] district court *of the United States*, within any circuit or district, respectively, wherein the unfair labor practice in question occurred or wherein such person resides or transacts business, for the enforcement of such order and for appropriate temporary relief or restraining order, and shall [certify and] file in the court [a transcript of] the [entire] record in the proceedings, [including the pleadings and testimony upon which such order was entered and the findings and order of the Board.] *as printed in section 2112 of Title 28.* Upon [such filing] *the filing of such petition*, the court shall cause notice thereof to be served upon such person, and thereupon shall have jurisdiction of the proceeding and of the question determined therein, and shall have power to grant such temporary relief or restraining order as it deems just and proper, and to make and enter [upon the pleadings, testimony, and proceedings set forth in such transcript] a decree enforcing, modifying, and enforcing as so modified, or setting aside in whole or in part the order of the Board. No objection that has not been urged before the Board, its member, agent, or agency, shall be considered by the court, unless the failure or neglect to urge such objection shall be excused because of extraordinary circumstances. The findings of the Board with respect to questions of fact

* The title "administrative law judge" was adopted in 5 U.S.C. § 3105, in 1972.

if supported by **substantial** evidence **on the record considered as a whole** shall be conclusive. If either party shall apply to the court for leave to adduce additional evidence and shall show to the satisfaction of the court that such additional evidence is material and that there were reasonable grounds for the failure to adduce such evidence in the hearing before the Board, its member, agent, or agency, the court may order such additional evidence to be taken before the Board, its member, agent, or agency, and to be made a part of [the transcript] *record.* The Board may modify its findings as to the facts, or make new findings, by reason of additional evidence so taken and filed, and it shall file such modified or new findings, which findings with respect to questions of fact if supported by **substantial** evidence **on the record considered as a whole** shall be conclusive, and shall file its recommendations, if any, for the modification or setting aside of its original order. *Upon the filing of the record with it* the jurisdiction of the court shall be exclusive and its judgment and decree shall be final, except that the same shall be subject to review by the appropriate circuit court of appeals if application was made to the district court as hereinabove provided, and by the Supreme Court of the United States upon writ of certiorari or certification as provided in section 1254 of Title 28.

(f) Any person aggrieved by a final order of the Board granting or denying in whole or in part the relief sought may obtain a review of such order in any United States court of appeals in the circuit wherein the unfair labor practice in question was alleged to have been engaged in or wherein such person resides or transacts business, or in the United States Court of Appeals for the District of Columbia, by filing in such court a written petition praying that the order of the Board be modified or set aside. A copy of such petition shall be forthwith [served upon the Board] *transmitted by the clerk of the court to the Board* and thereupon the aggrieved party shall file in the court [a transcript of] the [entire] record in the proceeding, certified by the Board, [including the pleading and testimony upon which the order complained of was entered, and the findings and order of the Board.] *as provided in section 2112 of Title 28.* Upon [such filing,] *the filing of such petition,* the court shall proceed in the same manner as in the case of an application by the Board under subsection (e) *of this section,* and shall have the same exclusive jurisdiction to grant to the Board such temporary relief or restraining order as it deems just and proper, and in like manner to make and enter a decree enforcing, modifying, and enforcing as so modified, or setting aside in whole or in part the order of the Board; the findings of the Board with respect to questions of fact if supported by **substantial** evidence **on the record considered as a whole** shall in like manner be conclusive.

(g) The commencement of proceedings under subsection (e) or (f) of this section shall not, unless specifically ordered by the court, operate as a stay of the Board's order.

(h) When granting appropriate temporary relief or a restraining order, or making and entering a decree enforcing, modifying, and enforcing as so modified, or setting aside in whole or in part an order of the Board, as provided in this section, the jurisdiction of courts sitting in equity shall not be limited by sections 101 to 115 of title 29, United States Code.*

(i) [Repealed.]

(j) The Board shall have power, upon issuance of a complaint as provided in subsection (b) charging that any person has engaged in or is engaging in an unfair labor practice, to petition any United States district court within any district wherein the unfair labor practice in question is alleged to have occurred or wherein such person resides or transacts business, for appropriate temporary relief or restraining order. Upon the filing of any such petition the court shall cause notice thereof to be served upon such person, and thereupon shall have jurisdiction to grant to the Board such temporary relief or restraining order as it deems just and proper.

(k) Whenever it is charged that any person has engaged in an unfair labor practice within the meaning of paragraph (4)(D) of section 8(b), the Board is empowered and directed to hear and determine the dispute out of which such unfair labor practice shall have arisen, unless, within ten days after notice that such charge has been filed, the parties to such dispute submit to the Board satisfactory evidence that they have adjusted, or agreed upon methods for the voluntary adjustment of, the dispute. Upon compliance by the parties to the dispute with the decision of the Board or upon such voluntary adjustment of the dispute, such charge shall be dismissed.

(*l*) Whenever it is charged that any person has engaged in an unfair labor practice within the meaning of paragraph (4)(A), (B), or (C) of section 8(b), *or section 8(e) or section 8(b)(7)* **the preliminary investigation of such charge shall be made forthwith and given priority over all other cases except cases of like character in the office where it is filed or to which it is referred. If, after such investigation, the officer or regional attorney to whom the matter may be referred has reasonable cause to believe such charge is true and that a complaint should issue, he shall, on behalf of the Board, petition any United States district court within any district where the unfair labor practice in question has occurred, is alleged to have occurred, or wherein such person resides or transacts business, for appropriate injunctive relief pending the final adjudication of the Board with respect to such matter. Upon the filing of any such petition the district**

* The Norris-LaGuardia Act of 1932.

court shall have jurisdiction to grant such injunctive relief or temporary restraining order as it deems just and proper, notwithstanding any other provision of law: *Provided further*, That no temporary restraining order shall be issued without notice unless a petition alleges that substantial and irreparable injury to the charging party will be unavoidable and such temporary restraining order shall be effective for no longer than five days and will become void at the expiration of such period[.]: *Provided further, That such officer or regional attorney shall not apply for any restraining order under section 8(b)(7) if a charge against the employer under section 8(a)(2) has been filed and after the preliminary investigation, he has reasonable cause to believe that such charge is true and that a complaint should issue.* **Upon filing of any such petition the courts shall cause notice thereof to be served upon any person involved in the charge and such person, including the charging party, shall be given an opportunity to appear by counsel and present any relevant testimony: *Provided further*, That for the purposes of this subsection district courts shall be deemed to have jurisdiction of a labor organization (1) in the district in which such organization maintains its principal office, or (2) in any district in which its duly authorized officers or agents are engaged in promoting or protecting the interests of employee members. The service of legal process upon such officer or agent shall constitute service upon the labor organization and make such organization a party to the suit. In situations where such relief is appropriate the procedure specified herein shall apply to charges with respect to sections 8(b)(4)(D).**

(m) Whenever it is charged that any person has engaged in an unfair labor practice within the meaning of subsection (a)(3) or (b)(2) of section 8, such charge shall be given priority over all other cases except cases of like character in the office where it is filed or to which it is referred and cases given priority under subsection (l) of this section.

INVESTIGATORY POWERS

Sec. 11. For the purpose of all hearings and investigations, which, in the opinion of the Board, are necessary and proper for the exercise of the powers vested in it by section 9 and section 10—

(1) The Board, or its duly authorized agents or agencies, shall at all reasonable times have access to, for the purpose of examination, and the right to copy any evidence of any person being investigated or proceeded against that relates to any matter under investigation or in question. The Board, or any member thereof, shall upon application of any party to such proceedings, forthwith issue to such party subpoenas requiring the attendance and testimony of witnesses or the production of any evidence in such proceeding or investigation requested in such application. **Within five days after the service of a subpoena on any person**

requiring the production of any evidence in his possession or under his control, such person may petition the Board to revoke, and the Board shall revoke, such subpoena if in its opinion the evidence whose production is required does not relate to any matter under investigation, or any matter in question in such proceedings, or if in its opinion such subpoena does not describe with sufficient particularity the evidence whose production is required. Any member of the Board, or any agent or agency designated by the Board for such purposes, may administer oaths and affirmations, examine witnesses, and receive evidence. Such attendance of witnesses and the production of such evidence may be required from any place in the United States or any Territory or possession thereof, at any designated place of hearing.

(2) In case of contumacy or refusal to obey a subpoena issued to any person, any district court of the United States or the United States courts of any Territory or possession, or the District Court of the United States for the District of Columbia, within the jurisdiction of which the inquiry is carried on or within the jurisdiction of which said person guilty of contumacy or refusal to obey is found or resides or transacts business, upon application by the Board shall have jurisdiction to issue to such person an order requiring such person to appear before the Board, its member, agent, or agency, there to produce evidence if so ordered, or there to give testimony touching the matter under investigation or in question; and any failure to obey such order of the court may be punished by said court as a contempt thereof.

[(3) No person shall be excused from attending and testifying or from producing books, records, correspondence, documents, or other evidence in obedience to the subpoena of the Board, on the ground that the testimony or evidence required of him may tend to incriminate him or subject him to a penalty or forfeiture; but no individual shall be prosecuted or subjected to any penalty or forfeiture for or on account of any transaction, matter, or thing concerning which he is compelled, after having claimed his privilege against self-incrimination, to testify or produce evidence, except that such individual so testifying shall not be exempt from prosecution and punishment for perjury committed in so testifying.]*

(4) Complaints, orders, and other process and papers of the Board, its member, agent, or agency, may be served either personally or by registered mail or by telegraph or by leaving a copy thereof at the principal office or place of business of the person required to be served. The verified return by the individual so serving the same setting forth the manner of such service shall be proof of the same, and the return post office receipt or telegraph receipt therefor when registered and mailed or telegraphed as aforesaid shall be proof of service of the same. Witnesses

* Section 11(3) was repealed in 1970, by 84 Stat. 930. Similar immunity provisions were substituted; see 18 U.S.C. §§ 6001, 6002, 6004 (1970).

summoned before the Board, its member, agent, or agency, shall be paid the same fees and mileage that are paid witnesses in the courts of the United States, and witnesses whose depositions are taken and the persons taking the same shall severally be entitled to the same fees as are paid for like services in the courts of the United States.

(5) All process of any court to which application may be made under this Act may be served in the judicial district wherein the defendant or other person required to be served resides or may be found.

(6) The several departments and agencies of the Government, when directed by the President, shall furnish the Board, upon its request, all records, papers, and information in their possession relating to any matter before the Board.

Sec. 12. Any person who shall willfully resist, prevent, impede, or interfere with any member of the Board or any of its agents or agencies in the performance of duties pursuant to this Act shall be punished by a fine of not more than $5,000 or by imprisonment for not more than one year, or both.

LIMITATIONS

Sec. 13. Nothing in this Act, **except as specifically provided for herein,** shall be construed so as either to interfere with or impede or diminish in any way the right to strike, **or to affect the limitations or qualifications on that right.**

Sec. 14. (a) Nothing herein shall prohibit any individual employed as a supervisor from becoming or remaining a member of a labor organization, but no employer subject to this Act shall be compelled to deem individuals defined herein as supervisors as employees for the purpose of any law, either national or local, relating to collective bargaining.

(b) Nothing in this Act shall be construed as authorizing the execution or application of agreements requiring membership in a labor organization as a condition of employment in any State or Territory in which such execution or application is prohibited by State or Territorial law.

(c)(1) The Board, in its discretion, may, by rule of decision or by published rules adopted pursuant to the Administrative Procedure Act, decline to assert jurisdiction over any labor dispute involving any class or category of employers, where, in the opinion of the Board, the effect of such labor dispute on commerce is not sufficiently substantial to warrant the exercise of its jurisdiction: Provided, That the Board shall not decline to assert jurisdiction over any labor dispute over which it would assert jurisdiction under the standards prevailing upon August 1, 1959.

(2) Nothing in this Act shall be deemed to prevent or bar any agency or the courts of any State or Territory (including the Commonwealth of Puerto Rico, Guam, and the Virgin Islands), from assuming and asserting

jurisdiction over labor disputes over which the Board declines, pursuant to paragraph (1) of this subsection, to assert jurisdiction.

Sec. 15. [Reference to repealed provisions of the Bankruptcy Act.]

Sec. 16. If any provision of this Act, or the application of such provision to any person or circumstances, shall be held invalid, the remainder of this Act, or the application of such provision to persons or circumstances other than those as to which it is held invalid, shall not be affected thereby.

Sec. 17. This Act may be cited as the "National Labor Relations Act."

Sec. 18. [This section, which refers to the now-repealed Sections 9(f), (g), (h), is omitted.]

INDIVIDUALS WITH RELIGIOUS CONVICTIONS

Sec. 19. Any employee who is a member of and adheres to established and traditional tenets or teachings of a bona fide religion, body, or sect which has historically held conscientious objections to joining or financially supporting labor organizations shall not be required to join or financially support any labor organization as a condition of employment; except that such employee may be required in a contract between such employee's employer and a labor organization in lieu of periodic dues and initiation fees, to pay sums equal to such dues and initiation fees to a nonreligious, nonlabor organization charitable fund exempt from taxation under section 501(c)(3) of title 26 of the Internal Revenue Code [section 501(c)(3) of title 26], chosen by such employee from a list of at least three such funds, designated in such contract or if the contract fails to designate such funds, then to any such fund chosen by the employee. If such employee who holds conscientious objections pursuant to this section requests the labor organization to use the grievance-arbitration procedure on the employee's behalf, the labor organization is authorized to charge the employee for the reasonable cost of using such procedure.*

* This section was added by Pub.L. 93–360, July 26, 1974, 88 Stat. 397, and amended, Pub.L. 96–593, Dec. 24, 1980, 94 Stat. 3452.

LABOR MANAGEMENT RELATIONS ACT

61 Stat. 136 (1947), as amended; 29 U.S.C. §§ 141–97 (1988).

SHORT TITLE AND DECLARATION OF POLICY

Sec. 1. (a) This Act may be cited as the "Labor Management Relations Act, 1947."

(b) Industrial strife which interferes with the normal flow of commerce and with the full production of articles and commodities for commerce, can be avoided or substantially minimized if employers, employees, and labor organizations each recognize under law one another's legitimate rights in their relations with each other, and above all recognize under law that neither party has any right in its relations with any other to engage in acts or practices which jeopardize the public health, safety, or interest.

It is the purpose and policy of this Act, in order to promote the full flow of commerce, to prescribe the legitimate rights of both employees and employers in their relations affecting commerce, to provide orderly and peaceful procedures for preventing the interference by either with the legitimate rights of the other, to protect the rights of individual employees in their relations with labor organizations whose activities affect commerce, to define and proscribe practices on the part of labor and management which affect commerce and are inimical to the general welfare, and to protect the rights of the public in connection with labor disputes affecting commerce.

TITLE I

AMENDMENT OF NATIONAL LABOR RELATIONS ACT

Sec. 101. The National Labor Relations Act is hereby amended to read as follows: [The text of the National Labor Relations Act as amended is set forth supra.]

TITLE II

CONCILIATION OF LABOR DISPUTES IN INDUSTRIES AFFECTING COMMERCE; NATIONAL EMERGENCIES

Sec. 201. That it is the policy of the United States that—

(a) sound and stable industrial peace and the advancement of the general welfare, health, and safety of the Nation and of the best interests of employers and employees can most satisfactorily be secured by the settlement of issues between employers and employees through the processes of conference and collective bargaining between employers and the representatives of their employees;

(b) the settlement of issues between employers and employees through collective bargaining may be advanced by making available full and adequate governmental facilities for conciliation, mediation, and voluntary arbitration to aid and encourage employers and the representatives of their employees to reach and maintain agreements concerning rates of pay, hours, and working conditions, and to make all reasonable efforts to settle their differences by mutual agreement reached through conferences and collective bargaining or by such methods as may be provided for in any applicable agreement for the settlement of disputes; and

(c) certain controversies which arise between parties to collective-bargaining agreements may be avoided or minimized by making available full and adequate governmental facilities for furnishing assistance to employers and the representatives of their employees in formulating for inclusion within such agreements provision for adequate notice of any proposed changes in the terms of such agreements, for the final adjustment of grievances or questions regarding the application or interpretation of such agreements, and other provisions designed to prevent the subsequent arising of such controversies.

Sec. 202. (a) There is hereby created an independent agency to be known as the Federal Mediation and Conciliation Service (herein referred to as the "Service," except that for sixty days after the date of the enactment of this Act such term shall refer to the Conciliation Service of the Department of Labor). The Service shall be under the direction of a Federal Mediation and Conciliation Director (hereinafter referred to as the "Director"), who shall be appointed by the President by and with the advice and consent of the Senate. The Director shall not engage in any other business, vocation, or employment.

(b) The Director is authorized, subject to the civil-service laws, to appoint such clerical and other personnel as may be necessary for the execution of the functions of the Service, and shall fix their compensation in accordance with chapter 51 and subchapter III of chapter 53 of title 5, and may, without regard to the provisions of the civil-service laws, appoint such conciliators and mediators as may be necessary to carry out the functions of the Service. The Director is authorized to make such expenditures for supplies, facilities, and services as he deems necessary. Such expenditures shall be allowed and paid upon presentation of itemized vouchers therefor approved by the Director or by any employee designated by him for that purpose.

(c) The principal office of the Service shall be in the District of Columbia, but the Director may establish regional offices convenient to localities in which labor controversies are likely to arise. The Director may by order, subject to revocation at any time, delegate any authority and discretion conferred upon him by this Act to any regional director, or other officer or employee of the Service. The Director may establish suitable procedures for cooperation with State and local mediation agencies. The Director shall make an annual report in writing to Congress at the end of the fiscal year.

(d) All mediation and conciliation functions of the Secretary of Labor or the United States Conciliation Service under section 8 of the Act entitled "An Act to create a Department of Labor," approved March 4, 1913 (U.S.C., title 29, sec. 51), and all functions of the United States Conciliation Service under any other law are transferred to the Federal Mediation and Conciliation Service, together with the personnel and records of the United States Conciliation Service. Such transfer shall take effect upon the sixtieth day after June 23, 1947. Such transfer shall not affect any proceedings pending before the United States Conciliation Service or any certification, order, rule, or regulation theretofore made by it or by the Secretary of Labor. The Director and the Service shall not be subject in any way to the jurisdiction or authority of the Secretary of Labor or any official or division of the Department of Labor.

FUNCTIONS OF THE SERVICE

Sec. 203. (a) It shall be the duty of the Service, in order to prevent or minimize interruptions of the free flow of commerce growing out of labor disputes, to assist parties to labor disputes in industries affecting commerce to settle such disputes through conciliation and mediation.

(b) The Service may proffer its services in any labor dispute in any industry affecting commerce, either upon its own motion or upon the request of one or more of the parties to the dispute, whenever in its judgment such dispute threatens to cause a substantial interruption of commerce. The Director and the Service are directed to avoid attempting to mediate disputes which would have only a minor effect on interstate commerce if State or other conciliation services are available to the parties. Whenever the Service does proffer its services in any dispute, it shall be the duty of the Service promptly to put itself in communication with the parties and to use its best efforts, by mediation and conciliation, to bring them to agreement.

(c) If the Director is not able to bring the parties to agreement by conciliation within a reasonable time, he shall seek to induce the parties voluntarily to seek other means of settling the dispute without resort to strike, lock-out, or other coercion, including submission to the employees in the bargaining unit of the employer's last offer of settlement for approval or rejection in a secret ballot. The failure or refusal of either party to agree to any procedure suggested by the Director shall not be deemed a violation of any duty or obligation imposed by this Act.

(d) Final adjustment by a method agreed upon by the parties is hereby declared to be the desirable method for settlement of grievance disputes arising over the application or interpretation of an existing collective-bargaining agreement. The Service is directed to make its conciliation and mediation services available in the settlement of such grievance disputes only as a last resort and in exceptional cases.

(e)* The Service is authorized and directed to encourage and support the establishment and operation of joint labor management activities conducted by plant, area, and industrywide committees designed to improve labor management relationships, job security and organizational effectiveness, in accordance with the provisions of section 205A.

Sec. 204. (a) In order to prevent or minimize interruptions of the free flow of commerce growing out of labor disputes, employers and employees and their representatives, in any industry affecting commerce, shall—

(1) exert every reasonable effort to make and maintain agreements concerning rates of pay, hours, and working conditions, including provision for adequate notice of any proposed change in the terms of such agreements;

(2) whenever a dispute arises over the terms or application of a collective-bargaining agreement and a conference is requested by a party or prospective party thereto, arrange promptly for such a conference to be held and endeavor in such conference to settle such dispute expeditiously; and

(3) in case such dispute is not settled by conference, participate fully and promptly in such meetings as may be undertaken by the Service under this Act for the purpose of aiding in a settlement of the dispute.

Sec. 205. (a) There is created a National Labor-Management Panel which shall be composed of twelve members appointed by the President, six of whom shall be selected from among persons outstanding in the field of management and six of whom shall be selected from among persons outstanding in the field of labor. Each member shall hold office for a term of three years, except that any member appointed to fill a vacancy occurring prior to the expiration of the term for which his predecessor was appointed shall be appointed for the remainder of such term, and the terms of office of the members first taking office shall expire, as designated by the President at the time of appointment, four at the end of the first year, four at the end of the second year, and four at the end of the third year after the date of appointment. Members of the panel, when serving on business of the panel, shall be paid compensation at the rate of $25 per day, and shall also be entitled to receive an allowance for actual and necessary travel and subsistence expenses while so serving away from their places of residence.

(b) It shall be the duty of the panel, at the request of the Director, to advise in the avoidance of industrial controversies and the manner in

---

* Subsection (e) was added in 1978, by Pub.L. 95–524, § 6(c)(1), 92 Stat. 2020.

which mediation and voluntary adjustment shall be administered, particularly with reference to controversies affecting the general welfare of the country.

Sec. 205A.* **(a)**(1) The Service is authorized and directed to provide assistance in the establishment and operation of plant, area and industrywide labor management committees which—

(A) have been organized jointly by employers and labor organizations representing employees in that plant, area, or industry; and

(B) are established for the purpose of improving labor management relationships, job security, organizational effectiveness, enhancing economic development or involving workers in decisions affecting their jobs including improving communication with respect to subjects of mutual interest and concern.

(2) The Service is authorized and directed to enter into contracts and to make grants, where necessary or appropriate, to fulfill its responsibilities under this section.

(b)(1) No grant may be made, no contract may be entered into and no other assistance may be provided under the provisions of this section to a plant labor management committee unless the employees in that plant are represented by a labor organization and there is in effect at that plant a collective bargaining agreement.

(2) No grant may be made, no contract may be entered into and no other assistance may be provided under the provisions of this section to an area or industrywide labor management committee unless its participants include any labor organizations certified or recognized as the representative of the employees of an employer participating in such committee. Nothing in this clause shall prohibit participation in an area or industrywide committee by an employer whose employees are not represented by a labor organization.

(3) No grant may be made under the provisions of this section to any labor management committee which the Service finds to have as one of its purposes the discouragement of the exercise of rights contained in section 7 of the National Labor Relations Act (29 U.S.C. § 157) [section 157 of this title], or the interference with collective bargaining in any plant, or industry.

(c) The Service shall carry out the provisions of this section through an office established for that purpose.

(d) There are authorized to be appropriated to carry out the provisions of this section $10,000,000 for the fiscal year 1979, and such sums as may be necessary thereafter.

* This section was added in 1978, by Pub.L. 95–524, § 6(c)(2), 92 Stat. 2020.

NATIONAL EMERGENCIES

Sec. 206. Whenever in the opinion of the President of the United States, a threatened or actual strike or lock-out affecting an entire industry or a substantial part thereof engaged in trade, commerce, transportation, transmission, or communication among the several States or with foreign nations, or engaged in the production of goods for commerce, will, if permitted to occur or to continue, imperil the national health or safety, he may appoint a board of inquiry to inquire into the issues involved in the dispute and to make a written report to him within such time as he shall prescribe. Such report shall include a statement of the facts with respect to the dispute, including each party's statement of its position but shall not contain any recommendations. The President shall file a copy of such report with the Service and shall make its contents available to the public.

Sec. 207. (a) A board of inquiry shall be composed of a chairman and such other members as the President shall determine, and shall have power to sit and act in any place within the United States and to conduct such hearings either in public or in private, as it may deem necessary or proper, to ascertain the facts with respect to the causes and circumstances of the dispute.

(b) Members of a board of inquiry shall receive compensation at the rate of $50 for each day actually spent by them in the work of the board, together with necessary travel and subsistence expenses.

(c) For the purpose of any hearing or inquiry conducted by any board appointed under this title, the provisions of sections 9 and 10 (relating to the attendance of witnesses and the production of books, papers, and documents) of the Federal Trade Commission Act of September 16, 1914, as amended (U.S.C. 19, title 15, secs. 49 and 50, as amended), are made applicable to the powers and duties of such board.

Sec. 208. (a) Upon receiving a report from a board of inquiry the President may direct the Attorney General to petition any district court of the United States having jurisdiction of the parties to enjoin such strike or lock-out or the continuing thereof, and if the court finds that such threatened or actual strike or lock-out—

(i) affects an entire industry or a substantial part thereof engaged in trade, commerce, transportation, transmission, or communication among the several States or with foreign nations, or engaged in the production of goods for commerce; and

(ii) if permitted to occur or to continue, will imperil the national health or safety, it shall have jurisdiction to enjoin any such strike or lock-out, or the continuing thereof, and to make such other orders as may be appropriate.

(b) In any case, the provisions of the Act of March 23, 1932, entitled "An Act to amend the Judicial Code and to define and limit the jurisdiction of courts sitting in equity, and for other purposes," shall not be applicable.

(c) The order or orders of the court shall be subject to review by the appropriate United States court of appeals and by the Supreme Court upon writ of certiorari or certification as provided in sections 239 and 240 of the Judicial Code, as amended (U.S.C., title 29, secs. 346 and 347).

Sec. 209. (a) Whenever a district court has issued an order under section 208 enjoining acts or practices which imperil or threaten to imperil the national health or safety, it shall be the duty of the parties to the labor dispute giving rise to such order to make every effort to adjust and settle their differences, with the assistance of the Service created by this Act. Neither party shall be under any duty to accept, in whole or in part, any proposal of settlement made by the Service.

(b) Upon the issuance of such order, the President shall reconvene the board of inquiry which has previously reported with respect to the dispute. At the end of a sixty-day period (unless the dispute has been settled by that time), the board of inquiry shall report to the President the current position of the parties and the efforts which have been made for settlement, and shall include a statement by each party of its position and a statement of the employer's last offer of settlement. The President shall make such report available to the public. The National Labor Relations Board, within the succeeding fifteen days, shall take a secret ballot of the employees of each employer involved in the dispute on the question of whether they wish to accept the final offer of settlement made by their employer as stated by him and shall certify the results thereof to the Attorney General within five days thereafter.

Sec. 210. Upon the certification of the results of such ballot or upon a settlement being reached, whichever happens sooner, the Attorney General shall move the court to discharge the injunction, which motion shall then be granted and the injunction discharged. When such motion is granted, the President shall submit to the Congress a full and comprehensive report of the proceedings, including the findings of the board of inquiry and the ballot taken by the National Labor Relations Board, together with such recommendations as he may see fit to make for consideration and appropriate action.

COMPILATION OF COLLECTIVE BARGAINING AGREEMENTS, ETC.

Sec. 211. (a) For the guidance and information of interested representatives of employers, employees, and the general public, the Bureau of Labor Statistics of the Department of Labor shall maintain a file of copies of all available collective-bargaining agreements and other available agreements and actions thereunder settling or adjusting labor disputes. Such file shall be open to inspection under appropriate conditions prescribed by the Secretary of Labor, except that no specific information submitted in confidence shall be disclosed.

(b) The Bureau of Labor Statistics in the Department of Labor is authorized to furnish upon request of the Service, or employers, employees, or their representatives, all available data and factual information which may aid in the settlement of any labor dispute, except that no specific information submitted in confidence shall be disclosed.

EXEMPTION OF RAILWAY LABOR ACT

Sec. 212. The provisions of this title shall not be applicable with respect to any matter which is subject to the provisions of the Railway Labor Act, as amended from time to time.

CONCILIATION OF LABOR DISPUTES IN THE HEALTH CARE INDUSTRY

Sec. 213. (a) If, in the opinion of the Director of the Federal Mediation and Conciliation Service a threatened or actual strike or lockout affecting a health care institution will, if permitted to occur or to continue, substantially interrupt the delivery of health care in the locality concerned, the Director may further assist in the resolution of the impasse by establishing within 30 days after the notice to the Federal Mediation and Conciliation Service under clause (A) of the last sentence of section 8(d) (which is required by clause (3) of such section 8(d)), or within 10 days after the notice under clause (B), an impartial Board of Inquiry to investigate the issues involved in the dispute and to make a written report thereon to the parties within fifteen (15) days after the establishment of such a Board. The written report shall contain the findings of fact together with the Board's recommendations for settling the dispute, with the objective of achieving a prompt, peaceful and just settlement of the dispute. Each such Board shall be composed of such number of individuals as the Director may deem desirable. No member appointed under this section shall have any interest or involvement in the health care institutions or the employee organizations involved in the dispute.

(b)(1) Members of any board established under this section who are otherwise employed by the Federal Government shall serve without compensation but shall be reimbursed for travel, subsistence, and other necessary expenses incurred by them in carrying out its duties under this section.

(2) Members of any board established under this section who are not subject to paragraph (1) shall receive compensation at a rate prescribed by the Director but not to exceed the daily rate prescribed for GS-18 of the General Schedule under section 5332 of title 5, United States Code, including travel for each day they are engaged in the performance of their duties under this section and shall be entitled to reimbursement for travel, subsistence, and other necessary expenses incurred by them in carrying out their duties under this section.

(c) After the establishment of a board under subsection (a) of this section and for 15 days after any such board has issued its report, no change in the status quo in effect prior to the expiration of the contract in the case of negotiations for a contract renewal, or in effect prior to the time of the impasse in the case of an initial bargaining negotiation, except by agreement, shall be made by the parties to the controversy.

(d) There are authorized to be appropriated such sums as may be necessary to carry out the provisions of this section.

TITLE III

SUITS BY AND AGAINST LABOR ORGANIZATIONS

Sec. 301. (a) Suits for violation of contracts between an employer and a labor organization representing employees in an industry affecting commerce as defined in this Act, or between any such labor organizations, may be brought in any district court of the United States having jurisdiction of the parties, without respect to the amount in controversy or without regard to the citizenship of the parties.

(b) Any labor organization which represents employees in an industry affecting commerce as defined in this Act and any employer whose activities affect commerce as defined in this Act shall be bound by the acts of its agents. Any such labor organization may sue or be sued as an entity and in behalf of the employees whom it represents in the courts of the United States. Any money judgment against a labor organization in a district court of the United States shall be enforceable only against the organization as an entity and against its assets, and shall not be enforceable against any individual member or his assets.

(c) For the purposes of actions and proceedings by or against labor organizations in the district courts of the United States, district courts shall be deemed to have jurisdiction of a labor organization (1) in the district in which such organization maintains its principal office, or (2) in any district in which its duly authorized officers or agents are engaged in representing or acting for employee members.

(d) The service of summons, subpoena, or other legal process of any court of the United States upon an officer or agent of a labor organization, in his capacity as such, shall constitute service upon the labor organization.

(e) For the purposes of this section, in determining whether any person is acting as an "agent" of another person so as to make such other person responsible for his acts, the question of whether the specific acts performed were actually authorized or subsequently ratified shall not be controlling.

RESTRICTIONS ON PAYMENTS TO EMPLOYEE REPRESENTATIVES

Sec. 302. (a) It shall be unlawful for any employer or association of employers or any person who acts as a labor relations expert, adviser, or consultant to an employer or who acts in the interest of an employer to pay, lend, or deliver, or agree to pay, lend, or deliver, any money or other thing of value—

(1) to any representative of any of his employees who are employed in an industry affecting commerce; or

(2) to any labor organization, or any officer or employee thereof, which represents, seeks to represent, or would admit to membership, any of the employees of such employer who are employed in an industry affecting commerce; or

(3) to any employee or group or committee of employees of such employer employed in an industry affecting commerce in excess of their normal compensation for the purpose of causing such employee or group or committee directly or indirectly to influence any other employees in the exercise of the right to organize and bargain collectively through representatives of their own choosing; or

(4) to any officer or employee of a labor organization engaged in an industry affecting commerce with intent to influence him in respect to any of his actions, decisions, or duties as a representative of employees or as such officer or employee of such labor organization.

(b)(1) It shall be unlawful for any person to request, demand, receive, or accept, or agree to receive or accept, any payment, loan or delivery of any money or other thing of value prohibited by subsection (a).

(2) It shall be unlawful for any labor organization, or for any person acting as an officer, agent, representative, or employee of such labor organization, to demand or accept from the operator of any motor vehicle (as defined in part II of the Interstate Commerce Act) employed in the transportation of property in commerce, or the employer of any such operator, any money or other thing of value payable to such organization or to an officer, agent, representative or employee thereof as a fee or charge for the unloading, or in connection with the unloading, of the cargo of such vehicle: *Provided*, That nothing in this paragraph shall be construed to make unlawful any payment by an employer to any of his employees as compensation for their services as employees.

(c) The provisions of this section shall not be applicable (1) in respect to any money or other thing of value payable by an employer to any of his employees whose established duties include acting openly for such employer in matters of labor relations or personnel administration or to any representative of his employees, or to any officer or employee of a labor organization, who is also an employee or former employee of such employer, as compensation for, or by reason of, his service as an employee of such employer; (2) with respect to the payment or delivery of any money or other thing of value in satisfaction of a judgment of any court or a decision or award of an arbitrator or impartial chairman or in compromise, adjustment, settlement, or release of any claim, complaint, grievance, or dispute in the absence of fraud or duress; (3) with respect to the sale or purchase of an article or commodity at the prevailing market price in the regular course of business; (4) with respect to money deducted from the wages of employees in payment of membership dues in a labor organization: *Provided*, That the employer has received from each employee, on whose account such deductions are made, a written assignment which shall not be irrevocable for a period of more than one year, or beyond the termination date of the applicable collective agreement, whichever occurs sooner; (5) with respect to money or other thing of value paid to a trust fund established by such representative, for the sole and exclusive benefit of the employees of such employer, and their families and dependents (or of such employees, families, and dependents jointly with the employees of other employers making similar payments, and their families and dependents): *Provided*, That (A) such payments are held in trust for the purpose of paying, either from principal or income or both, for the benefit of employees, their families and dependents, for medical or hospital care, pensions on retirement or death of employees, compensation for injuries or illness resulting from occupational activity or insurance to provide any of the foregoing, or unemployment benefits or life insurance, disability and sickness insurance, or accident insurance; (B) the detailed basis on which such payments are to be made is specified in a written agreement with the employer, and employees and employers are equally represented in the administration of such fund, together with such neutral persons as the representatives of the employers and the representatives of employees may agree upon and in the event the employer and employee groups deadlock on the administration of such fund and there are no neutral persons empowered to break such deadlock, such agreement provides that the two groups shall agree on an impartial umpire to decide such dispute, or in event of their failure to agree within a reasonable length of time, an impartial umpire to decide such dispute shall, on petition of either group, be appointed by the district court of the United States for the district where the trust fund has its principal office, and shall also contain provisions for an annual audit of the trust fund, a statement of the results of which shall be available for inspection by interested persons at the principal office of the trust fund and at such other places as may be designated in such written agreement; and (C) such payments as are intended to be used for the purpose of providing pensions or annuities for employees are made to a separate trust which provides that the funds held therein cannot be used for any purpose other than paying such pensions or annuities; (6) with respect to money or other thing of value paid by any employer to a trust fund established by such representative for the purpose of pooled vacation, holiday, severance or similar benefits, or defraying costs of apprenticeship or other training programs: *Provided*, That the requirements of clause (B) of the proviso to clause (5) of this subsection, shall apply to such trust funds; (7) with respect to money or other thing of value paid by any employer to a pooled or individual trust fund established by such representative for the purpose of (A) scholarships for the benefit of employees, their families, and dependents for study at educational institutions, (B) child care centers for pre-school and school age dependents of employees, or (C) financial assistance for employee housing: *Provided,* That no labor organization or employer shall be required to bargain on the establishment of any such trust fund, and refusal to do so shall not constitute an unfair labor practice: *Provided further,* That the requirements of clause (B) of the proviso to clause (5) of this subsection shall apply to such trust funds; (8) with respect to money or any other thing of value paid by any employer to a trust fund established by such representative for the purpose of defraying the costs of legal services for employees, their families, and dependents for counsel or plan of their choice: *Provided,* That the requirements of clause (B) of the proviso to clause (5) of this subsection shall apply to such trust funds: *Provided further,* That no such legal services shall be furnished: (A) to initiate any proceeding directed (i) against any such employer or its officers or agents except in workman's compensation cases, or (ii) against such labor organization, or its parent or subordinate bodies, or their officers or agents, or (iii) against any other employer or labor organization, or their officers or agents, in any matter arising under the National Labor Relations Act, as amended, or this Act; and (B) in any proceeding where a labor organization would be prohibited from defraying the costs of legal services by the provisions of the Labor-Management Reporting and Disclosure Act of 1959; or (9) with respect to money or other things of value paid by an employer to a plant, area or industry-wide labor management committee established for one or more of the purposes set forth in section 5(b) of the Labor Management Cooperation Act of 1978.*

(d)(1) Any person who participates in a transaction involving a payment, loan, or delivery of money or other thing of value to a labor organization in payment of membership dues or to a joint labor-management trust fund as defined by clause (B) of the proviso to clause (5) of subsection (c) of this section or to a plant, area, or industry-wide labor-management committee that is received and used by such labor organization, trust fund, or committee, which transaction does not satisfy all the applicable requirements of subsections (c)(4) through (c)(9) of this section, and willfully and with intent to benefit himself or to benefit other persons he knows are not permitted to receive a payment, loan, money, or other thing of value under subsections (c)(4) through (c)(9) violates this subsection, shall, upon conviction thereof, be guilty of a felony and be subject to a fine of not more than $15,000, or imprisoned for not more than five years, or both; but if the value of the amount of money or thing of value involved in any violation of the provisions of this section does not exceed $1,000, such person shall be guilty of a misdemeanor and be

* Sec. 302(c)(7) was added by Pub.L. 91–86, Oct. 14, 1969, 83 Stat. 133; Sec. 302(c)(8) by Pub.L. 93–95, Aug. 15, 1973, 87 Stat. 314; and Sec. 302(c)(9) by Pub.L. 95–524, Oct. 27, 1978, 92 Stat. 2021.

subject to a fine of not more than $10,000, or imprisoned for not more than one year, or both.

(2) Except for violations involving transactions covered by subsection (d)(1) of this section, any person who willfully violates this section shall, upon conviction thereof, be guilty of a felony and be subject to a fine of not more than $15,000 or imprisoned for not more than five years, or both; but if the value of the amount of money or thing of value involved in any violation of the provisions of this section does not exceed $1,000, such person shall be guilty of a misdemeanor and be subject to a fine of not more than $10,000, or imprisoned for not more than one year, or both.*

(e) The district courts of the United States and the United States courts of the Territories and possessions shall have jurisdiction, for cause shown, and subject to the provisions of section 17 (relating to notice to opposite party) of the Act entitled "An Act to supplement existing laws against unlawful restraints and monopolies, and for other purposes," approved October 15, 1914, as amended (U.S.C., title 28, section 381), to restrain violations of this section, without regard to the provisions of sections 6 and 20 of such Act of October 15, 1914, as amended (U.S.C., title 15, section 17, and title 29, section 52), and the provisions of the Act entitled "An Act to amend the Judicial Code and to define and limit the jurisdiction of courts sitting in equity, and for other purposes," approved March 23, 1932 (U.S.C., title 29, sections 101–115).

(f) This section shall not apply to any contract in force on the date of enactment of this Act, until the expiration of such contract, or until July 1, 1948, whichever first occurs.

(g) Compliance with the restrictions contained in subsection (c)(5)(B) upon contributions to trust funds, otherwise lawful, shall not be applicable to contributions to such trust funds established by collective agreement prior to January 1, 1946, nor shall subsection (c)(5)(A) be construed as prohibiting contributions to such trust funds if prior to January 1, 1947, such funds contained provisions for pooled vacation benefits.

BOYCOTTS AND OTHER UNLAWFUL COMBINATIONS

Sec. 303. (a) It shall be unlawful, for the purpose of this section only, in an industry or activity affecting commerce, for any labor organization to engage in any activity or conduct defined as an unfair labor practice in section 8(b)(4) of the National Labor Relations Act, as amended.

(b) Whoever shall be injured in his business or property by reason of any violation of subsection (a) may sue therefor in any district court of the United States subject to the limitations and provisions of section 301 hereof without respect to the amount in controversy, or in any other court

* Section 302(d) was amended by Pub.L. 98–473, Oct. 12, 1984, 98 Stat. 2131.

having jurisdiction of the parties, and shall recover the damages by him sustained and the cost of the suit.

Sec. 304. [Repealed.]

Sec. 305. [Repealed.]

TITLE IV

CREATION OF JOINT COMMITTEE TO STUDY AND REPORT ON BASIC PROBLEMS AFFECTING FRIENDLY LABOR RELATIONS AND PRODUCTIVITY

* * *

TITLE V

DEFINITIONS

Sec. 501. When used in this Act—

(1) The term "industry affecting commerce" means any industry or activity in commerce or in which a labor dispute would burden or obstruct commerce or tend to burden or obstruct commerce or the free flow of commerce.

(2) The term "strike" includes any strike or other concerted stoppage of work by employees (including a stoppage by reason of the expiration of a collective-bargaining agreement) and any concerted slow-down or other concerted interruption of operations by employees.

(3) The terms "commerce", "labor disputes", "employer", "employee", "labor organization", "representative", "person", and "supervisor" shall have the same meaning as when used in the National Labor Relations Act as amended by this Act.

SAVING PROVISION

Sec. 502. Nothing in this Act shall be construed to require an individual employee to render labor or service without his consent, nor shall anything in this Act be construed to make the quitting of his labor by an individual employee an illegal act; nor shall any court issue any process to compel the performance by an individual employee of such labor or service, without his consent; nor shall the quitting of labor by an employee or employees in good faith because of abnormally dangerous conditions for work at the place of employment of such employee or employees be deemed a strike under this Act.

SEPARABILITY

Sec. 503. If any provision of this Act, or the application of such provision to any person or circumstance, shall be held invalid, the remainder of this Act, or the application of such provision to persons or circumstances other than those as to which it is held invalid, shall not be affected thereby.

LABOR-MANAGEMENT REPORTING AND DISCLOSURE ACT OF 1959

73 Stat. 519 (1959), as amended; 29 U.S.C. §§ 401–531 (1988).

SHORT TITLE

Sec. 1. This Act may be cited as the "Labor-Management Reporting and Disclosure Act of 1959".

DECLARATION OF FINDINGS, PURPOSES, AND POLICY

Sec. 2. (a) The Congress finds that, in the public interest, it continues to be the responsibility of the Federal Government to protect employees' rights to organize, choose their own representatives, bargain collectively, and otherwise engage in concerted activities for their mutual aid or protection; that the relations between employers and labor organizations and the millions of workers they represent have a substantial impact on the commerce of the Nation; and that in order to accomplish the objective of a free flow of commerce it is essential that labor organizations, employers, and their officials adhere to the highest standards of responsibility and ethical conduct in administering the affairs of their organizations, particularly as they affect labor-management relations.

(b) The Congress further finds, from recent investigations in the labor and management fields, that there have been a number of instances of breach of trust, corruption, disregard of the rights of individual employees, and other failures to observe high standards of responsibility and ethical conduct which require further and supplementary legislation that will afford necessary protection of the rights and interests of employees and the public generally as they relate to the activities of labor organizations, employers, labor relations consultants, and their officers and representatives.

(c) The Congress, therefore, further finds and declares that the enactment of this Act is necessary to eliminate or prevent improper practices on the part of labor organizations, employers, labor relations consultants, and their officers and representatives which distort and defeat the policies of the Labor Management Relations Act, 1947, as amended, and the Railway Labor Act, as amended, and have the tendency or necessary effect of burdening or obstructing commerce by (1) impairing the efficiency, safety, or operation of the instrumentalities of commerce; (2) occurring in the current of commerce; (3) materially affecting, restraining, or controlling the flow of raw materials or manufactured or processed goods into or from the channels of commerce, or the prices of such materials or goods in commerce; or (4) causing diminution of employment and wages in such volume as substantially to impair or disrupt the market for goods flowing into or from the channels of commerce.

DEFINITIONS

Sec. 3. For the purposes of titles I, II, III, IV, V (except section 505), and VI of this Act—

(a) "Commerce" means trade, traffic, commerce, transportation, transmission, or communication among the several States or between any State and any place outside thereof.

(b) "State" includes any State of the United States, the District of Columbia, Puerto Rico, the Virgin Islands, American Samoa, Guam, Wake Island, the Canal Zone, and Outer Continental Shelf lands defined in the Outer Continental Shelf Lands Act (43 U.S.C. §§ 1331–1343).

(c) "Industry affecting commerce" means any activity, business, or industry in commerce or in which a labor dispute would hinder or obstruct commerce or the free flow of commerce and includes any activity or industry "affecting commerce" within the meaning of the Labor Management Relations Act, 1947, as amended, or the Railway Labor Act, as amended.

(d) "Person" includes one or more individuals, labor organizations, partnerships, associations, corporations, legal representatives, mutual companies, joint-stock companies, trusts, unincorporated organizations, trustees, trustees in bankruptcy, or receivers.

(e) "Employer" means any employer or any group or association of employers engaged in an industry affecting commerce (1) which is, with respect to employees engaged in an industry affecting commerce, an employer within the meaning of any law of the United States relating to the employment of any employees or (2) which may deal with any labor organization concerning grievances, labor disputes, wages, rates of pay, hours of employment, or conditions of work, and includes any person acting directly or indirectly as an employer or as an agent of an employer in relation to an employee but does not include the United States or any corporation wholly owned by the Government of the United States or any State or political subdivision thereof.

(f) "Employee" means any individual employed by an employer, and includes any individual whose work has ceased as a consequence of, or in connection with, any current labor dispute or because of any unfair labor practice or because of exclusion or expulsion from a labor organization in any manner or for any reason inconsistent with the requirements of this Act.

(g) "Labor dispute" includes any controversy concerning terms, tenure, or conditions of employment, or concerning the association or representation of persons in negotiating, fixing, maintaining, changing or seeking to arrange terms or conditions of employment, regardless of whether the disputants stand in the proximate relation of employer and employee.

(h) "Trusteeship" means any receivership, trusteeship, or other method of supervision or control whereby a labor organization suspends the autonomy otherwise available to a subordinate body under its constitution or bylaws.

(i) "Labor organization" means a labor organization engaged in an industry affecting commerce and includes any organization of any kind, any agency, or employee representation committee, group, association, or plan so engaged in which employees participate and which exists for the purpose, in whole or in part, of dealing with employers concerning grievances, labor disputes, wages, rates of pay, hours, or other terms or conditions of employment, and any conference, general committee, joint or system board, or joint council so engaged which is subordinate to a national or international labor organization, other than a State or local central body.

(j) A labor organization shall be deemed to be engaged in an industry affecting commerce if it—

(1) is the certified representative of employees under the provisions of the National Labor Relations Act, as amended, or the Railway Labor Act, as amended; or

(2) although not certified, is a national or international labor organization or a local labor organization recognized or acting as the representative of employees of an employer or employers engaged in an industry affecting commerce; or

(3) has chartered a local labor organization or subsidiary body which is representing or actively seeking to represent employees of employers within the meaning of paragraph (1) or (2); or

(4) has been chartered by a labor organization representing or actively seeking to represent employees within the meaning of paragraph (1) or (2) as the local or subordinate body through which such employees may enjoy membership or become affiliated with such labor organization; or

(5) is a conference, general committee, joint or system board, or joint council, subordinate to a national or international labor organization, which includes a labor organization engaged in an industry affecting commerce within the meaning of any of the preceding paragraphs of this subsection, other than a State or local central body.

(k) "Secret ballot" means the expression by ballot, voting machine, or otherwise, but in no event by proxy, of a choice with respect to any election or vote taken upon any matter, which is cast in such a manner that the person expressing such choice cannot be identified with the choice expressed.

(*l*) "Trust in which a labor organization is interested" means a trust or other fund or organization (1) which was created or established by a labor organization, or one or more of the trustees or one or more members of the governing body of which is selected or appointed by a labor organization, and (2) a primary purpose of which is to provide benefits for the members of such labor organization or their beneficiaries.

(m) "Labor relations consultant" means any person who, for compensation, advises or represents an employer, employer organization, or labor organization concerning employee organizing, concerted activities, or collective bargaining activities.

(n) "Officer" means any constitutional officer, any person authorized to perform the functions of president, vice president, secretary, treasurer, or other executive functions of a labor organization, and any member of its executive board or similar governing body.

(*o*) "Member" or "member in good standing", when used in reference to a labor organization, includes any person who has fulfilled the requirements for membership in such organization, and who neither has voluntarily withdrawn from membership nor has been expelled or suspended from membership after appropriate proceedings consistent with lawful provisions of the constitution and bylaws of such organization.

(p) "Secretary" means the Secretary of Labor.

(q) "Officer, agent, shop steward, or other representative", when used with respect to a labor organization, includes elected officials and key administrative personnel, whether elected or appointed (such as business agents, heads of departments or major units, and organizers who exercise substantial independent authority), but does not include salaried nonsupervisory professional staff, stenographic, and service personnel.

(r) "District court of the United States" means a United States district court and a United States court of any place subject to the jurisdiction of the United States.

TITLE I—BILL OF RIGHTS OF MEMBERS OF LABOR ORGANIZATIONS

BILL OF RIGHTS

Sec. 101. (a)(1) EQUAL RIGHTS.—Every member of a labor organization shall have equal rights and privileges within such organization to nominate candidates, to vote in elections or referendums of the labor organization, to attend membership meetings, and to participate in the deliberations and voting upon the business of such meetings, subject to reasonable rules and regulations in such organization's constitution and bylaws.

(2) FREEDOM OF SPEECH AND ASSEMBLY.—Every member of any labor organization shall have the right to meet and assemble freely with other members; and to express any views, arguments, or opinions; and to express at meetings of the labor organization his views, upon

candidates in an election of the labor organization or upon any business properly before the meeting, subject to the organization's established and reasonable rules pertaining to the conduct of meetings: *Provided*, That nothing herein shall be construed to impair the right of a labor organization to adopt and enforce reasonable rules as to the responsibility of every member toward the organization as an institution and to his refraining from conduct that would interfere with its performance of its legal or contractual obligations.

(3) DUES, INITIATION FEES, AND ASSESSMENTS.—Except in the case of a federation of national or international labor organizations, the rates of dues and initiation fees payable by members of any labor organization in effect on the date of enactment of this Act shall not be increased, and no general or special assessment shall be levied upon such members, except—

(A) in a case of a local labor organization, (i) by majority vote by secret ballot of the members in good standing voting at a general or special membership meeting, after reasonable notice of the intention to vote upon such question, or (ii) by majority vote of the members in good standing voting in a membership referendum conducted by secret ballot; or

(B) in the case of a labor organization, other than a local labor organization or a federation of national or international labor organizations, (i) by majority vote of the delegates voting at a regular convention, or at a special convention of such labor organization held upon not less than thirty days' written notice to the principal office of each local or constituent labor organization entitled to such notice, or (ii) by majority vote of the members in good standing of such labor organization voting in a membership referendum conducted by secret ballot, or (iii) by majority vote of the members of the executive board or similar governing body of such labor organization, pursuant to express authority contained in the constitution and bylaws of such labor organization: *Provided*, That such action on the part of the executive board or similar governing body shall be effective only until the next regular convention of such labor organization.

(4) PROTECTION OF THE RIGHT TO SUE.—No labor organization shall limit the right of any member thereof to institute an action in any court, or in a proceeding before any administrative agency, irrespective of whether or not the labor organization or its officers are named as defendants or respondents in such action or proceeding, or the right of any member of a labor organization to appear as a witness in any judicial, administrative, or legislative proceeding, or to petition any legislature or to communicate with any legislator: *Provided*, That any such member may be required to exhaust reasonable hearing procedures (but not to exceed a four-month lapse of time) within such organization, before instituting legal or administrative proceedings against such organizations or any officer thereof: *And provided further*, That no

interested employer or employer association shall directly or indirectly finance, encourage, or participate in, except as a party, any such action, proceeding, appearance, or petition.

(5) SAFEGUARDS AGAINST IMPROPER DISCIPLINARY ACTION.—No member of any labor organization may be fined, suspended, expelled, or otherwise disciplined except for nonpayment of dues by such organization or by any officer thereof unless such member has been (A) served with written specific charges; (B) given a reasonable time to prepare his defense; (C) afforded a full and fair hearing.

(b) Any provision of the constitution and bylaws of any labor organization which is inconsistent with the provisions of this section shall be of no force or effect.

CIVIL ENFORCEMENT

Sec. 102. Any person whose rights secured by the provisions of this title have been infringed by any violation of this title may bring a civil action in a district court of the United States for such relief (including injunctions) as may be appropriate. Any such action against a labor organization shall be brought in the district court of the United States for the district where the alleged violation occurred, or where the principal office of such labor organization is located.

RETENTION OF EXISTING RIGHTS

Sec. 103. Nothing contained in this title shall limit the rights and remedies of any member of a labor organization under any State or Federal law or before any court or other tribunal, or under the constitution and bylaws of any labor organization.

RIGHT TO COPIES OF COLLECTIVE BARGAINING AGREEMENTS

Sec. 104. It shall be the duty of the secretary or corresponding principal officer of each labor organization, in the case of a local labor organization, to forward a copy of each collective bargaining agreement made by such labor organization with any employer to any employee who requests such a copy and whose rights as such employee are directly affected by such agreement, and in the case of a labor organization other than a local labor organization, to forward a copy of any such agreement to each constituent unit which has members directly affected by such agreement; and such officer shall maintain at the principal office of the labor organization of which he is an officer copies of any such agreement made or received by such labor organization, which copies shall be available for inspection by any member or by any employee whose rights are affected by such agreement. The provisions of section 210 shall be applicable in the enforcement of this section.

INFORMATION AS TO ACT

Sec. 105. Every labor organization shall inform its members concerning the provisions of this Act.

TITLE II—REPORTING BY LABOR ORGANIZATIONS, OFFICERS AND EMPLOYEES OF LABOR ORGANIZATIONS, AND EMPLOYERS

REPORT OF LABOR ORGANIZATIONS

Sec. 201. (a) Every labor organization shall adopt a constitution and bylaws and shall file a copy thereof with the Secretary, together with a report, signed by its president and secretary or corresponding principal officers, containing the following information—

(1) the name of the labor organization, its mailing address, and any other address at which it maintains its principal office or at which it keeps the records referred to in this title;

(2) the name and title of each of its officers;

(3) the initiation fee or fees required from a new or transferred member and fees for work permits required by the reporting labor organization;

(4) the regular dues or fees or other periodic payments required to remain a member of the reporting labor organization; and

(5) detailed statements, or references to specific provisions of documents filed under this subsection which contain such statements, showing the provision made and procedures followed with respect to each of the following: (A) qualifications for or restrictions on membership, (B) levying of assessments, (C) participation in insurance or other benefit plans, (D) authorization for disbursement of funds of the labor organization, (E) audit of financial transactions of the labor organization, (F) the calling of regular and special meetings, (G) the selection of officers and stewards and of any representatives to other bodies composed of labor organizations' representatives, with a specific statement of the manner in which each officer was elected, appointed, or otherwise selected, (H) discipline or removal of officers or agents for breaches of their trust, (I) imposition of fines, suspensions and expulsions of members, including the grounds for such action and any provision made for notice, hearing, judgment on the evidence, and appeal procedures, (J) authorization for bargaining demands, (K) ratification of contract terms, (L) authorization for strikes, and (M) issuance of work permits. Any change in the information required by this subsection shall be reported to the Secretary at the time the reporting labor organization files with the Secretary the annual financial report required by subsection (b).

(b) Every labor organization shall file annually with the Secretary a financial report signed by its president and treasurer or corresponding principal officers containing the following information in such detail as may be necessary accurately to disclose its financial condition and operations for its preceding fiscal year—

(1) assets and liabilities at the beginning and end of the fiscal year;

(2) receipts of any kind and the sources thereof;

(3) salary, allowances, and other direct or indirect disbursements (including reimbursed expenses) to each officer and also to each employee who, during such fiscal year, received more than $10,000 in the aggregate from such labor organization and any other labor organization affiliated with it or with which it is affiliated, or which is affiliated with the same national or international labor organization;

(4) direct and indirect loans made to any officer, employee, or member, which aggregated more than $250 during the fiscal year, together with a statement of the purpose, security, if any, and arrangements for repayment;

(5) direct and indirect loans to any business enterprise, together with a statement of the purpose, security, if any, and arrangements for repayment; and

(6) other disbursements made by it including the purposes thereof;

all in such categories as the Secretary may prescribe.

(c) Every labor organization required to submit a report under this title shall make available the information required to be contained in such report to all of its members, and every such labor organization and its officers shall be under a duty enforceable at the suit of any member of such organization in any State court of competent jurisdiction or in the district court of the United States for the district in which such labor organization maintains its principal office, to permit such member for just cause to examine any books, records, and accounts necessary to verify such report. The court in such action may, in its discretion, in addition to any judgment awarded to the plaintiff or plaintiffs, allow a reasonable attorney's fee to be paid by the defendant, and costs of the action.

REPORT OF OFFICERS AND EMPLOYEES OF LABOR ORGANIZATIONS

Sec. 202. (a) Every officer of a labor organization and every employee of a labor organization (other than an employee performing exclusively clerical or custodial services) shall file with the Secretary a signed report listing and describing for his preceding fiscal year—

(1) any stock, bond, security, or other interest, legal or equitable, which he or his spouse or minor child directly or indirectly held in, and any income or any other benefit with monetary value (including reimbursed expenses) which he or his spouse or minor child derived directly or indirectly from, an employer whose employees such labor organization represents or is actively seeking

to represent, except payments and other benefits received as a bona fide employee of such employer;

(2) any transaction in which he or his spouse or minor child engaged, directly or indirectly, involving any stock, bond, security, or loan to or from, or other legal or equitable interest in the business of an employer whose employees such labor organization represents or is actively seeking to represent;

(3) any stock, bond, security, or other interest, legal or equitable, which he or his spouse or minor child directly or indirectly held in, and any income or any other benefit with monetary value (including reimbursed expenses) which he or his spouse or minor child directly or indirectly derived from, any business a substantial part of which consists of buying from, selling or leasing to, or otherwise dealing with, the business of an employer whose employees such labor organization represents or is actively seeking to represent;

(4) any stock, bond, security, or other interest, legal or equitable, which he or his spouse or minor child directly or indirectly held in, and any income or any other benefit with monetary value (including reimbursed expenses) which he or his spouse or minor child directly or indirectly derived from, a business any part of which consists of buying from, or selling or leasing directly or indirectly to, or otherwise dealing with such labor organization;

(5) any direct or indirect business transaction or arrangement between him or his spouse or minor child and any employer whose employees his organization represents or is actively seeking to represent, except work performed and payments and benefits received as a bona fide employee of such employer and except purchases and sales of goods or services in the regular course of business at prices generally available to any employee of such employer; and

(6) any payment of money or other thing of value (including reimbursed expenses) which he or his spouse or minor child received directly or indirectly from any employer or any person who acts as a labor relations consultant to an employer, except payments of the kinds referred to in section 302(c) of the Labor Management Relations Act, 1947, as amended.

(b) The provisions of paragraphs (1), (2), (3), (4), and (5) of subsection (a) shall not be construed to require any such officer or employee to report his bona fide investments in securities traded on a securities exchange registered as a national securities exchange under the Securities Exchange Act of 1934, in shares in an investment company registered under the Investment Company Act of 1940, or in securities of a public utility holding company registered under the Public Utility Holding Company Act of 1935, or to report any income derived therefrom.

(c) Nothing contained in this section shall be construed to require any officer or employee of a labor organization to file a report under subsection (a) unless he or his spouse or minor child holds or has held an interest, has received income or any other benefit with monetary value or a loan, or has engaged in a transaction described therein.

REPORT OF EMPLOYERS

Sec. 203. (a) Every employer who in any fiscal year made—

(1) any payment or loan, direct or indirect, of money or other thing of value (including reimbursed expenses), or any promise or agreement therefor, to any labor organization or officer, agent, shop steward, or other representative of a labor organization, or employee of any labor organization, except (A) payments or loans made by any national or State bank, credit union, insurance company, savings and loan association or other credit institution and (B) payments of the kind referred to in section 302(c) of the Labor Management Relations Act, 1947, as amended;

(2) any payment (including reimbursed expenses) to any of his employees, or any group or committee of such employees, for the purpose of causing such employee or group or committee of employees to persuade other employees to exercise or not to exercise, or as the manner of exercising, the right to organize and bargain collectively through representatives of their own choosing unless such payments were contemporaneously or previously disclosed to such other employees;

(3) any expenditure, during the fiscal year, where an object thereof, directly or indirectly, is to interfere with, restrain, or coerce employees in the exercise of the right to organize and bargain collectively through representatives of their own choosing, or is to obtain information concerning the activities of employees or a labor organization in connection with a labor dispute involving such employer, except for use solely in conjunction with an administrative or arbitral proceeding or a criminal or civil judicial proceeding;

(4) any agreement or arrangement with a labor relations consultant or other independent contractor or organization pursuant to which such person undertakes activities where an object thereof, directly or indirectly, is to persuade employees to exercise or not to exercise, or persuade employees as to the manner of exercising, the right to organize and bargain collectively through representatives of their own choosing, or undertakes to supply such employer with information concerning the activities of employees or a labor organization in connection with a labor dispute involving such employer, except information for use solely in conjunction with an administrative or arbitral proceeding or a criminal or civil judicial proceeding; or

(5) any payment (including reimbursed expenses) pursuant to an agreement or arrangement described in subdivision (4);

shall file with the Secretary a report, in a form prescribed by him, signed by its president and treasurer or corresponding principal officers showing in detail the date and amount of each such payment, loan, promise, agreement, or arrangement and the name, address, and position, if any, in any firm or labor organization of the person to whom it was made and a full explanation of the circumstances of all such payments, including the terms of any agreement or understanding pursuant to which they were made.

(b) Every person who pursuant to any agreement or arrangement with an employer undertakes activities where an object thereof is, directly or indirectly—

(1) to persuade employees to exercise or not to exercise, or persuade employees as to the manner of exercising, the right to organize and bargain collectively through representatives of their own choosing; or

(2) to supply an employer with information concerning the activities of employees or a labor organization in connection with a labor dispute involving such employer, except information for use solely in conjunction with an administrative or arbitral proceeding or a criminal or civil judicial proceeding;

shall file within thirty days after entering into such agreement or arrangement a report with the Secretary, signed by its president and treasurer or corresponding principal officers, containing the name under which such person is engaged in doing business and the address of its principal office, and a detailed statement of the terms and conditions of such agreement or arrangement. Every such person shall file annually, with respect to each fiscal year during which payments were made as a result of such an agreement or arrangement, a report with the Secretary, signed by its president and treasurer or corresponding principal officers, containing a statement (A) of its receipts of any kind from employers on account of labor relations advice or services, designating the sources thereof, and (B) of its disbursements of any kind, in connection with such services and the purposes thereof. In each such case such information shall be set forth in such categories as the Secretary may prescribe.

(c) Nothing in this section shall be construed to require any employer or other person to file a report covering the services of such person by reason of his giving or agreeing to give advice to such employer or representing or agreeing to represent such employer before any court, administrative agency, or tribunal of arbitration or engaging or agreeing to engage in collective bargaining on behalf of such employer with respect to wages, hours, or other terms or conditions of employment or the negotiation of an agreement or any question arising thereunder.

(d) Nothing contained in this section shall be construed to require an employer to file a report under subsection (a) unless he has made an expenditure, payment, loan, agreement, or arrangement of the kind described therein. Nothing contained in this section shall be construed to require any other person to file a report under subsection (b) unless he was a party to an agreement or arrangement of the kind described therein.

(e) Nothing contained in this section shall be construed to require any regular officer, supervisor, or employee of an employer to file a report in connection with services rendered to such employer nor shall any employer be required to file a report covering expenditures made to any regular officer, supervisor, or employee of an employer as compensation for service as a regular officer, supervisor, or employee of such employer.

(f) Nothing contained in this section shall be construed as an amendment to, or modification of the rights protected by, section 8(c) of the National Labor Relations Act, as amended.

(g) The term "interfere with, restrain, or coerce" as used in this section means interference, restraint, and coercion which, if done with respect to the exercise of rights guaranteed in section 7 of the National Labor Relations Act, as amended, would, under section 8(a) of such Act, constitute an unfair labor practice.

ATTORNEY-CLIENT COMMUNICATIONS EXEMPTED

Sec. 204. Nothing contained in this Act shall be construed to require an attorney who is a member in good standing of the bar of any State, to include in any report required to be filed pursuant to the provisions of this Act any information which was lawfully communicated to such attorney by any of his clients in the course of a legitimate attorney-client relationship.

REPORTS MADE PUBLIC INFORMATION

Sec. 205. (a) The contents of the reports and documents filed with the Secretary pursuant to sections 201, 202, 203, and 211 shall be public information, and the Secretary may publish any information and data which he obtains pursuant to the provisions of this title. The Secretary may use the information and data for statistical and research purposes, and compile and publish such studies, analyses, reports, and surveys based thereon as he may deem appropriate.

(b) The Secretary shall by regulation make reasonable provision for the inspection and examination, on the request of any person, of the information and data contained in any report or other document filed with him pursuant to section 201, 202, 203, or 211.

(c) The Secretary shall by regulation provide for the furnishing by the Department of Labor of copies of reports or other documents filed with the Secretary pursuant to this title, upon payment of a charge based upon the cost of the service. The Secretary shall make available without payment of a charge, or require any person to furnish, to such State agency as is designated by law or by the Governor of the State in which such person has his principal place of business or headquarters, upon request of the Governor of such State, copies of any reports and documents filed by such person with the Secretary pursuant to section 201, 202, 203, or 211, or of information and data contained therein. No person shall be required by reason of any law of any State to furnish to any officer or agency of such State any information included in a report filed by such person with the Secretary pursuant to the provisions of this title, if a copy of such report, or of the portion thereof containing such information, is furnished to such officer or agency. All moneys received in payment of such charges fixed by the Secretary pursuant to this subsection shall be deposited in the general fund of the Treasury.

RETENTION OF RECORDS

Sec. 206. Every person required to file any report under this title shall maintain records on the matters required to be reported which will provide in sufficient detail the necessary basic information and data from which the documents filed with the Secretary may be verified, explained or clarified, and checked for accuracy and completeness, and shall include vouchers, worksheets, receipts, and applicable resolutions, and shall keep such records available for examination for a period of not less than five years after the filing of the documents based on the information which they contain.

EFFECTIVE DATE

Sec. 207. (a) Each labor organization shall file the initial report required under section 201(a) within ninety days after the date on which it first becomes subject to this Act.

(b) Each person required to file a report under section 201(b), 202, 203(a), or the second sentence of 203(b), or section 211 shall file such report within ninety days after the end of each of its fiscal years; except that where such person is subject to section 201(b), 202, 203(a), the second sentence of 203(b), or section 211, as the case may be, for only a portion of such a fiscal year (because the date of enactment of this Act occurs during such person's fiscal year or such person becomes subject to this Act during its fiscal year) such person may consider that portion as the entire fiscal year in making such report.

RULES AND REGULATIONS

Sec. 208. The Secretary shall have authority to issue, amend, and rescind rules and regulations prescribing the form and publication of reports required to be filed under this title and such other reasonable rules and regulations (including rules prescribing reports concerning trusts in which a labor organization is interested) as he may find necessary to prevent the circumvention or evasion of such reporting requirements. In exercising his power under this section the Secretary shall prescribe by general rule simplified reports for labor organizations or employers for whom he finds that by virtue of their size a detailed report would be unduly burdensome, but the Secretary may revoke such provision for simplified forms of any labor organization or employer if he determines, after such investigation as he deems proper and due notice and opportunity for a hearing, that the purposes of this section would be served thereby.

CRIMINAL PROVISIONS

Sec. 209. (a) Any person who willfully violates this title shall be fined not more than $10,000 or imprisoned for not more than one year, or both.

(b) Any person who makes a false statement or representation of a material fact, knowing it to be false, or who knowingly fails to disclose a material fact, in any document, report, or other information required under the provisions of this title shall be fined not more than $10,000 or imprisoned for not more than one year, or both.

(c) Any person who willfully makes a false entry in or willfully conceals, withholds, or destroys any books, records, reports, or statements required to be kept by any provision of this title shall be fined not more than $10,000 or imprisoned for not more than one year, or both.

(d) Each individual required to sign reports under sections 201 and 203 shall be personally responsible for the filing of such reports and for any statement contained therein which he knows to be false.

CIVIL ENFORCEMENT

Sec. 210. Whenever it shall appear that any person has violated or is about to violate any of the provisions of this title, the Secretary may bring a civil action for such relief (including injunctions) as may be appropriate. Any such action may be brought in the district court of the United States where the violation occurred or, at the option of the parties, in the United States District Court for the District of Columbia.

SURETY COMPANY REPORTS

Sec. 211. Each surety company which issues any bond required by this Act or the Employee Retirement Income Security Act of 1974 shall file annually with the Secretary, with respect to each fiscal year during which any such bond was in force, a report, in such form and detail as he may prescribe by regulation, filed by the president and treasurer or corresponding principal officers of the surety company, describing its bond experience under each such Act, including information as to the premiums received, total claims paid, amounts recovered by way of subrogation, administrative and legal expenses and such related data and information as the Secretary shall determine to be necessary in the public interest and to carry out the policy of the Act. Notwithstanding the foregoing, if the Secretary finds that any such specific information cannot be practicably ascertained or would be uninformative, the Secretary may modify or waive the requirement for such information.

TITLE III—TRUSTEESHIPS

REPORTS

Sec. 301. (a) Every labor organization which has or assumes trusteeship over any subordinate labor organization shall file with the Secretary within thirty days after the date of the enactment of this Act or the imposition of any such trusteeship, and semiannually thereafter, a report, signed by its president and treasurer or corresponding principal officers, as well as by the trustees of such subordinate labor organization, containing the following information: (1) the name and address of the subordinate organization; (2) the date of establishing the trusteeship; (3) a detailed statement of the reason or reasons for establishing or continuing the trusteeship; and (4) the nature and extent of participation by the membership of the subordinate organization in the selection of delegates to represent such organization in regular or special conventions or other policy-determining bodies and in the election of officers of the labor organization which has assumed trusteeship over such subordinate organization. The initial report shall also include a full and complete account of the financial condition of such subordinate organization as of the time trusteeship was assumed over it. During the continuance of a trusteeship the labor organization which has assumed trusteeship over a subordinate labor organization shall file on behalf of the subordinate labor organization the annual financial report required by section 201(b) signed by the president and treasurer or corresponding principal officers of the labor organization which has assumed such trusteeship and the trustees of the subordinate labor organization.

(b) The provisions of sections 201(c), 205, 206, 208, and 210 shall be applicable to reports filed under this title.

(c) Any person who willfully violates this section shall be fined not more than $10,000 or imprisoned for not more than one year, or both.

(d) Any person who makes a false statement or representation of a material fact, knowing it to be false, or who knowingly fails to disclose a material fact, in any report required under the provisions of this section or willfully makes any false entry in or willfully withholds, conceals, or destroys any documents, books, records, reports, or statements upon which such report is based, shall be fined not more than $10,000 or imprisoned for not more than one year, or both.

(e) Each individual required to sign a report under this section shall be personally responsible for the filing of such report and for any statement contained therein which he knows to be false.

PURPOSES FOR WHICH A TRUSTEESHIP MAY BE ESTABLISHED

Sec. 302. Trusteeships shall be established and administered by a labor organization over a subordinate body only in accordance with the constitution and bylaws of the organization which has assumed trusteeship over the subordinate body and for the purpose of correcting corruption or financial malpractice, assuring the performance of collective bargaining agreements or other duties of a bargaining representative, restoring democratic procedures, or otherwise carrying out the legitimate objects of such labor organization.

UNLAWFUL ACTS RELATING TO LABOR ORGANIZATION UNDER TRUSTEESHIP

Sec. 303. (a) During any period when a subordinate body of a labor organization is in trusteeship, it shall be unlawful (1) to count the vote of delegates from such body in any convention or election of officers of the labor organization unless the delegates have been chosen by secret ballot in an election in which all the members in good standing of such subordinate body were eligible to participate, or (2) to transfer to such organization any current receipts or other funds of the subordinate body except the normal per capita tax and assessments payable by subordinate bodies not in trusteeship: *Provided,* That nothing herein contained shall prevent the distribution of the assets of a labor organization in accordance with its constitution and bylaws upon the bona fide dissolution thereof.

(b) Any person who willfully violates this section shall be fined not more than $10,000 or imprisoned for not more than one year, or both.

ENFORCEMENT

Sec. 304. (a) Upon the written complaint of any member or subordinate body of a labor organization alleging that such organization has violated the provisions of this title (except section 301) the Secretary shall investigate the complaint and if the Secretary finds probable cause to believe that such violation has occurred and has not been remedied he shall, without disclosing the identity of the complainant, bring a civil action in any district court of the United States having jurisdiction of the labor organization for such relief (including injunctions) as may be appropriate. Any member or subordinate body of a labor organization affected by any violation of this title (except section 301) may bring a civil action in any district court of the United States having jurisdiction of the labor organization for such relief (including injunctions) as may be appropriate.

(b) For the purpose of actions under this section, district courts of the United States shall be deemed to have jurisdiction of a labor organization (1) in the district in which the principal office of such labor organization is located, or (2) in any district in which its duly authorized officers or agents are engaged in conducting the affairs of the trusteeship.

(c) In any proceeding pursuant to this section a trusteeship established by a labor organization in conformity with the procedural requirements of its constitution and bylaws and authorized or ratified after a fair hearing either before the executive board or before such other body as may be provided in accordance with its constitution or bylaws shall be presumed valid for a period of eighteen months from the date of its establishment and shall not be subject to attack during such period except upon clear and convincing proof that the trusteeship was not established or maintained in good faith for a purpose allowable under section 302. After the expiration of eighteen months the trusteeship shall be presumed invalid in any such proceeding and its discontinuance shall be decreed unless the labor organization shall show by clear and convincing proof that the continuation of the trusteeship is necessary for a purpose allowable under section 302. In the latter event the court may dismiss the complaint or retain jurisdiction of the cause on such conditions and for such period as it deems appropriate.

REPORT TO CONGRESS

Sec. 305. The Secretary shall submit to the Congress at the expiration of three years from the date of enactment of this Act a report upon the operation of this title.

COMPLAINT BY SECRETARY

Sec. 306. The rights and remedies provided by this title shall be in addition to any and all other rights and remedies at law or in equity: *Provided,* That upon the filing of a complaint by the Secretary the jurisdiction of the district court over such trusteeship shall be exclusive and the final judgment shall be res judicata.

TITLE IV—ELECTIONS

TERMS OF OFFICE; ELECTION PROCEDURES

Sec. 401. (a) Every national or international labor organization, except a federation of national or international labor organizations, shall elect its officers not less often than once every five years either by secret ballot among the members in good standing or at a convention of delegates chosen by secret ballot.

(b) Every local labor organization shall elect its officers not less often than once every three years by secret ballot among the members in good standing.

(c) Every national or international labor organization, except a federation of national or international labor organizations, and every local labor organization, and its officers, shall be under a duty, enforceable at the suit of any bona fide candidate for office in such labor organization in the district court of the United States in which such labor organization maintains its principal office, to comply with all reasonable requests of any candidate to distribute by mail or otherwise at the candidate's expense campaign literature in aid of such person's candidacy to all members in good standing of such labor organization and to refrain from discrimination in favor of or against any candidate with respect to the use of lists of members, and whenever such labor organizations or its officers authorize the distribution by mail or otherwise to members of campaign literature on behalf of any candidate or of the labor organization itself with reference to such election, similar distribution at the request of any other bona fide candidate shall be made by such labor organization and its officers, with equal treatment as to the expense of such distribution. Every bona fide candidate shall have the right, once within 30 days prior to an election of a labor organization in which he is a candidate, to inspect a list containing the names and last known addresses of all members of the labor organization who are subject to a collective bargaining agreement requiring membership therein as a condition of employment, which list shall be maintained and kept at the principal office of such labor organization by a designated official thereof. Adequate safeguards to insure a fair election shall be provided, including the right of any candidate to have an observer at the polls and at the counting of the ballots.

(d) Officers of intermediate bodies, such as general committees, system boards, joint boards, or joint councils, shall be elected not less often than once every four years by secret ballot among the members in good standing or by labor organization officers representative of such members who have been elected by secret ballot.

(e) In any election required by this section which is to be held by secret ballot a reasonable opportunity shall be given for the nomination of candidates and every member in good standing shall be eligible to be a candidate and to hold office (subject to section 504 and to reasonable qualifications uniformly imposed) and shall have the right to vote for or otherwise support the candidate or candidates of his choice, without being subject to penalty, discipline, or improper interference or reprisal of any kind by such organization or any member thereof. Not less than fifteen days prior to the election notice thereof shall be mailed to each member at his last known home address. Each member in good standing shall be entitled to one vote. No member whose dues have been withheld by his employer for payment to such organization pursuant to his voluntary authorization provided for in a collective bargaining agreement, shall be declared ineligible to vote or be a candidate for office in such organization by reason of alleged delay or default in the payment of dues. The votes cast by members of each local labor organization shall be counted, and the results published, separately. The election officials designated in the constitution and bylaws or the secretary, if no other official is designated, shall preserve for one year the ballots and all other records pertaining to the election. The election shall be conducted in accordance with the constitution and bylaws of such organization insofar as they are not inconsistent with the provisions of this title.

(f) When officers are chosen by a convention of delegates elected by secret ballot, the convention shall be conducted in accordance with the constitution and bylaws of the labor organization insofar as they are not inconsistent with the provisions of this title. The officials designated in the constitution and bylaws or the secretary, if no other is designated, shall preserve for one year the credentials of the delegates and all minutes and other records of the convention pertaining to the election of officers.

(g) No moneys received by any labor organization by way of dues, assessment, or similar levy, and no moneys of an employer shall be contributed or applied to promote the candidacy of any person in an election subject to the provisions of this title. Such moneys of a labor organization may be utilized for notices, factual statements of issues not involving candidates, and other expenses necessary for the holding of an election.

(h) If the Secretary, upon application of any member of a local labor organization, finds after hearing in accordance with the Administrative Procedure Act that the constitution and bylaws of such labor organization do not provide an adequate procedure for the removal of an elected officer guilty of serious misconduct, such officer may be removed, for cause shown and after notice and hearing, by the members in good standing voting in a secret ballot conducted by the officers of such labor organization in accordance with its constitution and bylaws insofar as they are not inconsistent with the provisions of this title.

(i) The Secretary shall promulgate rules and regulations prescribing minimum standards and procedures for determining the adequacy of the removal procedures to which reference is made in subsection (h).

ENFORCEMENT

Sec. 402. (a) A member of a labor organization—

(1) who has exhausted the remedies available under the constitution and bylaws of such organization and of any parent body or

(2) who has invoked such available remedies without obtaining a final decision within three calendar months after their invocation,

may file a complaint with the Secretary within one calendar month thereafter alleging the violation of any provision of section 401 (including violation of the constitution and bylaws of the labor organization pertaining to the election and removal of officers). The challenged election shall be presumed valid pending a final decision thereon (as hereinafter provided) and in the interim the affairs of the organization shall be conducted by the officers elected or in such other manner as its constitution and bylaws may provide.

(b) The Secretary shall investigate such complaint and, if he finds probable cause to believe that a violation of this title has occurred and has not been remedied, he shall, within sixty days after the filing of such complaint, bring a civil action against the labor organization as an entity in the district court of the United States in which such labor organization maintains its principal office to set aside the invalid election, if any, and to direct the conduct of an election or hearing and vote upon the removal of officers under the supervision of the Secretary and in accordance with the provisions of this title and such rules and regulations as the Secretary may prescribe. The court shall have power to take such action as it deems proper to preserve the assets of the labor organization.

(c) If, upon a preponderance of the evidence after a trial upon the merits, the court finds—

(1) that an election has not been held within the time prescribed by section 401, or

(2) that the violation of section 401 may have affected the outcome of an election

the court shall declare the election, if any, to be void and direct the conduct of a new election under supervision of the Secretary and, so far as lawful and practicable, in conformity with the constitution and bylaws of the labor organization. The Secretary shall promptly certify to the court the names of the persons elected, and the court shall thereupon enter a decree declaring such persons to be the officers of the labor organization. If the proceeding is for the removal of officers pursuant to subsection (h) of section 401, the Secretary shall certify the results of the vote and the court shall enter a decree declaring whether such persons have been removed as officers of the labor organization.

(d) An order directing an election, dismissing a complaint, or designating elected officers of a labor organization shall be appealable in the same manner as the final judgment in a civil action, but an order directing an election shall not be stayed pending appeal.

APPLICATION OF OTHER LAWS

Sec. 403. No labor organization shall be required by law to conduct elections of officers with greater frequency or in a different form or manner than is required by its own constitution or bylaws, except as otherwise provided by this title. Existing rights and remedies to enforce the constitution and bylaws of a labor organization with respect to elections prior to the conduct thereof shall not be affected by the provisions of this title. The remedy provided by this title for challenging an election already conducted shall be exclusive.

EFFECTIVE DATE

Sec. 404. The provisions of this title shall become applicable—

(1) ninety days after the date of enactment of this Act in the case of a labor organization whose constitution and bylaws can lawfully be modified or amended by action of its constitutional officers or governing body, or

(2) where such modification can only be made by a constitutional convention of the labor organization, not later than the next constitutional convention of such labor organization after the date of enactment of this Act, or one year after such date, whichever is sooner. If no such convention is held within such one-

year period, the executive board or similar governing body empowered to act for such labor organization between conventions is empowered to make such interim constitutional changes as are necessary to carry out the provisions of this title.

TITLE V—SAFEGUARDS FOR LABOR ORGANIZATIONS

FIDUCIARY RESPONSIBILITY OF OFFICERS OF LABOR ORGANIZATIONS

Sec. 501. (a) The officers, agents, shop stewards, and other representatives of a labor organization occupy positions of trust in relation to such organization and its members as a group. It is, therefore, the duty of each such person, taking into account the special problems and functions of a labor organization, to hold its money and property solely for the benefit of the organization and its members and to manage, invest, and expend the same in accordance with its constitution and bylaws and any resolutions of the governing bodies adopted thereunder, to refrain from dealing with such organization as an adverse party or in behalf of an adverse party in any matter connected with his duties and from holding or acquiring any pecuniary or personal interest which conflicts with the interests of such organization, and to account to the organization for any profit received by him in whatever capacity in connection with transactions conducted by him or under his direction on behalf of the organization. A general exculpatory provision in the constitution and bylaws of such a labor organization or a general exculpatory resolution of a governing body purporting to relieve any such person of liability for breach of the duties declared by this section shall be void as against public policy.

(b) When any officer, agent, shop steward, or representative of any labor organization is alleged to have violated the duties declared in subsection (a) and the labor organization or its governing board or officers refuse or fail to sue or recover damages or secure an accounting or other appropriate relief within a reasonable time after being requested to do so by any member of the labor organization, such member may sue such officer, agent, shop steward, or representative in any district court of the United States or in any State court of competent jurisdiction to recover damages or secure an accounting or other appropriate relief for the benefit of the labor organization. No such proceeding shall be brought except upon leave of the court obtained upon verified application and for good cause shown which application may be made ex parte. The trial judge may allot a reasonable part of the recovery in any action under this subsection to pay the fees of counsel prosecuting the suit at the instance of the member of the labor organization and to compensate such member for any expenses necessarily paid or incurred by him in connection with the litigation.

(c) Any person who embezzles, steals, or unlawfully and willfully abstracts or converts to his own use, or the use of another, any of the moneys, funds, securities, property, or other assets of a labor organization of which he is an officer, or by which he is employed, directly or indirectly, shall be fined not more than $10,000 or imprisoned for not more than five years, or both.

BONDING

Sec. 502. (a) Every officer, agent, shop steward, or other representative or employee of any labor organization (other than a labor organization whose property and annual financial receipts do not exceed $5,000 in value), or of a trust in which a labor organization is interested, who handles funds or other property thereof shall be bonded to provide protection against loss by reason of acts of fraud or dishonesty on his part directly or through connivance with others. The bond of each such person shall be fixed at the beginning of the organization's fiscal year and shall be in an amount not less than 10 per centum of the funds handled by him and his predecessor or predecessors, if any, during the preceding fiscal year, but in no case more than $500,000. If the labor organization or the trust in which a labor organization is interested does not have a preceding fiscal year, the amount of the bond shall be, in the case of a local labor organization, not less than $1,000, and in the case of any other labor organization or of a trust in which a labor organization is interested, not less than $10,000. Such bonds shall be individual or schedule in form, and shall have a corporate surety company as surety thereon. Any person who is not covered by such bonds shall not be permitted to receive, handle, disburse, or otherwise exercise custody or control of the funds or other property of a labor organization or of a trust in which a labor organization is interested. No such bond shall be placed through an agent or broker or with a surety company in which any labor organization or any officer, agent, shop steward, or other representative of a labor organization has any direct or indirect interest. Such surety company shall be a corporate surety which holds a grant of authority from the Secretary of the Treasury under the Act of July 30, 1947 (6 U.S.C. 6–13), as an acceptable surety on Federal bonds: *Provided*, That when in the opinion of the Secretary a labor organization has made other bonding arrangements which would provide the protection required by this section at comparable cost or less, he may exempt such labor organization from placing a bond through a surety company holding such grant of authority.

(b) Any person who willfully violates this section shall be fined not more than $10,000 or imprisoned for not more than one year, or both.

MAKING OF LOANS; PAYMENT OF FINES

Sec. 503. (a) No labor organization shall make directly or indirectly any loan or loans to any officer or employee of such organization which results in a total indebtedness on the part of such officer or employee to the labor organization in excess of $2,000.

(b) No labor organization or employer shall directly or indirectly pay the fine of any officer or employee convicted of any willful violation of this Act.

(c) Any person who willfully violates this section shall be fined not more than $5,000 or imprisoned for not more than one year, or both.

PROHIBITION AGAINST CERTAIN PERSONS HOLDING OFFICE

Sec. 504.* (a) No person who is or has been a member of the Communist Party or who has been convicted of, or served any part of a prison term resulting from his conviction of, robbery, bribery, extortion, embezzlement, grand larceny, burglary, arson, violation of narcotics laws, murder, rape, assault with intent to kill, assault which inflicts grievous bodily injury, or a violation of subchapter III or IV of this chapter, any felony involving abuse or misuse of such person's position or employment in a labor organization or employee benefit plan to seek or obtain an illegal gain at the expense of the members of the labor organization or the beneficiaries of the employee benefit plan, or conspiracy to commit any such crimes or attempt to commit any such crimes, or a crime in which any of the foregoing crimes is an element, shall serve or be permitted to serve—

(1) as a consultant or adviser to any labor organization,

(2) as an officer, director, trustee, member of any executive board or similar governing body, business agent, manager, organizer, employee, or representative in any capacity of any labor organization,

(3) as a labor relations consultant or adviser to a person engaged in an industry or activity affecting commerce, or as an officer, director, agent, or employee of any group or association of employers dealing with any labor organization, or in a position having specific collective bargaining authority or direct responsibility in the area of labor-management relations in any corporation or association engaged in an industry or activity affecting commerce, or

(4) in a position which entitles its occupant to a share of the proceeds of, or as an officer or executive or administrative employee of, any entity whose activities are in whole or substantial part devoted to providing goods or services to any labor organization, or

(5) in any capacity, other than in his capacity as a member of such labor organization, that involves decisionmaking authority concerning, or decisionmaking authority over, or custody of, or control of the moneys, funds, assets, or property of any labor organization,

---

* This section was amended by Pub.L. 98–473, Title II, § 803, Oct. 12, 1984, 98 Stat. 2133.

during or for the period of thirteen years after such conviction or after the end of such imprisonment, whichever is later, unless the sentencing court on the motion of the person convicted sets a lesser period of at least three years after such conviction or after the end of such imprisonment, whichever is later, or unless prior to the end of such period, in the case of a person so convicted or imprisoned, (A) his citizenship rights, having been revoked as a result of such conviction, have been fully restored, or (B) the United States Parole Commission determines that such person's service in any capacity referred to in clauses (1) through (5) would not be contrary to the purposes of this chapter. Prior to making any such determination the Commission shall hold an administrative hearing and shall give notice of such proceeding by certified mail to the Secretary of Labor and to State, county, and Federal prosecuting officials in the jurisdiction or jurisdictions in which such person was convicted. The Commission's determination in any such proceeding shall be final. No person shall knowingly hire, retain, employ, or otherwise place any other person to serve in any capacity in violation of this subsection.

(b) Any person who willfully violates this section shall be fined not more than $10,000 or imprisoned for not more than five years, or both.

(c) For the purpose of this section—

(1) A person shall be deemed to have been "convicted" and under the disability of "conviction" from the date of the judgment of the trial court, regardless of whether that judgment remains under appeal.

(2) A period of parole shall not be considered as part of a period of imprisonment.

(d) Whenever any person—

(1) by operation of this section, has been barred from office or other position in a labor organization as a result of a conviction, and

(2) has filed an appeal of that conviction,

any salary which would be otherwise due such person by virtue of such office or position, shall be placed in escrow by the individual employer or organization responsible for payment of such salary. Payment of such salary into escrow shall continue for the duration of the appeal or for the period of time during which such salary would be otherwise due, whichever period is shorter. Upon the final reversal of such person's conviction on appeal, the amounts in escrow shall be paid to such person. Upon the final sustaining of such person's conviction on appeal, the amounts in escrow shall be returned to the individual employer or organization responsible for payments of those amounts. Upon final reversal of such person's conviction, such person shall no longer be barred by this statute from assuming any position from which such person was previously barred.

TITLE VI—MISCELLANEOUS PROVISIONS

INVESTIGATIONS

Sec. 601. (a) The Secretary shall have power when he believes it necessary in order to determine whether any person has violated or is about to violate any provision of this Act (except title I or amendments made by this Act to other statutes) to make an investigation and in connection therewith he may enter such places and inspect such records and accounts and question such persons as he may deem necessary to enable him to determine the facts relative thereto. The Secretary may report to interested persons or officials concerning the facts required to be shown in any report required by this Act and concerning the reasons for failure or refusal to file such a report or any other matter which he deems to be appropriate as a result of such an investigation.

(b) For the purpose of any investigation provided for in this Act, the provisions of sections 9 and 10 (relating to the attendance of witnesses and the production of books, papers, and documents) of the Federal Trade Commission Act of September 16, 1914, as amended (15 U.S.C. 49, 50), are hereby made applicable to the jurisdiction, powers, and duties of the Secretary or any officers designated by him.

EXTORTIONATE PICKETING

Sec. 602. (a) It shall be unlawful to carry on picketing on or about the premises of any employer for the purpose of, or as part of any conspiracy or in furtherance of any plan or purpose for, the personal profit or enrichment of any individual (except a bona fide increase in wages or other employee benefits) by taking or obtaining any money or other thing of value from such employer against his will or with his consent.

(b) Any person who willfully violates this section shall be fined not more than $10,000 or imprisoned not more than twenty years, or both.

RETENTION OF RIGHTS UNDER OTHER FEDERAL AND STATE LAWS

Sec. 603. (a) Except as explicitly provided to the contrary, nothing in this Act shall reduce or limit the responsibilities of any labor organization or any officer, agent, shop steward, or other representative of a labor organization, or of any trust in which a labor organization is interested, under any other Federal law or under the laws of any State, and, except as explicitly provided to the contrary, nothing in this Act shall take away any right or bar any remedy to which members of a labor organization are entitled under such other Federal law or law of any State.

(b) Nothing contained in titles I, II, III, IV, V, or VI of this Act shall be construed to supersede or impair or otherwise affect the provisions of the Railway Labor Act, as amended, or any of the obligations, rights, benefits, privileges, or immunities of any carrier, employee, organization, representative, or person subject thereto; nor shall anything contained in said titles (except section 505) of this Act be construed to confer any rights, privileges, immunities, or defenses upon employers, or to impair or otherwise affect the rights of any person under the National Labor Relations Act, as amended.

EFFECT ON STATE LAWS

Sec. 604. Nothing in this Act shall be construed to impair or diminish the authority of any State to enact and enforce general criminal laws with respect to robbery, bribery, extortion, embezzlement, grand larceny, burglary, arson, violation of narcotics laws, murder, rape, assault with intent to kill, or assault which inflicts grievous bodily injury, or conspiracy to commit any of such crimes.

STATE AUTHORITY TO ENACT AND ENFORCE LEGISLATION

Sec. 604a. Notwithstanding this or any other Act regulating labor-management relations, each State shall have the authority to enact and enforce, as part of a comprehensive statutory system to eliminate the threat of pervasive racketeering activity in an industry that is, or over time has been, affected by such activity, a provision of law that applies equally to employers, employees, and collective bargaining representatives, which provision of law governs service in any position in a local labor organization which acts or seeks to act in that State as a collective bargaining representative pursuant to the National Labor Relations Act [29 U.S.C.A. § 151 et seq.], in the industry that is subject to that program.*

SERVICE OF PROCESS

Sec. 605. For the purposes of this Act, service of summons, subpoena, or other legal process of a court of the United States upon an officer or agent of a labor organization in his capacity as such shall constitute service upon the labor organization.

ADMINISTRATIVE PROCEDURE ACT

Sec. 606. The provisions of the Administrative Procedure Act shall be applicable to the issuance, amendment, or rescission of any rules or regulations, or any adjudication, authorized or required pursuant to the provisions of this Act.

OTHER AGENCIES AND DEPARTMENTS

Sec. 607. In order to avoid unnecessary expense and duplication of functions among Government agencies, the Secretary may make such arrangements or agreements for cooperation or mutual assistance in the performance of his functions under this Act and the functions of any such agency as he may find to be practicable and consistent with law. The Secretary may utilize the facilities or services of any department, agency,

---

* Pub.L. 98–473, Title II, § 2201, Oct. 12, 1984, 98 Stat. 2192.

or establishment of the United States or of any State or political subdivision of a State, including the services of any of its employees, with the lawful consent of such department, agency, or establishment; and each department, agency, or establishment of the United States is authorized and directed to cooperate with the Secretary and, to the extent permitted by law, to provide such information and facilities as he may request for his assistance in the performance of his functions under this Act. The Attorney General or his representative shall receive from the Secretary for appropriate action such evidence developed in the performance of his functions under this Act as may be found to warrant consideration for criminal prosecution under the provisions of this Act or other Federal law.

CRIMINAL CONTEMPT

Sec. 608. No person shall be punished for any criminal contempt allegedly committed outside the immediate presence of the court in connection with any civil action prosecuted by the Secretary or any other person in any court of the United States under the provisions of this Act unless the facts constituting such criminal contempt are established by the verdict of the jury in a proceeding in the district court of the United States, which jury shall be chosen and empaneled in the manner prescribed by the law governing trial juries in criminal prosecutions in the district courts of the United States.

PROHIBITION ON CERTAIN DISCIPLINE BY LABOR ORGANIZATION

Sec. 609. It shall be unlawful for any labor organization, or any officer, agent, shop steward, or other representative of a labor organization, or any employee thereof to fine, suspend, expel, or otherwise discipline any of its members for exercising any right to which he is entitled under the provisions of this Act. The provisions of section 102 shall be applicable in the enforcement of this section.

DEPRIVATION OF RIGHTS UNDER ACT BY VIOLENCE

Sec. 610. It shall be unlawful for any person through the use of force or violence, or threat of the use of force or violence, to restrain, coerce, or intimidate, or attempt to restrain, coerce, or intimidate any member of a labor organization for the purpose of interfering with or preventing the exercise of any right to which he is entitled under the provisions of this Act. Any person who willfully violates this section shall be fined not more than $1,000 or imprisoned for not more than one year, or both.

SEPARABILITY PROVISIONS

Sec. 611. If any provision of this Act, or the application of such provision to any person or circumstances, shall be held invalid, the remainder of this Act or the application of such provision to persons or circumstances other than those as to which it is held invalid, shall not be affected thereby.

WORKER ADJUSTMENT AND RETRAINING NOTIFICATION ACT

102 Stat. 890 (1988), 29 U.S.C. §§ 2101–2109 (1988).

§ 2101. Definitions; exclusions from definition of loss of employment

(a) Definitions.—As used in this chapter—

(1) the term "employer" means any business enterprise that employs—

(A) 100 or more employees, excluding part-time employees; or

(B) 100 or more employees who in the aggregate work at least 4,000 hours per week (exclusive of hours of overtime);

(2) the term "plant closing" means the permanent or temporary shutdown of a single site of employment, or one or more facilities or operating units within a single site of employment, if the shutdown results in an employment loss at the single site of employment during any 30-day period for 50 or more employees excluding any part-time employees;

(3) the term "mass layoff" means a reduction in force which—

(A) is not the result of a plant closing; and

(B) results in an employment loss at the single site of employment during any 30-day period for—

(i)(I) at least 33 percent of the employees (excluding any part-time employees); and

(II) at least 50 employees (excluding any part-time employees); or

(ii) at least 500 employees (excluding any part-time employees);

(4) the term "representative" means an exclusive representative of employees within the meaning of section 158(f) or 159(a) of this title or section 152 of Title 45;

(5) the term "affected employees" means employees who may reasonably be expected to experience an employment loss as a consequence of a proposed plant closing or mass layoff by their employer;

(6) subject to subsection (b) of this section the term "employment loss" means (A) an employment termination, other than a discharge for cause, voluntary departure, or retirement, (B) a layoff exceeding 6 months, or (C) a reduction in hours of work of more than 50 percent during each month of any 6-month period;

(7) the term "unit of local government" means any general purpose political subdivision of a State which has the power to levy taxes and spend funds, as well as general corporate and police powers; and

(8) the term "part-time employee" means an employee who is employed for an average of fewer than 20 hours per week or who has been employed for fewer than 6 of the 12 months preceding the date on which notice is required.

(b) Exclusions from definition of employment loss.—(1) In the case of a sale of part or all of an employer's business, the seller shall be responsible for providing notice for any plant closing or mass layoff in accordance with section 2102 of this title, up to and including the effective date of the sale. After the effective date of the sale of part or all of an employer's business, the purchaser shall be responsible for providing notice for any plant closing or mass layoff in accordance with section 2102 of this title. Notwithstanding any other provision of this chapter, any person who is an employee of the seller (other than a part-time employee) as of the effective date of the sale shall be considered an employee of the purchaser immediately after the effective date of the sale.

(2) Notwithstanding subsection (a)(6) of this section, an employee may not be considered to have experienced an employment loss if the closing or layoff is the result of the relocation or consolidation of part or all of the employer's business and, prior to the closing or layoff—

(A) the employer offers to transfer the employee to a different site of employment within a reasonable commuting distance with no more than a 6-month break in employment; or

(B) the employer offers to transfer the employee to any other site of employment regardless of distance with no more than a 6-month break in employment, and the employee accepts within 30 days of the offer or of the closing or layoff, whichever is later.

§ 2102. Notice required before plant closings and mass layoffs

(a) Notice to employees, state dislocated worker units, and local governments.—An employer shall not order a plant closing or mass layoff until the end of a 60-day period after the employer serves written notice of such an order—

(1) to each representative of the affected employees as of the time of the notice or, if there is no such representative at that time, to each affected employee; and

(2) to the State dislocated worker unit (designated or created under title III of the Job Training Partnership Act [29 U.S.C.A.

§ 1651 et seq.]), and the chief elected official of the unit of local government within which such closing or layoff is to occur.

If there is more than one such unit, the unit of local government which the employer shall notify is the unit of local government to which the employer pays the highest taxes for the year preceding the year for which the determination is made.

(b) Reduction of notification period.—(1) An employer may order the shutdown of a single site of employment before the conclusion of the 60-day period if as of the time that notice would have been required the employer was actively seeking capital or business which, if obtained, would have enabled the employer to avoid or postpone the shutdown and the employer reasonably and in good faith believed that giving the notice required would have precluded the employer from obtaining the needed capital or business.

(2)(A) An employer may order a plant closing or mass layoff before the conclusion of the 60-day period if the closing or mass layoff is caused by business circumstances that were not reasonably foreseeable as of the time that notice would have been required.

(B) No notice under this chapter shall be required if the plant closing or mass layoff is due to any form of natural disaster, such as a flood, earthquake, or the drought currently ravaging the farmlands of the United States.

(3) An employer relying on this subsection shall give as much notice as is practicable and at that time shall give a brief statement of the basis for reducing the notification period.

(c) Extension of layoff period.—A layoff of more than 6 months which, at its outset, was announced to be a layoff of 6 months or less, shall be treated as an employment loss under this chapter unless—

(1) the extension beyond 6 months is caused by business circumstances (including unforeseeable changes in price or cost) not reasonably foreseeable at the time of the initial layoff; and

(2) notice is given at the time it becomes reasonably foreseeable, that the extension beyond 6 months will be required.

(d) Determinations with respect to employment loss.—For purposes of this section, in determining whether a plant closing or mass layoff has occurred or will occur, employment losses for 2 or more groups at a single site of employment, each of which is less than the minimum number of employees specified in section 2101(a)(2) or (3) of this title but which in the aggregate exceed that minimum number, and which occur within any 90-day period shall be considered to be a plant closing or mass layoff unless the employer demonstrates that the employment losses are the result of separate and distinct actions and causes and are not an attempt by the employer to evade the requirements of this chapter.

§ 2103. Exemptions

This chapter shall not apply to a plant closing or mass layoff if—

(1) the closing is of a temporary facility or the closing or layoff is the result of the completion of a particular project or undertaking, and the affected employees were hired with the understanding that their employment was limited to the duration of the facility or the project or undertaking; or

(2) the closing or layoff constitutes a strike or constitutes a lockout not intended to evade the requirements of this chapter. Nothing in this chapter shall require an employer to serve written notice pursuant to section 2102(a) of this title when permanently replacing a person who is deemed to be an economic striker under the National Labor Relations Act [29 U.S.C.A. § 151 et seq.]: *Provided,* That nothing in this chapter shall be deemed to validate or invalidate any judicial or administrative ruling relating to the hiring of permanent replacements for economic strikers under the National Labor Relations Act.

§ 2104. Administration and enforcement of requirements

(a) Civil actions against employers.—(1) Any employer who orders a plant closing or mass layoff in violation of section 2102 of this title shall be liable to each aggrieved employee who suffers an employment loss as a result of such closing or layoff for—

(A) back pay for each day of violation at a rate of compensation not less than the higher of—

(i) the average regular rate received by such employee during the last 3 years of the employee's employment; or

(ii) the final regular rate received by such employee; and

(B) benefits under an employee benefit plan described in section 1002(3) of this title, including the cost of medical expenses incurred during the employment loss which would have been covered under an employee benefit plan if the employment loss had not occurred.

Such liability shall be calculated for the period of the violation, up to a maximum of 60 days, but in no event for more than one-half the number of days the employee was employed by the employer.

(2) The amount for which an employer is liable under paragraph (1) shall be reduced by—

(A) any wages paid by the employer to the employee for the period of the violation;

(B) any voluntary and unconditional payment by the employer to the employee that is not required by any legal obligation; and

(C) any payment by the employer to a third party or trustee (such as premiums for health benefits or payments to a defined contribution pension plan) on behalf of and attributable to the employee for the period of the violation.

In addition, any liability incurred under paragraph (1) with respect to a defined benefit pension plan may be reduced by crediting the employee with service for all purposes under such a plan for the period of the violation.

(3) Any employer who violates the provisions of section 2102 of this title with respect to a unit of local government shall be subject to a civil penalty of not more than $500 for each day of such violation, except that such penalty shall not apply if the employer pays to each aggrieved employee the amount for which the employer is liable to that employee within 3 weeks from the date the employer orders the shutdown or layoff.

(4) If an employer which has violated this chapter proves to the satisfaction of the court that the act or omission that violated this chapter was in good faith and that the employer had reasonable grounds for believing that the act or omission was not a violation of this chapter the court may, in its discretion, reduce the amount of the liability or penalty provided for in this section.

(5) A person seeking to enforce such liability, including a representative of employees or a unit of local government aggrieved under paragraph (1) or (3), may sue either for such person or for other persons similarly situated, or both, in any district court of the United States for any district in which the violation is alleged to have occurred, or in which the employer transacts business.

(6) In any such suit, the court, in its discretion, may allow the prevailing party a reasonable attorney's fee as part of the costs.

(7) For purposes of this subsection, the term, "aggrieved employee" means an employee who has worked for the employer ordering the plant closing or mass layoff and who, as a result of the failure by the employer to comply with section 2102 of this title, did not receive timely notice either directly or through his or her representative as required by section 2102 of this title.

(b) Exclusivity of remedies.—The remedies provided for in this section shall be the exclusive remedies for any violation of this chapter. Under this chapter, a Federal court shall not have authority to enjoin a plant closing or mass layoff.

§ 2105. Procedures in addition to other rights of employees

The rights and remedies provided to employees by this chapter are in addition to, and not in lieu of, any other contractual or statutory rights and remedies of the employees, and are not intended to alter or affect such rights and remedies, except that the period of notification required by this chapter shall run concurrently with any period of notification required by contract or by any other statute.

§ 2106. Procedures encouraged where not required

It is the sense of Congress that an employer who is not required to comply with the notice requirements of section 2102 of this title should, to the extent possible, provide notice to its employees about a proposal to close a plant or permanently reduce its workforce.

§ 2107. Authority to prescribe regulations

(a) The Secretary of Labor shall prescribe such regulations as may be necessary to carry out this chapter. Such regulations shall, at a minimum, include interpretative regulations describing the methods by which employers may provide for appropriate service of notice as required by this chapter.

(b) The mailing of notice to an employee's last known address or inclusion of notice in the employee's paycheck will be considered acceptable methods for fulfillment of the employer's obligation to give notice to each affected employee under this chapter.

§ 2108. Effect on other laws

The giving of notice pursuant to this chapter, if done in good faith compliance with this chapter, shall not constitute a violation of the National Labor Relations Act [29 U.S.C.A. § 151 et seq.] or the Railway Labor Act [45 U.S.C.A. 151 et seq.].

§ 2109. Report on employment and international competitiveness

Two years after Aug. 4, 1988, the Comptroller General shall submit to the Committee on Small Business of both the House and Senate, the Committee on Labor and Human Resources, and the Committee on Education and Labor a report containing a detailed and objective analysis of the effect of this chapter on employers (especially small- and medium-sized businesses), the economy (international competitiveness), and employees (in terms of levels and conditions of employment). The Comptroller General shall assess both costs and benefits, including the effect on productivity, competitiveness, unemployment rates and compensation, and worker retraining and readjustment.

Collective Bargaining Agreement

PREAMBLE

This Agreement is made and entered into by and between the MAJOR CONTAINER COMPANY ("Company"), their successors or assigns, and the UNITED PAPERWORKERS INTERNATIONAL UNION, AFL-CIO ("Union").

I. PURPOSE

Section 1. WITNESSETH, whereas the parties hereto have reached agreement as a result of collective bargaining for the purpose of facilitating the peaceful adjustment of differences which may arise from time to time between this Company and the Union, and to promote harmony and efficiency and to the end that the employees and the Company and the general public may mutually benefit, the parties hereto contract and agree with each other as follows:

II. RECOGNITION AND UNION SECURITY

Section 1. The Company recognizes the Union as the sole agency for collective bargaining on behalf of all employees, with the exception of timekeepers, clerks, office employees, watchmen and non-working foremen and non-working supervisors, in charge of any classes of labor.

Section 2. This recognition is interpreted by the parties to apply to any transfer or relocation of the Company's present facility to another location within or outside of the metropolitan area, which are an accretion to the existing bargaining unit, where the jobs performed are substantially the same as are covered by the present Agreement.

Section 3. All employees with the exceptions noted in Section 1 who are members of the Union in good standing on the effective date of this Agreement, shall as a condition of continued employment, maintain their membership in good standing in the Union. All employees, who on the effective date of this Agreement, are not as yet members in good standing of the Union, shall become members of the Union in good standing by no later than thirty (30) days following the effective date of this Agreement and shall maintain membership in good standing in the Union in order to continue in employment. All new employees, shall as a condition of continued employment, become members and maintain membership in good standing in the Union by no later than thirty (30) days following the date of their employment or the effective date of this Agreement, whichever is the later.

Section 4. The Company agrees to discharge any employee who does not join or maintain his membership in good standing in the Union within seven (7) calendar days after receipt of written notice from the Union that such employee is delinquent in initiation fee or dues. The Union will indemnify and save harmless the Company against any and all claims, demands, or suits that may arise out of the discharge of any employee under this section.

Section 5. During the term of this Agreement, and at the written request of the Union, the Company will deduct from their wages and remit promptly to the Union the regular monthly membership dues and/or initiation fees established by the Union in accordance with the Constitution and By-Laws of the Union for all employees who have executed and caused to be delivered to the Company a written authorization for such deductions, on a form in conformity with the applicable statutes, which shall not be irrevocable for a period of more than one (1) year, or the termination date of this Agreement, whichever occurs sooner.

III. MANAGEMENT RIGHTS

Section 1. It is understood and agreed that the management of the Plant and the direction of the work force, including but not limited to the right to hire, suspend, transfer or discharge for proper cause and the right to relieve employees from duty because of lack of work, the right to establish, determine, and maintain reasonable standards of production, to introduce new and improved methods, materials, equipment or facilities and change or eliminate methods, materials, equipment or facilities are vested exclusively in the Company, subject to the provisions of this Agreement.

IV. DISCRIMINATION

Section 1. No employee shall be discriminated against by the Company for activity in or on behalf of the Union, but shall not be exempted from discipline that is not discriminatory.

Section 2. The Company and the Union agree that there shall be no discrimination in regard to hiring, tenure of employment or any condition of employment, or in regard to membership in the Union, because of race, color, religion, sex, age, disability, national origin, marital status, sexual orientation, veteran status, or any other classification protected by law.

Section 3. The parties recognize that in complying with this Article they are subject to the specific provisions and exemptions of Title VII of the Civil Rights Act of 1964, the Age Discrimination in Employment Act of 1967, the Americans with Disabilities Act, as well as the specific statutes of the various states and pertinent Executive Orders issued by the President of the United States.

V. WAGES

Section 1. The schedule of rates attached hereto as "Exhibit A" shall become a part of this Agreement and they shall be the minimum rates of pay to be paid by the Company to its employees for the duration of this Agreement.

Section 2. All employees shall receive their pay weekly.

VI. HOURS OF WORK; OVERTIME

Section 1. Eight (8) consecutive hours, shall constitute a normal day's work; five (5) days, shall constitute a normal work week. Employees assigned to work days will be granted an unpaid lunch period of thirty (30) minutes. Shift employees will be granted a paid twenty (20) minutes lunch period during the shift, when operating requirements permit. Any employee who works over eight (8) hours in any twenty-four (24) hour period, or forty (40) hours (for which overtime has not previously been paid) in any one work week, shall be paid at the rate of time and a half. This provision shall not be construed to guarantee any specific hours or days of work.

Any employee who works over sixty (60) hours (for which double-time has not previously been paid) in any one work week shall be paid at the rate of double-time.

Section 2. Overtime shall be distributed as equitably as possible among the employees who can perform the work. The Company shall maintain open overtime records for the purpose of distributing over time equitably.

Section 3. All work performed on Sundays and holidays shall be paid for at the rate of double time.

Section 4. All work performed on Saturdays shall be paid for at the rate of time and one-half.

Section 5. Employees working on second shift shall receive a shift premium of fifteen (15) cents per hour.

Section 6. Employees working on third shift shall receive a shift premium of twenty-five (25) cents per hour.

VII. HOLIDAYS

Section 1. The following holidays or days celebrated in place thereof shall be observed and shall be paid for even though not worked at eight hours of the regular hourly rate of pay for all employees who have worked sixty (60) days or more in the Company. Holidays falling on Sunday shall be observed on the following Monday.

New Year's Day

Decoration Day

Fourth of July

Good Friday

Labor Day

Employee's Birthday

Thanksgiving Day

Day after Thanksgiving

Christmas Day

Christmas Eve Day

New Year's Eve Day

Section 2. Any employee entitled to a holiday with pay shall not be required to work on said holiday.

Section 3. It is agreed that to qualify for such holiday pay an employee shall have worked the regular scheduled work day immediately preceding and succeeding said holiday, provided work is available unless excused from such work by the plant management.

VIII. VACATIONS

Section 1. Vacation pay shall be computed on the basis of regular hourly rates of pay.

Section 2. The following schedule shall be the method of application of vacation periods and vacation pay.

Length of Service	Vacation Periods	Vacation Pay at Regular Hourly Rates of Pay
1 Year	1	42 Hours Pay
3 Years	2	84 Hours Pay
8 Years	3	126 Hours Pay
15 Years	4	168 Hours Pay
20 Years	5	210 Hours Pay
25 Years	6	252 Hours Pay

Section 3. The Company may shut down the plant completely or partially to grant vacations to all or part of the employees at one time provided it shall notify the employees of such a plan at least sixty (60) days before a vacation commences. Otherwise, vacations will be scheduled according to employees' desires, subject to the exclusive right of the Company to change vacation periods to assure orderly and efficient operation of the Plant. In the event of a dispute between two or more employees as to the time of their vacations, the employee with the greatest seniority with the Company shall receive the preference.

Section 4. Any employee eligible for a vacation, who is severed from the payroll of the Company in any calendar year before having taken his or her vacation, except one who is discharged for cause or who quits without two weeks' notice, shall receive vacation pay.

IX. SENIORITY

Section 1. Seniority is defined as the length of an employee's service with the Company within the bargaining unit; it shall apply plant-wide.

Section 2. The Company agrees to draw up a plant-wide Seniority list as of June 1st of each year, which shall be posted in a location available to all employees.

Section 3. The Union may select from the employees covered by this Agreement a Steward who has been employed by the Company for a period of at least one (1) year, whose duty it is to see that this contract is not broken by either the employees or the Employer. The Union shall notify the Company, in writing, of the name of the Shop Steward.

Section 4. In the event of layoff, all Union officers, shop stewards, and shop committee members shall have seniority during their terms of office only, over other employees of the Company provided they have at least one (1) year service with the Company.

Section 5. Production foremen, or other non-bargaining unit employees, shall not do any work, the performance of which, would cause any employee to suffer lay-off or loss of overtime.

Section 6. An employee shall be terminated and shall lose all accumulated seniority when he or she:

a) quits

b) is discharged

c) is laid off for lack of work for a continuous period of 15 calendar months or a period of time equal to the employee's plant seniority, whichever comes first

d) fails to return to work within four (4) days of notice to return to work, unless such failure to return is for reason satisfactory to the Company

e) engages in gainful employment during a leave of absence except in cases where such leave of absence is expressly granted for this purpose

f) fails to return to work within three (3) working days from the date of expiration of his leave of absence

g) is absent due to non-industrial accident or illness for a period of two (2) years

h) is retired under the Company's Pension Plan.

X. PERMANENT VACANCIES

Section 1. Each permanent job vacancy and each permanent new job which falls within the scope of the Union's certification shall be filled as follows:

(a) Notice of such job shall be posted in the plant for two (2) days. Such job postings shall include the job classification, department, and the shift on which the new job or vacancy exists. Any employee who wishes to bid for such jobs shall sign the posting. Job postings shall be placed in three locations throughout the plant for official signing in the presence of a member of management, who will initial the posting. Two postings will be provided in the supervisory offices assigned in the plant; a third posting will be placed in the Human Resources office for signing. At all posting locations, job descriptions for all jobs will be available for review. At the end of the two (2) days, the Company shall remove the posting.

(b) Where skill and ability are relatively equal, seniority shall prevail, providing the employee is physically able to perform the work without endangering his or her health or safety. The most senior qualified employee will be awarded the job and be notified by the Human Resources office within five (5) days after removal of the posting. The Company will transfer the employee awarded the vacancy hereunder to the new job within fifteen (15) calendar days, provided the release of the employee does not interfere with the efficient operations of the department. Multiple postings will be awarded from the highest pay grade posting to the lowest pay grade posting.

(c) An employee awarded the vacancy hereunder shall be given up to sixteen (16) working days in which to demonstrate his or her ability to perform the work involved. In some circumstances, extensions may be required, not to exceed sixteen (16) additional workdays. During the qualifying period, employees are unable to bid. During this period, the Company may remove the employee from the job if the Company considers the employee's work to be unsatisfactory. The employee may then bid on any other vacancy. An employee disqualified from a job will be unable to bid that job for a period of three (3) months.

Section 2. The Union and the Company may, by mutual agreement, provide rules whereby disabled employees may be assigned to jobs which they are able to satisfactorily perform without regard to this Article. When the Union and the Company agree to placement of an employee hereunder, the conditions pertaining to that placement shall be reduced to writing and signed by the parties.

XI. LAYOFF AND RECALL

Section 1. If the Company decides to reduce the number of employees in a job classification in a department, and the reduction is expected to continue for more than four (4) days, the reduction shall be made as follows:

(a) The least senior employee or employees shall be removed from the classification provided the skill and ability of the employees in the classification are relatively equal.

(b) An employee removed from his or her classification and/or shift pursuant to (a) shall be afforded the opportunity to move into a job classification in an equal or lower labor grade on any shift provided he or she has the proven skill and ability to perform such work which is held by an employee with less seniority. An employee displaced from his job classification by the exercise of the seniority rights granted in this paragraph shall also be afforded the opportunity to displace other employees in accordance with this paragraph and the exercise of seniority hereunder.

(c) In the operation of (a) and (b) above, a senior employee has the prerogative of accepting layoff instead of displacing a junior employee, if he or she so desires.

(d) The Company will post a notice of layoff expected to last more than four (4) days at least ten (10) days in advance of such layoff, unless the conditions leading to such layoff resulted from an Act of God, labor dispute, or other condition beyond the control of the Company.

Section 2. (a) Employees affected by a reduction of forces shall be recalled to their regular job classification and department in the inverse order of the force reduction. If the employee refuses such recall, he will be terminated as a voluntary quit. Employees recalled to their regular job classification and department, but not to their regular shift, shall be returned to their regular shift in order of seniority as openings occur.

(b) When a vacancy exists after exhausting paragraph (a), the job will be posted for bid according to the bidding procedure. If no employee is awarded such job vacancy, the most senior employee on layoff shall be afforded the vacancy providing he or she has the skill and ability to perform the work.

Section 3. Nothing in this Agreement shall prohibit the Company's laying off the employees for the purpose of taking inventory and offering the work available during such period to the senior qualified employees in the department.

XII. EMPLOYEE SAFETY

Section 1. The Company agrees to provide a place of employment which shall be safe for the employees therein, shall furnish and use safety devices and safeguards, and shall adopt and use methods and processes adequate to render such places of employment safe. The term "safe" or "safety" as applied to employment or place of employment shall include conditions and methods of sanitation and hygiene necessary for the protection of life, health and safety of the employees.

Section 2. The Company agrees that all machinery, equipment and facilities the Company furnishes shall meet with all required legal standards of safety and sanitation. Accident records shall be kept and maintained by the Company and shall be made available on request to the Safety Committee.

Section 3. The Company agrees to maintain a Joint Labor-Management Safety Committee. The Safety Committee shall be composed of at least two (2) representatives of Management and at least two (2) representatives of the Union. The Union representatives shall be selected by the local Union. The Safety Committee shall be able to sit in on any safety investigation when any employee is questioned and shall:

Meet at least once every month on definitely established dates;

Make inspections of the plant at least once every month;

Make recommendations for the correction of unsafe or harmful work practices;

Review and analyze all reports of industrial injury and illness, investigate causes of same and recommend rules and procedures for the prevention of accidents and disease and for the promotion of health and safety of employees;

Promote health and safety education.

Section 4. All disputes and disagreements brought to the attention of the Safety Committee, arising under the Safety clause of this contract, if not disposed of by the Safety Committee, shall be subject to the Grievance Procedure.

Section 5. In the event of special circumstances, the Safety Committee may seek advice, opinion and suggestions of experts and authorities on safety matters. Such experts shall have access to the plant for the purpose of applying this article at any time upon providing reasonable notice. The Personnel Manager or his/her designee and a Union designee shall accompany the Safety representative.

Section 6. Employees injured in the plant shall be furnished medical aid or treatment on Company time, and shall receive full pay for the shift on which they were working when injured.

Section 7. The Union agrees to participate on the Safety Committee and will endeavor to have its members observe all safety rules and use all equipment and safeguards provided. The Union representative on the Safety Committee, upon request, shall be allowed to leave his or her work during working hours for the purpose of performing his or duties as outlined in this Article without loss of time or pay.

XIII. DISCIPLINE

Section 1. The Employer may not discipline or discharge except for just cause and only after due regard for principles of progressive discipline, except as specified otherwise herein.

Section 2. The following shall be causes for immediate discharge:

(a) Bringing intoxicants, narcotics or other dangerous drugs into or consuming intoxicants or such narcotics or drugs in the plant or on the plant premises.

(b) Reporting for duty under the influence of liquor, narcotics, or drugs.

(c) Smoking while on duty or in prohibited areas.

(d) Deliberate destruction or removal of Company's or another employee's property.

(e) Refusal to comply with Company rules, provided that such rules shall be posted in a conspicuous place where they may be read by all employees; and further provided that no changes in present rules or no additional rules shall be made that are inconsistent with this Agreement.

(f) Disorderly conduct.

(g) Sleeping on duty.

(h) Giving or taking a bribe of any nature, as an inducement to obtaining work or retaining a position.

(i) Failure to report for duty without bona fide reasons.

(j) Reading of books, magazines or newspapers while on duty except where required in line of duty.

(k) Unsanitary practice endangering the health of others.

(*l*) Gambling during working hours.

Section 3. Except for the infractions noted in Section 2, above, the Employer shall not discharge or suspend an employee without first having discussed such action with the employee and Shop Steward or, in absence of both, having given notice to the Union. Such notice may be by telephone, telegram, or letter, and such notice must include the reason or reasons for an employee's discharge or suspension.

Section 4. No employee in the bargaining unit shall be required to take any polygraph test, but an employee may, of his own volition, take such a test.

XIV. GRIEVANCE PROCEDURE

Section 1. Should grievances arise, a diligent effort shall be made to settle all grievances as soon as possible after they have been presented either by the Union or an employee.

Any employee having a grievance shall submit same in writing as promptly as possible after its occurrence but no grievance shall be valid if not presented within fifteen (15) days from the time the cause for complaint became known to the employee.

If at any time a grievance remains at any step below Step 4 for more than seven (7) working days, the Local Union may, by written notice to local management, request that such grievance be heard at the next step.

Section 2. When grievances arise, the following steps shall be followed, each to be exhausted before resorting to the next:

Step 1. Between the immediate supervisor and the aggrieved employee; the appropriate Union representative shall be given an opportunity to be present.

Step 2. Between the Production Superintendent and the Union Committee.

Step 3. Between the Operations Manager and the Union Committee.

Step 4. Between the Divisional Vice President of the Company, or his representative, and the President of the International Union, or his representative.

XV. ARBITRATION

Section 1. In the event that a grievance based upon the interpretation, application or compliance with the terms of this Agreement shall not have been satisfactorily settled, the Union within thirty (30) days after the Company's answer to the last step in the grievance procedure may submit the matter to the American Arbitration Association under their rules then in effect. Expenses of the arbitrator shall be shared equally by the Company and the Union. The decision of the arbitrator shall be binding upon both parties to this Agreement. Such decision shall be within the scope and terms of this Agreement, but shall not change any of its terms or conditions.

XVI. STRIKES AND LOCKOUTS

Section 1. The Union and the Company agree that there shall be no strikes, sympathy strikes, boycotts, lockouts or general slowing down of production by employees, during the life of this Agreement, and that in the event differences should arise between the Company and the Union or its members employed by the Company, as to the meaning and application of this Agreement, or should any local trouble of any kind arise in the plant, there shall be no suspension of work by the employees on account of such differences.

XVII. EMPLOYEE BENEFITS

The benefits as shown in this section shall continue in effect during the life of this Agreement.

Medical Insurance: Blue Cross Preferred Comprehensive; Blue Shield, 100; and Major Medical Insurance shall continue to be provided at Company expense for employees until age 70. The Major Medical Insurance referred to herein shall be provided on the basis of $20,000 maximum; $200 deductible per person, and 80/20 participation.

A Blue Shield Eye Examination and Refraction Program shall be provided for employees and certain of their dependents at Company expense as promptly as arrangements can be made.

Dental Insurance: A dental insurance plan to be agreed upon by the parties shall be effective April 1, 2023. This plan shall provide dental benefits for employees and their covered dependents. Company shall contribute $40.00 per month per covered employee toward the cost of this coverage and any excess cost shall be made up by employee contributions.

Death in Family: Should death occur to the Mother, Father, Stepmother, Stepfather, Wife, Children, Stepchildren, Sister or Brother of any employee, he or she shall be entitled to a three-day leave of absence and should death occur to the Grandparent of any employee he or she shall be entitled to a one-day leave of absence. For all such leaves of absence the employee will be paid at his or her straight-time rate provided the leave is taken during the normal week, i.e., Monday through Friday.

Jury Duty: The Company agrees to pay to any employee who shall serve on a bona fide jury panel an amount equal to the difference between the employee's earnings from such service and his or her regular eight (8) hours straight time pay for the days, not in excess of fifteen days for any single period of jury service, during which the employee shall be absent and on jury service.

Sick Benefits: Provision is made for the payment of Sick Benefits to hourly paid employees who have been on the payroll for not less than one year immediately prior to the event of sickness.

On presentation of a licensed physician's, dentist's, chiropodist's, or chiropractor's certificate, an employee who has been ill seven (7) or more consecutive days is entitled to an amount equal to fifty (50) percent of his or her forty-hour weekly wages or the amount to which the employee would be entitled under the State Temporary Disability Law, whichever is greater, from the day he became ill, for a period not in excess of twenty-six weeks in any twelve-month period.

Sick benefits have no connection with illness due to injury in the plant. Disabilities due to injuries in the plant are compensated for under Employers' Liability Insurance in accordance with State regulations.

Retirement: All employees covered by this Agreement are also covered by the Pension Plan which went into operation July 1, 2000, as amended: This is a funded pension plan.

A copy of the Summary Plan Description will be regularly furnished to each new employee. Additional copies may be obtained upon request at the Personnel Office.

Life Insurance: A group life insurance policy will be purchased by the Company so that each employee with one or more years of continuous service with the Company shall have life insurance protection in the amount of $20,000 in the event such employee shall die while employed by the Company and before such employee's retirement. Beneficiary designations shall be made by each such employee in accordance with the provisions of such group policy.

XVIII. NEW EMPLOYEES

Section 1. New employees shall be considered probationary employees and shall not rank for seniority until they shall have been in the employ of the Company for sixty (60) calendar days, unless otherwise extended by mutual agreement. After the expiration of the sixty (60) day period, they shall cease to be probationary employees and rates of pay and all other provisions of this Agreement shall be applicable to them. They shall then rank for seniority from the date of original hiring in the plant. During the probationary period the Company may pay the employee the regular job wage rate.

XIX. SCOPE OF WORK; NEW TECHNOLOGIES

Section 1. It is the intent of the parties to permit the Company to remain technologically competitive and to meet its customer's needs so long as work opportunities now and in the future are preserved for the employees within the bargaining unit identified in Article II. As new technologies develop, the parties pledge their best efforts to fully train and include bargaining unit employees in the implementation of such technologies.

Section 2. In furtherance of the parties' intent, a technology committee consisting of two (2) Union and two (2) Company representatives shall be established and shall meet at the request of either the Union or the Company. The committee shall be empowered to investigate and discuss all issues involving the impact of new technology on bargaining unit work. The committee shall reach agreement on issues investigated and discussed.

Section 3. The Company shall provide training, if required, on any new technology used to perform bargaining unit work. The Company will not permit its proprietary or licensed software, data, hardware, equipment or facilities to be used by others to perform work or functions that replace work or functions being performed by bargaining unit employees.

XX. COMPLETE AGREEMENT

Section 1. The parties hereto acknowledge that, during the negotiations which resulted in this Agreement, each had the unlimited right and opportunity to make demands and proposals with respect to any subject or matter not removed by law from the area of collective bargaining, and that the understandings and Agreements arrived at by the parties after the exercise of the right and opportunity are set forth in this Agreement. Therefore, the parties hereto, for the life of this Agreement, each voluntarily and unqualifiedly waives the right, and each expressly agrees that the other shall not be obligated, to bargain collectively with respect to any subject or matter referred to, or covered or not specifically referred to or covered in the Agreement, even though such subject or matter may not have been within the knowledge or contemplation of either or both of the parties at the time that they negotiated or signed this Agreement.

Section 2. The parties hereto expressly agree that this contract is the sole and complete Agreement between them and that any other previous understandings or Agreements, oral or written (inconsistent with the provisions of this Agreement), are superseded and are of no effect during the term of this Agreement (except as elsewhere provided in the Agreement).

XXI. TERM OF AGREEMENT

Section 1. This Agreement shall be effective April 1, 2024, and shall continue in full force and effect to and including March 31, 2027, and from year to year after the latter date, unless and until either of the parties hereto shall give to the other three (3) months' written notice prior to the end of the original term, or three (3) months' written notice prior to the end of any subsequent year, of an intention to modify or terminate at the end of the original term or of the then current year.

XXII. SUCCESSORS AND ASSIGNS

Section 1. This Agreement shall be binding upon the successors, purchasers, transferees and assignees of the Company.

Section 2. The Company shall give notice of the existence of this Agreement to any successor, purchaser, transferee or assignee. Such notice shall be in writing, with a copy to the Union, at least sixty (60) days in advance of the effective date of transfer. After such notice is given, upon the request of either party, the parties shall bargain in good faith about any matter not covered by this Agreement.

Exhibit A

All incumbent employees shall receive the following wages:

Effective June 1, 2024

Work Level A	Start	$17.71	–$21.06
Work Level B	Start	$18.64	–$22.02
Work Level C	Start	$19.53	–$23.48
Work Level D	Start	$20.01	–$23.96
Work Level E	Start	$22.15	–$26.10

Effective June 1, 2025

Work Level A	Start	$17.88	–$21.34
Work Level B	Start	$18.83	–$22.32
Work Level C	Start	$19.74	–$23.81
Work Level D	Start	$20.23	–$24.30
Work Level E	Start	$22.41	–$25.48

Effective June 1, 2026

Work Level A	Start	$18.20	–$21.84
Work Level B	Start	$19.18	–$22.86
Work Level C	Start	$20.12	–$24.40
Work Level D	Start	$20.62	–$24.91
Work Level E	Start	$22.88	–$27.16

MEMORANDUM OF UNDERSTANDING #1
ABSENTEE CONTROL PROGRAM

Executed by Company and Union on June 1, 2011

The Company shall have the sole option of placing an employee on the absentee watch list by issuing a written notice to the employee, with a copy to the Union. The Company's decision to place an employee on the absentee watch list shall not be subject to the grievance or arbitration provisions of the contract.

Once an employee is placed on the absentee watch list, termination will take place in the event there are two (2) unexcused absences or four (4) tardinesses, or any combination thereof in any rolling 90-calendar day period. An unexcused absence is defined as *any* absence that is not approved by the Company in writing and signed by the Company President or a designee. In the event a termination based upon absenteeism or tardiness is processed to arbitration, the arbitrator shall be limited to determining whether or not an individual had two (2) or more unexcused absences or four (4) or more tardinesses, or any combination thereof, in the rolling 90-day period. It is further understood that an individual placed on the absentee watch list shall remain on that list for 300 calendar days provided there is no intervening unexcused absence or tardiness and otherwise for 365 calendar days from the date of written notice provided for above.

MEMORANDUM OF UNDERSTANDING #2
CHEMICAL SUBSTANCE ABUSE POLICY

Executed by Company and Union on October 15, 2023

1. An employee who is found or reasonable believed to be under the influence of alcohol, drugs or an intoxicant in the employee's system during the course of business on Company premises or when conducting Company business *at any time* will be subject to discipline including discharge, or may be referred to the Employee Assistance Program. Being "under the influence" of alcohol is defined as a blood alcohol content of .04 or higher; and being "under the influence" of an unauthorized controlled substance, illegal drug, prescription, or non-prescription drug is defined as testing positive at specified ng/ml levels.

2. It is the responsibility of each employee to report promptly to the Medical Department the use or possession of any prescribed medication which may affect judgment, performance, or behavior. No prescription drug will be brought on the Company premises or business in any manner, combination, or quantity other than that prescribed by a licensed physician. Failure to comply may result in discipline, including discharge, or the employee may be referred to the Employee Assistance Program.

3. All new hires will be tested for the use of drugs, alcohol, and intoxicating substances. Refusal to submit to testing, or testing positive, will result in rejection of employment by the Company. Applicants who

are denied employment because of a positive test result may reapply for employment and be re-tested after one year from the time of initial rejection.

4. If Management has reasonable suspicion (as herein defined) that an employee is under the influence or, impaired by, or unfit for work due to a chemical substance, including but not limited to a drug, alcohol, or intoxicating substance, or in the event of an accident when the cause may be human error, the subject employee shall be required to submit to medical chemical screening, which may include breath, saliva, urine, and/or blood specimen testing. Positive test results may result in the employee being disciplined, up to and including discharge, or the employee may be referred to the Employee Assistance Program.

5. "Reasonable suspicion" means objective belief based upon reasonable, individualized suspicion that can be described with particularity that a specific employee may be under the influence of alcohol, drugs, or other intoxicating substances based on direct observation by a supervisor or management representative.

PART ONE

THE EVOLUTION OF LABOR RELATIONS LAWS

II. JURISDICTION, ORGANIZATION AND PROCEDURE OF THE NLRB

A. NLRB JURISDICTION

Page 54. Add at the end of the last full paragraph:

In St. Leo University, Inc., 373 N.L.R.B. No. 121 (2024), despite General Counsel's urging, the Biden Board refused to overturn *Bethany College* and return to the more particularized inquiry regarding the religious character of the instruction the Board had articulated in *Pacific Lutheran University*, 361 N.L.R.B. 1404 (2014).

3. EXCLUDED EMPLOYEES

Page 73. Add to end of last full paragraph:

On February 14, 2025, NLRB Acting General Counsel William B. Cowen issued a memo to all field offices rescinding this memo. *See* GC Mem 25-05.

Page 74. Add at the end of the first (carryover) paragraph:

The Dartmouth players abandoned their unionization effort in December 2024, reportedly because of the election and the flipping of the Board to one likely to be less friendly to this effort. *See, e.g.*, Jimmy Golen, *Dartmouth basketball players end their unionization attempt in anticipation of shifting NLRB*, Associated Press (December 31, 2024).

B. NLRB ORGANIZATION AND PROCEDURE

Page 77. Add after the second paragraph:

In the course of or after the conclusion of the hearing, it is possible for the case to be resolved short of the ALJ's decision. On this, the Board has distinguished a "settlement," which is an agreement acceptable to the respondent and the General Counsel and/or the charging party, and what is oddly called a "consent order" approved by the ALJ and the respondent, but by no other party. For some time the latter required the order to provide a "full remedy" for the alleged unfair labor practices. The Trump Labor Board changed the standard to one of "reasonableness." UPMC, 365 N.L.R.B. 418 (2017). The Biden Board returned to the prior standard. Metro Health, Inc., 373 N.L.R.B. No. 89 (2024) (Member Kaplan dissenting).

Page 83. Add at the end of the first (carryover) paragraph:

Whether an election should go forward when an unfair labor practice has been charged has long been a subject of contest which eventually was resolved by a rulemaking that such a charge could block the conduct of an election. *See* 89 Fed. Reg. 62952, 62987 (July 26, 2024) (codified at 29 C.F.R. § 103.20).

Page 83. Add after first full paragraph:

Member Prouty broached the following on the location of representation elections usually held on the employer's premises due to voter accessibility:

> While I agree that the decision on the election's location is appropriately left to the Regional Director's discretion, I believe that the standards applied in exercising that discretion should be more weighted toward acceptance of neutral offsite election locations.
>
> This principle is especially significant in cases where one party to the election, the employer, has utilized its advantages over other parties available through its control of the premises, and where another party, usually the union, is objecting to holding the election on the employer's premises. While the Board has set forth the factors that must be considered by the Regional Director when determining the site of a *rerun* election [*citing* Austral USA, LLC, 357 NLRB 329, 331 (2011)] and while the Regional Director did consider these factors here in determining the site for this decertification election, I believe that Regional Directors should consider and give appropriate weight to these factors in *every type* of representation election when determining the location at which they are to be held.

Omnisource, LLC, 373 N.L.R.B. No. 134 (2024) (emphasis in original).

C. THE SITUATION OF THE NLRB GOING FORWARD

Page 93. Add after first full paragraph:

However, following President Trump's Inauguration, the pendulum quickly swung back. On February 14, 2025, President Trump's Acting General Counsel, William B. Cowen, issued a memo to all field offices rescinding this and a number of other memos issued by former General Counsel Abruzzo. *See* GC Memorandum 25-05. Among these are the following:

- GC 21-02 Rescission of Certain General Counsel Memoranda
- GC 21-03 Effectuation of the National Labor Relations Act Through Vigorous Enforcement of the Mutual Aid or Protection and Inherently Concerted Doctrines

- GC 21-08 Statutory Rights of Players at Academic Institutions (Student-Athletes) Under the National Labor Relations Act
- GC 22-06 Update on Efforts to Secure Full Remedies in Settlements (Revised Attachment)
- GC 23-02 Electronic Monitoring and Algorithmic Management of Employees Interfering with the Exercise of Section 7 Rights
- GC-23-04 Status Update on Advice Submissions Pursuant to GC Memo 21-04
- GC 23-05 Guidance in Response to Inquiries about the *McLaren Macomb* Decision
- GC 23-08 Non-Compete Agreements that Violate the National Labor Relations Act
- GC 24-04 Securing Full Remedies for All Victims of Unlawful Conduct
- GC 24-05 Section 10(j) Injunctive Relief and the U.S. Supreme Court's Decision in *Starbucks Corp. v. McKinney*
- GC 25-01 Remedying the Harmful Effects of Non-Compete and "Stay-or-Pay" Provisions that Violate the National Labor Relations Act
- GC 25-02 Ensuring Settlement Agreements Adequately Address the Public Rights at Issue in the Underlying Unfair Labor Practice Allegations

The following Memoranda also were rescinded pending further guidance:

- GC 21-05 Utilization of Section 10(j) Proceedings
- GC 21-06 Seeking Full Remedies
- GC 21-07 Full Remedies in Settlement Agreements
- GC 22-01 Ensuring Rights and Remedies for Immigrant Workers Under the NLRA
- GC 22-02 Seeking 10(j) Injunctions in Response to Unlawful Threats or Other Coercion During Union Organizing Campaigns
- GC 22-03 Inter-agency Coordination
- GC 23-01 Settling the Section 10(j) Aspect of Cases Warranting Interim Relief
- GC 24-01 (Revised) Guidance in Response to Inquiries about the Board's Decision in Cemex Construction Materials Pacific, LLC

References to this memo and its implications are included in other appropriate locations in this update.

Page 93. Add after the last paragraph:

After several district courts preliminarily enjoined the Board, the Fifth Circuit affirmed in a consolidated appeal. Space Exploration Technologies Corp. v. NLRB (SpaceX), 151 F.4th 761 (5th Cir. 2025). The panel concluded that the lower courts' injunctions were warranted because the Norris-LaGuardia Act does not divest federal courts of jurisdiction in these circumstances; the employers were likely to succeed on their claim that statutory removal restrictions for NLRB administrative law judges violated President's power of removal; the employers were likely to succeed on their claim that statutory removal restrictions for NLRB board members violated President's power of removal; the employers faced irreparable harm in absence of preliminary injunction; and the balance of equities and public interest favored issuance of a preliminary injunction.

But, so far, the Fifth Circuit stands alone. The Ninth and Third Circuits have held to the contrary, determining that the federal courts cannot enjoy Board proceedings on such grounds because of the Labor Act's displacement of the federal judiciary's power to issue injunctive relief in cases involving or arising out of a labor dispute. Amazon.com Services, LLC v. Teamsters, 163 F.4th 624 (9th Cir. 2025); Spring Creek Rehabilitation & Nursing Center v. NLRB, 160 F.4th 380 (3d Cir. 2025). In addition, the Second Circuit held an injunction could not issue for the want of a showing of irreparable harm. CareOne, LLC v. NLRB, 166 F.4th 335 (2nd Cir. 2026). Further, the Ninth Circuit has found that an employer subject to an unfair labor practice complaint could not show any requisite harm flowing from the alleged constitutional infirmity in the removal provision for Administrative Law Judges. NLRB v. North Mountain Foothills Apartments, 157 F.4th 1089 (9th Cir. 2025).

Page 93. Add at the end of the section:

In 2024, the Supreme Court handed down two decisions, by vote of six to three, worthy of note. Loper Bright Enterprises v. Raimondo, 603 U.S. 369 (2024), took up a challenge to the *Chevron* doctrine, deriving from a 1984 Supreme Court decision, that required courts to defer to an agency's interpretation of its organic statute when it was susceptible to differing reasonable constructions. The Court overruled the decision: "Courts must exercise their independent judgment in deciding whether an agency has acted within its statutory authority . . . . Careful attention to the judgment of the Executive Branch may help inform that inquiry." Slip op. at 19.

The decision would not appear to affect the future relationship of the courts to the NLRB's reading of the Act. The NLRB has not relied on *Chevron* in its decisions nor has *Chevron* featured much if at all in Court of Appeals review of Board decisions. In fact, the *Loper Bright* majority relies on two of the Court's labor law decisions—NLRB v. Hearst Pub.,

Inc., 322 U.S. 111 (1944), and Allentown Mack Sales & Services, Inc. v. NLRB, 522 U.S. 359 (1998)—as capturing the judiciary's independent, non-*Chevron* role even as these decisions defer to the NLRB's judgment.

The Court's other recent decision, SEC v. Jarkesy, 603 U.S. 109 (2024), concerned the constitutionality of the repose of power to enforce securities fraud violations in the hands of the Securities and Exchange Commission's Administrative Law Judges (ALJs). It held that the power could not be so reposed.

The Seventh Amendment provides that, "In Suits at common law, where the value in controversy shall exceed twenty dollars, the right of trial by jury shall be preserved. . . ." The statutory action at issue in the case, the imposition of penalties for securities fraud, was "modeled on common law fraud" and the remedies provided for "was available only in law courts." Slip. op. at 13. The Court therefore held that "This is a common law suit in all but name. And such suits typically must be adjudicated in Article III courts." *Id.*

The government had relied on the "public rights" exception which the Court had applied in Atlas Roofing Co. v. Occupational Safety and Health Review Comm'n, 430 U.S. 442 (1977). The Court distinguished *Atlas Roofing* as the statutory standards there "bring no common law soil with them." Slip. op. at 13. In "concept and creation" the Occupational Safety and Health Act was "self-consciously novel."

Justices Gorsuch and Thomas concurred but wrote separately and extensively on separation of powers issues the other four in the majority did not reach. Justices Sotomayor, Kagan, and Jackson dissented at length, differing on the majority's treatment of the meaning of the "public rights" exception and especially on *Atlas Roofing*, noting in passing that decision's reference to the NLRA.

Again, it is not obvious that the holding would support a successful assault on the Labor Act, which scheme had no roots in the common law and whose remedial purposes were equitable, not punitive, though the opinion may cast a shadow over the Board's adoption of new "compensatory" remedies dealt with at page 476. Justice Gorsuch's and Thomas's concurrence may anticipate their thinking on the arguments being mounted against the Act's constitutionality on separation of powers grounds noted in the last paragraph of this section.

A NOTE ON BOARD MAKEUP AND STATUS IN THE TRUMP II ADMINISTRATION

Shortly after taking office the second time, President Trump moved then-sitting NLRB Member Marvin Kaplan into the position of Chair, replacing Member Wilcox. On January 27, 2025, the President terminated Member Wilcox from her position on the Board via an email sent shortly before 11:00 PM, authored by the Deputy Director of the White House Presidential Personnel Office. The termination was not preceded by notice and a hearing, nor was any "neglect of duty or malfeasance" identified, despite the restrictions to removal of a Board member in Section 3(a) of NLRA ("Any member of the Board may be removed by the President, upon notice and hearing, for neglect of duty or malfeasance in office, but for no other cause."). The email instead stated that plaintiff does not share the objectives of the President's administration, and asserted that the restriction on the President's removal authority is unconstitutional as "inconsistent with the vesting of the executive Power in the President." This is the first time in the history of the Board that a president has removed a sitting Board member.

The NLRB's Director of Administration, who reports to Member Kaplan, began the termination process, eliminating Member Wilcox's access to her accounts and instructing her to clean out her office. The Board already had two vacancies, and, without Member Wilcox, was reduced to only two sitting members—one short of the three-member quorum required to operate.

Member Wilcox filed suit in the District of the District of Columbia, challenging her removal and requesting injunctive relief against the President and Member Kaplan so that she could resume her role on the Board. Member Wilcox argued that the termination is unlawful under the Act. The District Court granted summary judgment and permanent injunctive relief in Wilcox's favor, ordering that she be reinstated. *See* Wilcox v. Trump, 775 F. Supp. 3d 215 (D.D.C. 2025). In so doing, the court relied on Humphrey's Executor v. United States, 295 U.S. 602 (1935), which had upheld removal protections for multiple-member boards or commissions. The court concluded that *Humphrey's Executor* remains good law and is well-reasoned in terms of the balance of power it strikes between the political branches of government. The court also rejected the argument that NLRB members fall within the limitations on *Humphrey's Executor* the Supreme Court had recently articulated in Seila Law LLC v. Consumer Financial Protection Bureau, 591 U.S. 197 (2020).

On appeal, a panel of the D.C. Circuit stayed the order in this matter and the consolidated challenge by Cathy Harris, a member of the Merit Systems Protection Board, whom the President also had terminated. *See* Harris v. Bessent, 2025 WL 980278 (D.C. Cir. March 28, 2025). Among other things, the panel members determined that the district court had read *Humphrey's Executor* too broadly, and that, under *Seila Law*, a removal restriction is valid only if it applies to a "multimember expert agenc[y], balanced along partisan lines" that does not "wield substantial executive power." This disposition did not last long. On April 7, 2025, the full D.C. Circuit vacated the panel's stay in a 7–4 decision. *See* Harris v. Bessent, 2025 WL 1021435 (D.C. Cir. April 7, 2025) (*en banc*). In so doing, the majority principally relied on the fact that *Seila Law* had stated that

Humphrey's Executor remains good law, and that the decision in *Seila Law* does not apply in this circumstance.

However, on May 22, the Supreme Court granted the government's emergency application for a stay of the D.C. Circuit order in a 6–3 decision. Trump v. Wilcox, 145 S.Ct. 1415 (2025). The majority concluded as follows:

> Because the Constitution vests the executive power in the President, see Art. II, § 1, cl. 1, he may remove without cause executive officers who exercise that power on his behalf, subject to narrow exceptions recognized by our precedents, see *Seila Law LLC v. Consumer Financial Protection Bureau*, 591 U.S. 197, 215–218 (2020). The stay reflects our judgment that the Government is likely to show that both the NLRB and MSPB exercise considerable executive power. But we do not ultimately decide in this posture whether the NLRB or MSPB falls within such a recognized exception; that question is better left for resolution after full briefing and argument. The stay also reflects our judgment that the Government faces greater risk of harm from an order allowing a removed officer to continue exercising the executive power than a wrongfully removed officer faces from being unable to perform her statutory duty.

Although its disposition is expressly tentative, the Court's reasoning strongly suggests that it ultimately will conclude that the President has unlimited authority to terminate NLRB members, contrary to the language of the statute. Notably, the Court went out of its way to distinguish the Federal Reserve, stating that "the Federal Reserve is a uniquely structured, quasi-private entity that follows in the distinct historical tradition of the First and Second Banks of the United States."

In a lengthier dissent, Justice Kagan (joined by Justices Sotomayor and Jackson) emphasizes that *Humphrey's Executor* has stood as precedent for 90 years and "undergirds a significant feature of American governance: bipartisan administrative bodies carrying out expertise-based functions with a measure of independence from presidential control." The NLRB and Merit Systems Protection Board (MSPB) are but two such agencies. The dissent then criticizes the majority for using the emergency docket to overrule or revise existing law. "And nowhere is short-circuiting our deliberative process less appropriate than when the ruling requested would disrespect—by either overturning or narrowing—one of this Court's longstanding precedents, like our nearly century-old *Humphrey's* decision." In the dissent's view, this case is easy under *Humphrey's*, and the President therefore has no right to relief.

For these reasons, the dissent finds the majority's order granting the President's request for a stay ill-conceived and extraordinary, in essence acquiescing to the President's decision not to follow existing precedent while purporting not to reach the merits. It also criticizes the majority for its approach to balancing the interests, which, in its view, mischaracterizes what is being balanced and distorts the interest in preventing Wilcox and Harris from continuing in office: that interest is only the President's, not the government's, since Congress (through its enactment of the underlying statutes limiting dismissal of these members) is on the other side. Finally, the dissent takes the majority to task for, "out of the blue" and without any real basis, seemingly excepting the Federal Reserve from its undoing of *Humphrey's*, chiding "If the idea is to reassure the markets, a simpler—and more judicial—approach would have been to deny the President's application for a stay on the continued authority of *Humphrey's*."

The implications of this decision potentially are far-reaching. But one immediate effect was that the Board lacked a quorum for many months.

THE STATE OF AFFAIRS: JUNE 2026

As this Supplement goes to press, the Board consists of two Republicans and one Democrat, one vote short of the three necessary to overrule precedent were the Board to adhere to historical practice which, thus far, it has. A Republican nominee is up for committee vote. Given the hiatus in Board decision-making due to the lack of a quorum, the current Board confronts a significant case backlog. Robert Iafolla, *NLRB Has 17,000 Open Unfair Labor Practice Cases, Operations Chief Says*, BLOOMBERG LAW NEWS (March 6, 2026). It also faces the consequences of a divided judiciary on the courts of appeals; *i.e.*, the Board fares better among judges appointed by Democrats than Republicans. Robert Iafolla, *Growing Judicial Polarization Complicates NLRB's Court Tests*, BLOOMBERG LAW NEWS (April 3, 2026). Union representation election success declined in 2025 with overall union density remaining flat, George Weykamp, *Unionizing Set to Fall Due to Economic, Political Headwinds*, BLOOMBERG LAW NEWS (Feb. 6, 2026), even as unions now face a Labor Board set on curtailing union (and worker) favorable doctrines.

A NOTE ON THE UNITARY EXECUTIVE THEORY

In February 2025, President Trump issued Executive Order 14215, "Ensuring Accountability For All Agencies." All executive agencies, including "*so-called* 'independent regulatory agencies'" (emphasis added), are accountable to the President. All agency actions have to be vetted with the Office of Management and Budget; the chairs of independent regulatory agencies ("so-called") are to "coordinate their policies and priorities with the White House." The Order continues as follows:

> The President and the Attorney General, subject to the President's supervision and control, shall provide authoritative interpretations of law for the executive branch [including the

> "so-called" independent regulatory agencies]. The President and the Attorney General's opinions on questions of law are controlling on all employees in the conduct of their official duties. No employee of the executive branch acting in their official capacity may advance an interpretation of the law as the position of the United States that contravenes the President or the Attorney General's opinion on a matter of law, including but not limited to the issuance of regulations, guidance, and positions advanced in litigation, unless authorized to do so by the President or in writing by the Attorney General.

The Executive Order pursues the theory of a "unitary executive." There is a good deal of recent constitutional scholarship on the concept; but, for present purposes, the Executive Order rests on the idea that when Art. II says, "The executive Power shall be vested in a President . . .," it means all power, undivided, in one individual, "a" President. By this reading all appointees in the Executive branch are the President's subordinates; they must do his bidding. There are no agencies independent of his will.

The implications of the theory are illuminated in a letter of April 3, 2025, from an anti-union organization to the Attorney General asking her to direct the National Labor Relations Board forthwith to abrogate a list of ten labor-favorable decision of the Biden Board, *e.g.* protecting the wearing of a union button, forbidden captive audition, collectively advocating for non-employees, etc. *Letter of the Coalition for a Democratic Workplace* (April 3, 2025). The letter invokes the Executive Order as authorizing the Attorney General so to act.

In considering the theory on which the Executive Order rests, the student might consider this: there seems to be no question that the Board's General Counsel (GC) serves at the President's pleasure. Further, the Supreme Court has repeatedly said that the GC has "unreviewable" authority over the issuance of unfair labor practice complaints. Vaca v. Sipes, 386 U.S. 171, 182 (1967) (". . . the Board's General Counsel has unreviewable discretion to refuse to institute an unfair labor practice complaint"), *reiterated in* NLRB v. Sears, Roebuck & Co., 421 U.S. 132, 138 (1975). Tesla has been the object of numerous unfair labor practice charges. Assume one were to be for the discharge of a worker for wearing a union button. Could the President direct the GC to issue no complaint for the discharge of an employee for wearing a union button? In practical effect, the law will be as the President directs, just as the Executive Order asserts, without need for any action of the Labor Board. May the President so direct? If not, why?

PART TWO

The Establishment of the Collective Bargaining Relationship

I. Protection of the Right of Self-Organization

A. Interference, Restraint and Coercion

1. Restrictions on Solicitation and Distribution

Page 105. In the last citation at the end of Problem 6, replace "Bosch" with "Boch."

Page 105. Add to Problems for Discussion:

8. The Garçons-Limonadiers (GL), a union of waitstaff and bartenders, has been attempting to unionize an outlet of the Rumsford Café chain—the first in the company to unionize, if it does. Charles Rumsford, the CEO, has hosted a "collaborative session" for the staff to "co-create improvements in working conditions." Bernard Bailey, a bartender active on the organizing committee was in attendance and produced a list of grievances that, he announced to the group, could not be soon addressed without a union. In response, Rumsford said: "If you're not happy you can work for another company." Has Rumsford committed an unfair labor practice? Starbucks Corp., 373 N.L.R.B. No. 123 (2024); *compare* Community Organized Relief Effort, 373 N.L.R.B. No. 106 (2024) (on the consistency of the Board's approach).

Page 122. Add at the end of the first full paragraph:

On February 14, 2025, Acting General Counsel William B. Cowen issued a memo to all field offices rescinding this and a number of other memos issued by former General Counsel Abruzzo. *See* GC Mem 25-05.

Page 123. Add at the end of Problem 4:

Or the following prohibitions:

13. Failure to obtain permission to leave work for any reason during normal working hours.
15. Causing, creating or participating in a disruption of any kind during working hours on Company/client property.
20. Wearing extreme, unprofessional or inappropriate styles of dress or hair while working.

Pro Residential Services, Inc., 373 N.L.R.B. No. 100 (2024).

Page 124. Add at end of Discussion:

On April 7, 2026, the three-Member Board, two Republicans and one Democrat, sustained the application of *McLaren Macomb,* the two Republicans noting that they were "open to reconsideration" but could not overrule it absent a three member majority. Prime Communication, LP., 374 N.L.R.B. No. 88 (2026).

Page 134. Add to *Cedar Point Nursery* discussion:

The student will profit by engaging with the following thoughtful discussion of the case: Cynthia Estlund, *Showdown at* Cedar Point: *"Sole and Despotic Domination" Gains Ground,* 4 Sup. Ct. Rev. 125 (2021) and Eric Freyfogle, *The Democratic Forebodings of the "Right to Exclude",* 2025 U. Ill. L. Rev. 169 (2025).

Page 142. Add at the end of Problem 2:

In July, 2025, the Acting General Counsel issued "Guidance for Investigating Salting Cases" emphasizing the investigatory obligation before a complaint is filed to assure two components: (1) of a bona fide application; and (2) that it "reflected a genuine interest in becoming" the employer's employee. The GC requires that the Regions "deeply probe" the charging party, the applicant, about the legitimacy of the claim:

> In addition to affidavit testimony, Regions should also request that the charging party produce relevant documentary evidence pertaining to the genuine interest issue, including applications, resumes, social media posts, emails and other written communications between the applicant and employer, and those between the applicant and the union, that discuss, refer to or mention the employer and the application process. These documents should be closely scrutinized for signs that would indicate a lack of genuine interest in employment.

GC Memorandum 25-08 (July 24, 2025).

In investigating a charge to see if a complaint should issue one would expect due diligence on the Region's part to assure that what it will allege can be proven. Does this Guidance do more?

Page 144. Add after *Peerless Plywood* discussion:

Amazon Services LLC

373 N.L.R.B. No. 136 (2024).

[The General Counsel argued that the Board should reconsider the law and hold that the holding of employees as a captive audience to entertain an employer's position on unionization—most commonly hostile—but that in the speech itself contained no promise of benefit or threat of reprisal under § 8(e) in violation of section 8(a)(1). The Board, by vote of three to one, agreed. Before reaching its analysis, the Board detailed the history of its treatment of the issue from 1938 to *Livingston Shirt* and *Peerless Plywood* in 1953.]

* * *

Analysis

* * *

1. Section 8(a)(1)

Section 7 of the Act provides, in most relevant part, that employees "shall have the right to self-organization, to form, join, or assist labor organizations, to bargain collectively through representatives of their own choosing, and to engage in other concerted activities for the purpose of collective bargaining or other mutual aid or protection, and shall also have the right to refrain from any or all of such activities." 29 U.S.C. § 157. Section 8(a)(1) enforces Section 7 by making it unlawful for an employer "to interfere with, restrain, or coerce employees in the exercise of the rights guaranteed in section [7]." Id. § 158(a)(1). "The broad purpose of [Section] 8(a)(1) is to establish 'the right of employees to organize for mutual aid without employer interference.'" *Exchange Parts*, 375 U.S. at 409 (quoting *Republic Aviation Corp. v. NLRB*, 324 U.S. 793, 798 (1945)). Accordingly, "[t]he basic test for an 8(a)(1) violation . . . is whether—regardless of intent—the employer engaged in conduct that reasonably tends to interfere with the free exercise of employee rights under the Act." *MEI-GSR Holdings, LLC d/b/a Grand Sierra Resort & Casino/HG Staffing, LLC*, 365 NLRB 751, 752 (2017).

The Board's traditional interpretation of the statutory phrase "interfere with" is consistent with its ordinary meaning. See, e.g., *Standard-Coosa-Thatcher Co.*, 85 NLRB 1358, 1360 (1949) ("Inherent in the very nature of the rights protected by Section 7 is the concomitant right of privacy in their enjoyment—'full freedom' from employer intermeddling, intrusion, or even knowledge."). Accordingly, with judicial approval, the Board has long and consistently found that employers violate Section 8(a)(1) when they intrude on the privacy and autonomy of employees by, for instance, surveilling, interrogating, or polling them with regard to their exercise of Section 7 rights. These protections for employees' privacy and autonomy are necessary to make Section 7 rights meaningful, given the power that employers have over employees in the workplace—power that the Act and the Supreme Court explicitly recognize.

Captive-audience meetings intrude on this protected sphere of employee privacy and autonomy and reasonably tend to interfere with employees' exercise of Section 7 rights in at least three distinct ways. First, captive-audience meetings impinge on an employee's "Section 7 right to choose, free from any employer coercion, the degree to which [they] will participate in the debate concerning representation," which is an aspect of the employee's more fundamental right to be let alone with respect to the exercise of rights under the Act. Second, captive-audience meetings can readily serve as a mechanism for employers to observe and surveil employees as they address the exercise of employees' Section 7 rights. Finally, because the employer has compelled employees to attend captive-audience meetings on pain of discipline or discharge, the employer's message in the meeting urging rejection of or support for the union is reasonably likely to take on a similarly coercive character. Just as employees may reasonably conclude that they have no real choice but to attend the meeting, so may employees reasonably conclude that, in fact, they do not have free choice concerning union representation. The employer's ability to require attendance at the meeting demonstrates the employer's economic power over the employees and reasonably tends to inhibit them from acting freely.

To begin, when employers compel employees to attend captive-audience meetings under threat of discipline or discharge, they force them to participate, at least as listeners, in the debate concerning union representation. The power to compel attendance at captive-audience meetings is not an incident of Section 8(c)'s protection of employers' speech. Instead, exercising the power to compel attendance is quintessentially conduct by which employers "interfere with" employees' exercise of their own Section 7 rights. To be sure, an employer generally has the prerogative to dictate the work tasks and activities that fill its employees' working time, see, e.g., *Peyton Packing Co.*, 49 NLRB 828, 843 (1943) ("Working time is for work."), enfd. 142 F.2d 1009 (5th Cir. 1944), but when an employer compels its employees to attend a captive-audience meeting, it is not exercising that prerogative. Rather, it is meddling in the decision-making sphere that, under the Act, belongs exclusively to employees: namely, whether, when, and how employees choose to exercise their Section 7 rights or to refrain from doing so. It is well established that an employer may not "condition[ ] an employee's continued employment on the employee's abandonment of [their] Section 7 rights." *Intercon I (Zercom)*, 333 NLRB 223, 223 fn. 4 (2001). To hold otherwise would be to eviscerate the rights granted by the Act. Compelling employees to attend a captive-audience meeting effectively conditions their employment on the abandonment of their Section 7 rights.

As the Supreme Court has explained, Section 7 guarantees "workers' right to organize freely for collective bargaining," and that right "comprehends whatever may be appropriate and lawful to accomplish and maintain such organization," including the "right fully and freely to discuss and be informed concerning this choice." *Thomas*, 323 U.S. at 533–534. A captive-audience meeting overrides employees' right to *freely* be informed about unionization—or not. In the context of a political election, being compelled to attend a party's campaign meeting would rightly be denounced as antithetical to voters' freedom of choice. The same should be true in the context of union representation elections, not least because, as the Supreme Court has recognized, employees are vulnerable in a way that typical independent voters are not, given employees' economic dependence on the employer. See, e.g., *Gissel*, 395 U.S. at 617–618.

The compelled participation that the Act specifically protects against is also irreconcilable with American law's more general focus on protecting the "unwilling listener's interest in avoiding unwanted communication," despite the communicators' wish to express their views. *Hill v. Colorado*, 530 U.S. 703, 716–717 (2000) (upholding state law preventing protesters from approaching entrants to health clinic). That interest "is an aspect of the broader 'right to be let alone' " that Justice Brandeis characterized as " 'the most comprehensive of rights and the right most valued by civilized men.' " Id. at 717 (quoting *Olmstead v. United States*, 277 U.S. 438, 478 (1928) (Brandeis, J., dissenting)). Thus, while the "right to persuade" is an essential right "protected by the First Amendment, as well as by federal statutes," id. at 717–718 (internal citation omitted), like the Act's Section 8(c), it remains the case that " 'no one has a right to press even 'good' ideas on an unwilling recipient,' " id. at 718 (quoting *Rowan v. U.S. Post Office Dept.*, 397 U.S. 728, 738 (1970)). Accordingly, where " 'the degree of captivity makes it impractical for the unwilling viewer or auditor to avoid exposure,' " the need to protect such unwilling listeners is at its zenith. Id. (citing *Erznoznik v. City of Jacksonville*, 422 U.S. 205, 209 (1975); *Lehman v. Shaker Heights*, 418 U.S. 298 (1974)). By contrast, when a person is not captive—like the pedestrian who can readily walk away or the television viewer who can easily change the channel—"the burden normally falls upon the [person] to 'avoid further bombardment.' " *Erznoznik*, 422 U.S. at 210–211 (quoting *Cohen v. California*, 403 U.S. 15, 21 (1971)). In light of Section 7's guarantees, employees in the workplace have a legitimate interest in avoiding unwanted communication concerning the exercise of their Section 7 rights. Captive-audience meetings are particularly powerful tools to force a message onto unwilling listeners. Employees summoned by their employer to such meetings cannot simply walk away to avoid hearing views that they would rather not hear, unless they are prepared to lose their jobs or suffer other discipline. Under the Act and the First Amendment, employers undoubtedly have the right to persuade, but that right must accommodate employees' right to be left alone in the sphere protected by the Act, just as in other settings the right of a speaker does not override the right of an unwilling listener. Employers may express their views on unionization, but they may not compel employees to listen to them.

Captive-audience meetings intrude on employees' private sphere surrounding Section 7 rights in a second way by enabling employers to observe and monitor employees in a series of employer-structured events.[29] To begin, employees directed to attend a captive-audience

[29] For an example of such observation and monitoring, see *Sysco Grand Rapids, LLC*, 367 NLRB No. 111, slip op. at 14 (2019) (employer "convened mandatory small group meetings every week or every other week" and "[e]mployees' reactions at these meetings"—including "employee

meeting must choose whether or not to comply with the employer's order. This puts employees to the sort of employer-compelled "observable choice" concerning union support that the Board has prohibited in a variety of settings.[30] Next, captive-audience meetings let employers observe the behavior of employees in an employer-controlled setting that will reasonably tend to reveal their sentiments concerning unionization. Obviously, employees who speak out in opposition to the employer's views—perhaps because they feel pressure to do so[31]—will be noticed by the employer, as will employees who ask questions. In turn, employees who speak might well fear that they have exposed themselves to reprisal because they have frustrated the employer's expression of its own views, to which employees have been compelled to listen. But even employees who do not speak are subject to observation at the meeting—a meeting they must attend. An employer might monitor where employees sit (for instance, whether someone sits and talks with known union supporters or opponents) and other nonverbal behaviors (like raised eyebrows, rolled eyes, or darting glances) in response to the employer's statements. In sum, captive-audience meetings subject employees to the employer's scrutiny, as employees surely understand. Such scrutiny tends to interfere with the exercise of Section 7 rights.

Finally, the Supreme Court's recognition in *Gissel*, 395 U.S. at 617, that a realistic appraisal of an employer's communications about unionization must account for "the economic dependence of the employees on their employers" and "the necessary tendency of the former, because of that relationship, to pick up intended implications of the latter that might be more readily dismissed by a more disinterested ear" applies with particular force to statements made during a captive-audience meeting. The directive to attend the meeting, on pain of discipline or discharge, necessarily drives home to employees that the employer controls their participation in the election campaign by means of its economic power over them. The captive-audience context, in turn, clearly

---

demeanor and reactions to supervisors' statements"—"were recorded in a Company database"), enfd. in part mem. 825 Fed.Appx. 348 (6th Cir. 2020).

[30] See, e.g., *Allegheny Ludlum*, 333 NLRB at 740 (employers' request that employees participate in antiunion campaign videotape); *Smithfield Packing*, 344 NLRB at 3–4 (employee handed "Vote No" stamp to mark employer's product); *Dawson Construction*, 320 NLRB at 117 (employee ordered by employer to hold "reserve gate" sign indicating employer's view concerning jobsite picket of another employer); *Scientific Atlanta, Inc.*, 278 NLRB 467, 467 (1986) (employer required employees to disseminate antiunion literature).

[31] As already observed, a captive-audience meeting effectively forces employees to participate in the debate over unionization, under terms dictated by the employer. The pressures created by a captive-audience meeting are not hard to grasp.

First, the employer's expression of views might be provocative, even deliberately so, to supporters of the union, and so they may reactively speak out. The desire to speak may be especially strong because employees have no comparable power to summon their coworkers to a meeting, at work or otherwise. Thus, the occasion created by an employer's captive-audience meeting might be viewed by union supporters as a rare opportunity to rebut the employer's views in the workplace. Meanwhile, a supporter's silence might be seen by coworkers as reflecting a lack of courage or conviction, creating pressure on supporters to speak out. In these respects, it is the employer's decision to compel attendance at the meeting that tends to interfere with employees' ability to choose when, how, and to what degree to exercise their Sec. 7 rights.

communicates to employees that they lack the genuine freedom to choose whether, when, and how to participate in the choice concerning union representation, just as they lacked the freedom to choose whether to attend the meeting. This context, then, implicates the Supreme Court's distinction between free speech and coercive speech in the labor context. As the Court has observed, an employer's expression of views is not protected when to "persuasion other things are added which bring about coercion, or give it that character." *Thomas*, 323 U.S. at 537. Compelling employees to listen to the employer's views adds coercion to persuasion.

For each of these reasons, captive-audience meetings violate Section 8(a)(1) of the Act. They impermissibly demonstrate to employees that their employer's power over them in the workplace extends to the denial of the exercise of the rights guaranteed by Section 7.

2. Free-speech principles

A careful examination of Section 8(c) of the Act—which the *Babcock & Wilcox* Board failed to do—demonstrates that it does not immunize employers who conduct captive-audience meetings. The Supreme Court has repeatedly held that "people are entitled to rely on the law as written," such that "when the meaning of the statute's terms is plain," the analysis "is at an end." *Bostock v. Clayton County*, 590 U.S. 644, 673–674 (2020).

Below, we first explain that the analysis here appropriately starts and ends with the text of Section 8(c). Its plain meaning is that employers may noncoercively express their views on unionization, but they may not coerce employees to listen to them. We then explain that even if Section 8(c)'s legislative history is consulted, it confirms that Section 8(c) was not intended to shield employers from liability under Section 8(a)(1) for compelling attendance at a captive-audience meeting. Instead, it was intended to prevent the Board from using the content of an employer's lawful expression of its views as evidence of an unlawful motive in connection with an unfair labor practice, like unlawful retaliation under Section 8(a)(3) that, unlike unlawful interference under Section 8(a)(1), requires proof of motive. Last, we explain that, like Section 8(c), the First Amendment does not shield employers from liability under Section 8(a)(1) for compelling attendance at a captive-audience meeting. As the Supreme Court has explained, "[a]ny assessment of the precise scope of employer expression, of course, must be made in the context of its labor relations setting," and, "[t]hus, an employer's rights cannot outweigh the equal rights of the employees to associate freely." *Gissel*, 395 U.S. at 617. Prohibiting captive-audience meetings ensures the proper balance by not interfering with employers' right to express their views on unionization, while protecting employees' right to decide, for themselves, whether, when, and how to engage with those views.

a. Section 8(c)'s text

Section 8(c), as noted, provides:

> The expressing of any views, argument, or opinion, or the dissemination thereof, whether in written, printed, graphic, or visual form, shall not constitute or be evidence of an unfair labor practice under any of the provisions of this subchapter, if such expression contains no threat of reprisal or force or promise of benefit.

29 U.S.C. § 158(c). Section 8(c)'s unambiguous meaning is that employers may noncoercively *express* their views on unionization, but they may not *compel* employees to listen to them. On its face, Section 8(c) does not address captive-audience meetings. That fact is telling. When an employer compels its employees to attend a meeting, it is not "expressing" or "disseminating" any "views, argument, or opinion" in the "ordinary, contemporary, common meaning" of those words. *Star Athletica, L.L.C. v. Varsity Brands, Inc*, 580 U.S. 405, 414 (2017) (internal quotation marks omitted).[35] As the Supreme Court's cases in the free speech context illustrate, expressing or disseminating a view is distinct from compelling someone to listen to it. Prohibiting compulsion does not impermissibly interfere with expression or dissemination. Had Congress intended not only to protect employers' freedom to express their views, but also to immunize them from unfair labor practice liability for compelling employees to listen to their views, it surely would have said so specifically.

An employer's act of compelling employees to attend a captive-audience meeting is thus not Section 8(c)-protected expressive speech. This distinction between coercive conduct prohibited by Section 8(a)(1) and speech protected by Section 8(c) has been explicitly or implicitly drawn by the Board in analogous contexts, with judicial approval. In *Allegheny Ludlum*, for instance, the employer, as part of its antiunion campaign, prepared a video "as to why employees should vote against representation." 333 NLRB at 735. Under Section 8(c), the Board observed, "employers have the right to present noncoercively their position regarding a union organizing campaign, including through the use of antiunion campaign videotapes[.]" Id. at 738. But the employer crossed the line when it coerced employees, including by individually soliciting them, to appear in the video. Id. at 740–743. This was a straightforward manifestation of the Supreme Court's rule that "[a]ny assessment of the precise scope of employer expression . . . must be made

[35] The ordinary meaning of the words used in Sec. 8(c) supports our understanding of what that section protects and what it does not. A "view" is a "[m]ode of looking at anything; esp., manner of regarding any subject of thought; conception; opinion; judgment; as, to state one's *views* of a debated policy." *View*, Webster's New International Dictionary 2842 (2d ed. 1934). An "argument" is "[a] reason or reasons offered in proof, to induce belief, convince the mind, or persuade to action; reasoning expressed in words; as, an *argument about, concerning,* or *regarding* a proposition, *for* or *in favor of* it, or *against* it." *Argument*, Webster's New International Dictionary 147 (2d ed. 1934). An "opinion" is "[t]hat which is opined; belief stronger than impression, less strong than positive knowledge; settled judgment in regard to any point; a notion or conviction founded on probable evidence; a belief; a view; a judgment; as, based only on *opinion*; imprisoned for one's *opinions*." *Opinion*, Webster's New International Dictionary 1708 (2d ed. 1934).

in the context of its labor relations setting," such that "an employer's rights cannot outweigh the equal rights of the employees to associate freely[.]" *Gissel*, 395 U.S. at 617. Accordingly, the Third Circuit, in affirming the Board's decision, found that it "reasonably balance[d] the rights created under sections 8(a)(1) and 8(c)." *Allegheny Ludlum*, 301 F.3d at 179. We strike that same balance in prohibiting captive audience meetings.

Finding a violation of Section 8(a)(1) based on compelling employees to attend a captive-audience meeting does not require the Board to rely on the employer's expression of views, argument, or opinion as "evidence of" the unfair labor practice. That prohibition, as the Supreme Court has explained, is intended "to prevent the Board from attributing antiunion motive to an employer based on [its] past statements." *Linn*, 383 U.S. at 62 fn. 5 (citing Conference Report at 45, reprinted in 1 LMRA Hist. at 549). Such a motive is required to prove only certain violations, like an employer's retaliation, in violation of Section 8(a)(3), for an employee's exercise of Section 7 rights. The test for interference and coercion under Section 8(a)(1), by contrast, "does not turn on the employer's motive." *American Freightways*, 124 NLRB at 147. Accordingly, in cases such as *Allegheny Ludlum*, the violation of Section 8(a)(1) was based not on the employer's expression of views—whether in a video, literature, or paraphernalia—but rather on its pressuring and coercing employees to participate in or accept the expression. In the captive-audience context, similarly, the Section 8(a)(1) violation turns not on the substance of the employer's views, but rather on the employer's use of compulsion: the threat, whether explicit or implicit, that employees will suffer discipline, discharge, or some other adverse consequence if they fail to attend the meeting. Employers retain full freedom to express their views on unionization to employees in the workplace, provided that they do not compel employees to listen to them.

Moreover, for the reasons articulated above, an employer's message in a captive-audience meeting cannot meet the explicit requirement of Section 8(c) that, to be protected, an employer's views must "contain[ ] no threat of reprisal." As explained, by compelling employees to attend a captive-audience meeting and communicating its own message there, the employer creates a reasonable tendency that economically dependent employees will feel inhibited from exercising free choice as to whether, when, and how to participate in the decision concerning union representation. This tendency is eliminated if the employer expresses its views to employees who voluntarily choose to attend such a meeting, because such a meeting does not carry the threat of discipline or discharge for not attending.

b. Section 8(c)'s legislative history

Because the language of Section 8(c) is unambiguous, as we have shown, there is no need to consider its legislative history. . . . But even if we were to consider the legislative history, as a whole it confirms that

Section 8(c) was *not* intended to shield employers from liability under Section 8(a)(1) for compelling attendance at a captive-audience meeting. Rather, Section 8(c) was intended to prevent the Board from using the content of an employer's lawful expression of views as evidence of an unlawful motive in connection with an unfair labor practice that, unlike unlawful interference under Section 8(a)(1), requires proof of motive. The sole piece of legislative history that even mentions *Clark Bros.* suggests only an intent to overrule that case in part unrelated to the issue of compelling attendance at captive-audience meetings.

The Conference Report, which "next to the statute itself [ ] is the most persuasive evidence of congressional intent," *Demby v. Schweiker*, 671 F.2d 507, 510 (D.C. Cir. 1981), does not mention captive-audience meetings. Instead, it describes what Section 8(c) *was* designed to address: "The practice which the Board has had in the past of using speeches and publications of employers concerning labor organizations and collective-bargaining agreements as evidence, no matter how irrelevant or immaterial, that some later act of the employer had an illegal purpose gave rise to the necessity for this change in the law." Conference Report at 45, reprinted in 1 LMRA Hist. at 549. In other words, Section 8(c) was intended to prevent the Board from ascribing an antiunion motive to an employer in connection with an alleged unfair labor practice that requires proof of motive—such as a retaliatory discharge of employees for union activities, in violation of Section 8(a)(3)—based on the substance of the employer's earlier lawful statement of opposition to unionization. The Supreme Court has thus observed that the "congressional intent" was "to prevent the Board from attributing antiunion motive to an employer on the basis of [its] past statements." *Linn*, 383 U.S. at 62 fn. 5 (citing Conference Report at 45, reprinted in 1 LMRA Hist. at 549).

Moreover, the Conference Report makes clear that Section 8(c) was principally derived from the free speech provision of the House bill rather than from the corresponding provision in the Senate bill. Conference Report at 45, reprinted in 1 LMRA Hist. at 549. The House Report accompanying that House bill, like the Conference Report, makes no mention of captive-audience meetings. Instead, like the Conference Report, it describes the type of Board decisions that Section 8(c) was intended to "correct[ ]," such as when the Board infers from an employer's past criticism of a union that a foreman's later discharge of a union official for gross misconduct "was for union activity." House Report at 33, reprinted in 1 LMRA Hist. at 324.

Senator Taft, the principal sponsor of the legislation, placed a statement in the Congressional Record, which, with reference to the Section 8(c) that emerged from the Conference, expressed a substantially similar view to that of the Conference and House Reports:

> The conferees had in mind a number of Board decisions in which because of the fact that an employer has at some time committed an unfair labor practice a speech by him, innocuous in itself, has

> been held not to be privileged .... There have also been a number of decisions by the Board in which discharges of employees, even though there was no evidence in the surrounding circumstances of discrimination, have been deemed unfair labor practices simply because at one time or another the employer has expressed himself as not in favor of unionization of his employees. The object of this section, therefore, is to make it clear that decisions of this sort cannot be made under the conference bill.

93 Cong. Rec. 7002 (June 12, 1947), reprinted in 2 LMRA Hist. at 1624. Senator Taft also confirmed what is plain from the statutory text: "[T]he privilege of this subsection is limited to expression of 'views, arguments, or opinion,' " such that "[i]t has no application to statements which are acts in themselves or contain directions or instructions." Id. An employer's directive to employees requiring them to attend a captive-audience meeting clearly falls into this category of statements to which Section 8(c) does *not* apply.

The Senate Report accompanying the Senate bill is the only piece of legislative history that even mentions *Clark Bros.* It states:

> Another amendment to this section would insure both to employers and labor organizations full freedom to express their views to employees on labor matters, refrain from threats of violence, intimation of economic reprisal, or offers of benefit. The Supreme Court in *Thomas v. Collins* (323 U.S. 516) held, contrary to some earlier decisions of the Labor Board, that the Constitution guarantees freedom of speech on either side in labor controversies and approved the doctrine of the *American Tube Bending* case (134 F. (2d) 993). The Board has placed a limited construction upon these decisions by holding such speeches by employers to be coercive if the employer was found guilty of some other unfair labor practice, even though severable or unrelated (*Monumental Life Insurance*, 69 N. L. R. B. 247) or if the speech was made in the plant on working time (*Clark Brothers*, 70 N.L.R.B. [No.] 60). The committee believes these decisions to be too restrictive and, in this section, provides that if, under all the circumstances, there is neither an expressed or implied threat of reprisal, force, or offer of benefit, the Board shall not predicate any finding of unfair labor practice upon the statement. The Board, of course, will not be precluded from considering such statements as evidence.

Senate Report at 23–24, reprinted in 1 LMRA Hist. at 429–430.

The reference to *Clark Bros.* having been "too restrictive" would seem to be the unspecified "legislative history" that the *Babcock & Wilcox* Board relied on—along with the equally unexamined "language of Section 8(c)"—to conclude that Section 8(c) gives employers a right to hold captive-audience meetings. *See Babcock & Wilcox*, 77 NLRB at 578.

The *Babcock & Wilcox* Board ignored that Section 8(c) was principally derived from the House bill, not the Senate's bill discussed in the Senate Report, and ignored the rest of the legislative history, which, as explained, nowhere suggests that Congress intended to address the captive-audience issue.

In any event, the Senate Report itself does not demonstrate a clear intention to immunize employers who hold captive-audience meetings. Although it refers to the Board's decision in *Clark Bros.* as "too restrictive," the Report's description of that decision suggests that the Senate Committee intended simply to ensure that employers were free to express their constitutionally protected views on Section 7 activity in a "speech" "made in the plant on working time." Senate Report at 23, reprinted in 1 LMRA Hist. at 429. *Clark Bros.*, as noted, had broadly held such a speech to be unlawful. 70 NLRB at 804. But that decision had "also" and "independently" held that "the conduct of the [employer] in compelling its employees to listen to a speech on self-organization" was *separately* unlawful. Id. The Senate Report does not address this second, separate holding. For the Board to hold that an employer may not *compel* employees to attend a captive-audience meeting does not prevent the employer from making the type of speech that the Senate Report actually addressed—one that is "in the plant" and "on working time," provided that attendance is voluntary. In the case of the compelled meeting, the unfair labor practice is in no sense "predicate[d]" on any employer "statement" made in the speech, see Senate Report at 24, reprinted in 1 LMRA Hist. at 430, but rather is based entirely on the employer's requirement that employees attend the speech on pain of discipline or discharge. Moreover, there is no suggestion in the sole Supreme Court decision cited by the Senate Report, *Thomas v. Collins*, that the free speech rights of employers and unions entail a right to compel others to listen. In fact, as we have pointed out, *Thomas* strongly suggests the opposite. In light of these considerations, the Senate Report simply cannot bear the weight that *Babcock & Wilcox* apparently placed on it.

c. *First Amendment*

The First Amendment likewise does not entitle employers to hold captive-audience meetings. Not only would such a constitutional entitlement conflict with the general rule that the First Amendment gives " 'no one . . . a right to press even 'good' ideas on an unwilling recipient,' " *Hill*, 530 U.S. at 718 (quoting *Rowan*, 397 U.S. at 738), it would also ignore the Supreme Court's admonition that "[a]ny assessment of the precise scope of employer expression . . . must be made in the context of its labor relations setting," such that "an employer's rights cannot outweigh the equal rights of the employees to associate freely." *Gissel*, 395 U.S. at 617. In the "labor relations setting," the First Amendment comfortably accommodates an employer's robust right to express its views on unionization with an employee's right to decline to listen to those views.

3. Lawful voluntary meetings

* * *

To provide clear guidance for employers, we have decided to establish a safe harbor from liability for employers who wish to express their views concerning unionization in a workplace, work-hours meeting with employees. Thus, an employer will not be found to have violated Section 8(a)(1) if, reasonably in advance of the meeting, it informs employees that:

1. The employer intends to express its views on unionization at a meeting at which attendance is voluntary;

2. Employees will not be subject to discipline, discharge, or other adverse consequences for failing to attend the meeting or for leaving the meeting; and

3. The employer will not keep records of which employees attend, fail to attend, or leave the meeting.

An employer may avail itself of this "safe harbor" by giving employees these assurances. Then, of course, the employer must also follow through on these assurances to stay on the right side of the law. When an employer both gives these assurances and follows through on them, it may lawfully hold voluntary meetings with its employees on company time in order to noncoercively express its views on unionization. We do not hold, however, that the failure to give these assurances will itself result in a violation of Section 8(a)(1).

We add a few additional points of clarification. An employer will be found to have compelled attendance at a meeting concerning the employer's union views if, under all the circumstances, employees could reasonably conclude that attendance at the meeting is required as part of their job duties or could reasonably conclude that their failure to attend or remain at the meeting could subject them to discharge, discipline, or any other adverse consequences. An express order from a supervisor, manager, or other agent of the employer to attend such a meeting is sufficient, but not always necessary, to establish a violation. Moreover, attendance at a meeting that is included on employees' work schedules, as communicated by a supervisor, manager, or other agent of the employer, will be considered to be compelled. Compliance with the steps outlined above will ensure that the holding of the meeting itself is lawful, but it does not, of course, otherwise immunize employer and employee conduct or statements made during that meeting.

* * *

[Member Kaplan dissented resting on three lines of argument, that: (A) Congress and the courts have rejected the Board's efforts to restrict non-coercive speech; (B) captive audience meetings are insulated by section 8(c) and do not interfere in section 7 rights; and (C) the doctrine of the avoidance of a confrontation with the First Amendment requires the Board to step back. The majority responded to each to which Member Kaplan rejoined. The majority's response is reflective of the dissent's contentions and glosses its reasoning. It is set out below. The further texture of the dissent's criticism is taken up in the Questions for Discussion that will follow the conclusion of the case.]

. . . [O]ur colleague's argument . . . reflect a misunderstanding of our position here, of the Board's jurisprudence under Section 8(a)(1), of Section 8(c) and the Supreme Court's relevant decisions, and of the Act's legislative history, among other key considerations. Our colleague, in short, does not supply the reasoned basis for concluding that captive-audience meetings must be permitted that the Board failed to provide in *Babcock & Wilcox* many years ago. We cannot agree that the Board's perfunctory decision there demonstrates the "considered judgment" that our colleague claims for it.

We start with the dissent's repeated claim that permitting captive-audience meetings promotes the Act's policy of encouraging free debate in the workplace. By definition, captive-audience meetings are unfree. They demonstrate, to employees, the power of the employer to *control* the debate. Not only are employees forced to assemble and listen to their employer's views, but they may also be prevented from expressing their own views—all on pain of discipline or discharge. Indeed, our dissenting colleague himself cites a Board decision he joined, which found that "[i]t is lawful for an employer to conduct a captive-audience meeting to persuade employees not to unionize while refusing to allow others to express their opposing, prounion viewpoints during the meeting," including by ordering the assembled employees to "shut up" and having that order followed. *Electrolux Home Products*, 368 NLRB No. 34, slip op. at 4 & fns. 13–14. Our holding today, of course, permits employers to express their view at voluntary meetings in the workplace—and such meetings do a much better job fostering the uninhibited and free debate that our dissenting colleague purports to champion.

Our colleague's contention that captive-audience meetings comport with Section 8(a)(1) is similarly untenable. He insists that if captive-audience meetings are prohibited, "then there would appear to be no principled basis for not similarly prohibiting *any* mandatory meeting at which an employer states its position on *any* term or condition of employment—such as a new safety rule or work process—or, indeed, any subject that affects employees' interests as employees." (Emphasis in dissent; internal quotations omitted.) But the meetings he refers to—which fall outside the definition of a captive-audience meeting used here—do not implicate the Section 7 concerns we address. Our colleague does not persuasively explain how, when an employer conducts an everyday workplace meeting and "states its position on [a] term or condition of employment" (whatever this may mean), the Section 7 rights of employees are implicated in any way, much less interfered with.[40] As explained, our decision today prohibits only mandatory meetings where an employer expresses its views for or against unionization to its employees.

The dissent relatedly argues that because "an employer has the right to determine what work employees will be required to perform during working time . . . [i]t follows that, during working time, an employer may lawfully require employees to attend meetings about unionization as well." This argument is circular. It assumes that a captive-audience meeting may be regarded as "working time" consistent with the Act simply because the employer has imposed a requirement on employees to attend.[41] Certainly, attending a captive-audience meeting is distinct from an employee's ordinary work duties, for which the employee was hired. Nor may an employer create work duties that infringe on Section 7 rights. We do not understand our colleague to argue that an employer lawfully could determine that a nonsupervisory employee's work duties included wearing an antiunion button, soliciting other employees to oppose the union, distributing the employer's campaign literature, or reporting on other employees' union activity—and then direct the employee to do so or be fired. The fundamental purpose of the Act, rather, is to limit the traditional power of employers to command and control their employees by carving out a space for employees to engage in protected concerted activity—even at work, during the workday. An employer's authority

[40] The Board decisions our dissenting colleague cites—which are not based on the Board's traditional view that captive-audience meetings are lawful—demonstrate as much. In *Daisy's Originals, Inc., of Miami*, the employer had convened a mandatory meeting to announce its position that it had a basis to withdraw recognition from the incumbent union. 187 NLRB 251, 253–255 (1970). In *Addressograph-Multigraph Corp.*, the employer had convened a mandatory meeting to announce a new work procedure for certain union-represented employees. 228 NLRB 6, 6–9 (1977). The Board's conclusion in both cases—that the mandatory meetings did not constitute unlawful retaliation against protected activity in violation of Sec. 8(a)(3) of the Act—would be unaffected by our decision today. That a captive-audience meeting interferes with and is coercive as to employees' Sec. 7 right to decide whether, when, and how to engage with their employer's union views has no bearing on the legality of a meeting announcing withdrawal of union recognition or changes in work procedures.

[41] Our dissenting colleague is incorrect when he insists that a "captive audience meeting . . . is . . . a routine application of the longstanding rule that 'working time is for work.' " Neither the Board, nor the courts, have ever deemed captive-audience meetings to be "work." Our colleague's view, in turn, illustrates the threat posed by captive-audience meetings to the goals of the Act. If such meetings are lawful, for the reasons our colleague insists, then there can be no limiting principle on their use. An employer would be free to require employees to attend captive-audience meetings for the entire workday, over a period as long as the employer wishes, until the employer was satisfied that employees had adopted its view as their own—and this, of course, has been the law until today. See, e.g., *International Baking Co.*, 342 NLRB 136, 138 (2004) (employer's "managers and supervisors held approximately 80 meetings" with petitioned-for unit of 331 employees and "during each week of the campaign a particular subject or subjects were covered in all the meetings held that week"), enfd. mem. 185 Fed.Appx. 691 (9th Cir. 2006); .*Andel Jewelry Corp*, 326 NLRB 507, 507 (1998) (Member Fox, dissenting) (employer "repeatedly held captive audience meetings with employees," including "daily meetings during working time with employees in each of the Employer's departments"); *Giant Eagle, Inc.*, 06–CA–188991, 2018 WL 1325594, slip op. at 1, 3–4 (NLRB Div. of Judges 2018) (in three-week period before election for a petitioned-for unit of just seven employees, employer held meetings that "generally lasted three hours" in both the morning and the afternoon on five different days); *Rugby Manufacturing Co.*, 18–CA–15802–1, 2002 WL 2029505 (NLRB Div. of Judges 2002) (employer gave "daily anti-union speeches" at its facility).

over its employees must be balanced against employees' Section 7 rights. Our decision today strikes such a balance.

Our dissenting colleague also unpersuasively argues that there is "no meaningful difference" between "the distribution of employer campaign literature," which the Board has held does not violate Section 8(a)(1), and "attendance at a captive-audience speech." We disagree. Distribution merely requires employees "to *receive* the [employer's] campaign literature." (Emphasis added by dissent, quoting *Intermet Stevensville*, 350 NLRB 1349, 1356 (2007).) Once employees have received the literature—which takes but an instant—they are free to read it or not, as and when they choose, consistent with their Section 7 rights. A captive-audience meeting is very different. It is a time-consuming affair, which employees are compelled to attend and where they must listen to their employer's views on unionization. The more apt analogy with employer distribution of campaign literature is provided by the *voluntary* meetings that our decision today expressly authorizes and protects.

Our dissenting colleague's arguments related to Section 8(c) are no more persuasive. To begin, his position on the text's meaning is inconsistent.[43] At one point he argues that Section 8(c) narrowly "focus[es] on the content of the employer['s] or union['s] 'expression' itself rather than on the circumstances surrounding it." But elsewhere, he says, instead, that a captive-audience meeting "is, by its very nature, 'the dissemination' of the employer's views" that Section 8(c) explicitly protects. Neither of these interpretations advances his position here. We *agree* that Section 8(c) protects the content of an employer's speech, but not the circumstances surrounding the speech. As we have explained, our prohibition of captive-audience meetings is based not on the employer views expressed at the meeting—whether for or against unionization—but on the surrounding circumstances: that employees are compelled to attend the meeting, on pain of discipline or discharge. We disagree, however, with our colleague's suggestion that an employer's order to attend a meeting is itself a protected "dissemination" of the employer's views under Section 8(c). As we have explained, such a directive does not communicate a view. Neither does the directive—which, of course, comes *before* the meeting—disseminate the employer's view to be

[43] Meanwhile, our colleague's claim that compelled attendance at a captive-audience meeting does not implicate the Sec. 7 right to refrain from protected concerted activity is meritless. Our colleague says that employees are not engaged in protected activity "when they are required to sit in a room while an employer gives a speech opposing unionization,"" but surely he would agree that an employer could not fire employees for sitting and listening to a speaker advocate for the union, instead of getting up and walking away. Just as mistaken is our colleague's statement that a captive-audience meeting somehow furthers employees' right to receive antiunion information. Sec. 7, rather, grants employees the right to choose whether, when, and how to receive information related to unionization: they may not be coerced to receive it. Recall that Sec. 8(c) provides that: "The expressing of any views, argument, or opinion, or the dissemination thereof, whether in written, printed, graphic, or visual form, shall not constitute or be evidence of an unfair labor practice under any of the provisions of this subchapter, if such expression contains no threat of reprisal or force or promise of benefit."

communicated at the meeting, consistent with the ordinary meaning of "dissemination" as the spreading of a view.[44] But even if one could view an employer's directive as "dissemination" in the statutory sense, Section 8(c) protects only a "dissemination" that "contains no threat of reprisal." 29 U.S.C. § 158(c). A directive to attend a captive-audience meeting, on pain of discipline or discharge, obviously contains a "threat of reprisal."

Our dissenting colleague's assessment of Section 8(c)'s legislative history is similarly unconvincing. He concedes that neither the Conference Report nor the House Report addresses captive-audience meetings. He emphasizes that the House Report indicates an intent to allow the Board to only prohibit a statement that "by its own express terms" constitutes a threat, House Report at 33, reprinted in 1 LMRA Hist. at 324, but he ignores that that language was *not included* in the enacted text of Section 8(c). And he draws from the Conference Report that the "purpose [of Section 8(c)] is to protect the right of free speech," Conference Report at 45, reprinted in 1 LMRA Hist. at 549, but points to nothing in the Conference Report suggesting that compelling employees to listen to the employer's views is encompassed within that right, contrary to general free-speech principles. At bottom, what our dissenting colleague has engaged in is an exercise of "looking over a crowd and picking out [his] friends." *Exxon Mobil*, 545 U.S. at 568 (internal quotations omitted). He has found just one "friend"—the Senate Report—but, for the reasons we have explained, that Report is not friendly to his position.

Finally, our dissenting colleague contends that a prohibition on captive-audience meetings raises "serious constitutional problems" under the First Amendment and so, under the doctrine of constitutional avoidance, the Board must interpret the Act to permit such meetings. We are not persuaded. As explained, our focus is on the employer's requirement that employees attend the meeting and listen to the employer's views. An employer's implicit or explicit statement to employees that they must attend a captive-audience meeting or face job consequences is plainly a threat of reprisal. Such threats explicitly fall outside the protection of Section 8(c), and Section 8(c), as the Supreme Court has observed, "implements the First Amendment." *Gissel*, 395 U.S. at 617.

We see no serious constitutional problem, then, in prohibiting captive-audience meetings while permitting employers to express their views in voluntary meetings. We do not understand our colleague to argue that employers even arguably have the First Amendment right to threaten employees at a captive-audience meeting or to promise them benefits. He fails to see, however, that an employer's use of coercion to compel attendance at a captive audience meeting is not immunized

---

[44] *Disseminate*, Webster's New International Dictionary 753 (2d ed. 1934).

because the meeting involves the employer's expression of views.[45] Rather, in the Supreme Court's words, the First Amendment permits the Board to find an unfair labor practice when "to this persuasion other things are added which bring about coercion, or give it that character." *Thomas*, 323 U.S. at 537–538. Of course, the Supreme Court has made clear that the Board has the authority to find unfair labor practices that are based on speech itself, if the speech amounts to a threat of reprisal, as in *Gissel*, or a promise of benefit, as in *Exchange Parts*, 375 U.S. at 408. Finding captive-audience meetings unlawful does not turn on the employer's speech at the meeting, or on the viewpoint expressed there, but rather on the employer's directive to attend the meeting—which may be speech, but which is undeniably coercive as well. An employer's First Amendment rights are not meaningfully diminished if the employer is forbidden from using its power over employees to compel them to listen to its views, while retaining the ability to express those views to employees willing to listen to them.

Relying principally on the Eleventh Circuit's recent decision in *Honeyfund.com Inc. v. Governor, State of Florida*, 94 F.4th 1272 (11th Cir. 2024), the dissent contends that prohibition of captive-audience meetings raises serious First Amendment questions because it "singles out captive-audience speeches about unionization for prohibition while permitting mandatory meetings on other subjects" and, as such, is an impermissible content-based restriction. We have carefully considered the *Honeyfund.com* decision but conclude that it is distinguishable. Nor does our colleague's assertion that we are impermissibly "singling out" captive-audience speeches from all other employer-mandated subjects have any merit.

In *Honeyfund.com*, the Eleventh Circuit granted a preliminary injunction against enforcement of a newly enacted Florida statute—the Stop W.O.K.E. Act, also known as the Individual Freedom Act—under the First Amendment. The court observed that Florida sought

> to bar employers from holding mandatory meetings for their employees if those meetings endorse viewpoints the state finds offensive. But meetings on those same topics *are* allowed if speakers endorse viewpoints the state agrees with, or at least does not object to. This law, as Florida concedes, draws its distinctions based on viewpoint—the most pernicious of dividing lines under the First Amendment.

94 F.4th at 1275 (emphasis in original). The court went on to hold that "[b]y limiting its restrictions to a list of ideas designated as offensive, the [Stop W.O.K.E.] Act targets speech based on its content" and "by barring

[45] In a similar regard, the fact that a speaker intends to communicate a message protected by the First Amendment does not entitle them to use the threat of violence to force others to listen to them. In the labor relations setting, a coercive threat of discipline or discharge is similarly unprotected.

only speech that endorses any of those ideas, it penalizes certain viewpoints—the greatest First Amendment sin." Id. at 1277.[46]

Our holding today makes no distinctions based on viewpoint. An employer may not require employees to attend a captive-audience meeting regardless of the view that the employer expresses—whether it urges employees to vote against the union, to vote for the union, or simply to refrain from exercising their Section 7 rights altogether. None of these viewpoints is "offensive" to the Act. What is offensive to the Act, rather, is the employer's use of its power to require employees to listen to its views—whatever they are. The Act is intended to protect employee free choice from precisely such coercion.

Contrary to our dissenting colleague's assertion, no serious First Amendment issue is posed here because we prohibit captive-audience meetings (as defined) and not all employer-mandated meetings in the workplace. This distinction is entirely a function of the Act's protection of Section 7 rights—and the *Gissel* Court has made clear that the First Amendment must be understood in the "context of [the] labor relations setting" in which the Board regulates. *Gissel*, 395 U.S. at 617.[48] Where an employer-mandated meeting does not impinge on employees' Section 7 rights, the Board has no basis to regulate it. If our colleague's criticism of our holding were valid, in turn, it would undermine the Board's ability to effectively administer and enforce the Act. The Board necessarily "singles out" employer statements and actions that implicate Section 7, while ignoring others.[49] An employer's threat of reprisal for supporting a union violates the Act; a threat for supporting a political candidate does not. An employer's statement prohibiting employees from talking about wages violates the Act; a statement prohibiting discussion about foreign policy does not. An employer's promise of benefits if employees vote against the union violates the Act; a promise of benefits for attending religious services does not. An employer's requirement that employees

---

[46] It was in this context that the Eleventh Circuit rejected Florida's argument that the Stop W.O.K.E. Act was regulating conduct, not speech. The court observed that the "fact that only mandatory meetings *that convey a particular message and viewpoint* are prohibited makes quick work of Florida's conduct-not-speech defense." 94 F.4th at 1278 (emphasis in original). As the court explained:

> If Florida disapproves of the message, the meeting cannot be required. This is a direct penalty on certain viewpoints—because the conduct and the speech are so intertwined, regulating the former means restricting the latter. In short, the disfavored "conduct" cannot be identified apart from the disfavored speech.

Id. Here, in contrast, our holding does not reflect disapproval of the employer's message, but of the employer's coercion of employees as a means of ensuring that they will listen to the employer's message.

[48] The context in which this case arises, of course, differs dramatically from the context of *Honeyfund.com*, in which (as the Eleventh Circuit pointed out) Florida was unable to demonstrate any legitimate interest, predicated on some other existing statute or policy, for prohibiting and penalizing the meetings targeted by the Stop W.O.K.E. Act. 94 F.4th at 1280–1282.

[49] For example, as discussed above, the Board's discrimination standard under *Register Guard*, 351 NLRB at 1118, requires the Board to distinguish between statements and actions that implicate Sec. 7 and those that do not.

wear t-shirts communicating its anti-union message violates the Act; an employer's requirement that employees wear t-shirts communicating a message opposing climate change does not. These distinctions reflect the provisions of the Act, not the Board's impermissible content-based regulation of employer speech. In straining to find serious constitutional issues presented here, our colleague turns the doctrine of constitutional avoidance into its opposite, a doctrine of "constitutional collision." *United States v. Hansen*, 599 U.S. 762, 781 (2023).[50] The Supreme Court, however, has made clear that "[w]hen legislation and the Constitution brush up against each other, our task is to seek harmony, not to manufacture conflict." Id.

* * *

QUESTIONS FOR DISCUSSION

1. Member Kaplan argues that § 8(c)'s conferral of a right to express views "in written, printed, graphic, or visual form" includes the right to choose the place and captive manner in which non-coercive views may be expressed. The majority sees that as a separate matter not encompassed by § 8(c). As a matter of plain text, which is more persuasive?

2. Member Kaplan lays weight on the judicial rejection of the Board's efforts in the 1950s to impose an "equal time" rule, citing NLRB v. F.W. Woolworth Co., 214 F.2d 78 (6th Cir. 1954) and the Supreme Court's first amendment decision, Miami Herald Pub. Co. v. Tornillo, 418 U.S. 241 (1974). In the former, the Court of Appeals rejected the Board's approach: that when an employer imposes a lawful non-solicitation rule on the workforce—working time is for work and cannot be used for union solicitations—but then disregards it for its own solicitations it must allow the union equal workplace access. Is there a principled difference between a rule that prohibits compulsory audition and one that requires union access to the premises? *Tornillo* was a "right of reply law" imposed on the editorial page of a newspaper. The Court held that the state may not commandeer a publisher's press; such abridges the freedom of the press as expressly assured under the First Amendment. How does *Tornillo* apply to a prohibition on captive audition?

3. Once it has a quorum and the issue of whether captive audience meetings violate the Act comes before it, the Trump II Board is very likely to overturn this decision. Leaving aside for the moment the First Amendment issues, which side has the better argument on this question as a matter of statutory interpretation and application? Once the Board has done so, there are additional implications because a number of states have enacted statutes seeking to ban captive audience meetings. The preemption and First

[50] In any event, even if our prohibition were to trigger strict scrutiny, this should be the rare case where the regulation would withstand such scrutiny because it is "narrowly tailored to serve a compelling interest." See *Williams-Yulee v. Florida Bar*, 575 U.S. 433, 444 (2015). Ensuring employees' full freedom to decide whether, when, and how to exercise their organizational rights is a compelling interest given our Congressional charge of "protecting the exercise by workers of full freedom of association, self-organization, and designation of representatives of their own choosing." 29 U.S.C. § 151.

Amendment issues related to these bans are discussed in the updates to Part Eight, *infra*.

Page 164. Add at the end of Discussion of *Bell-Aerospace:*

In the ensuing half century the Labor Board has continued to abrogate policies and to announce new or modified policies by adjudication. It had never been held to have so abused its discretion in that regard as to require its action to be set aside; never, that is, until the Sixth Circuit's decision in *Brown-Forman v. NLRB*, 169 F.4th 646 (6th Cir. 2026). In this case, the two-judge majority held that the Board's newly announced rule governing when a bargaining order can issue to remedy unfair labor practices—*Cemex Construction Materials Pacific, LLC* set out in the casebook at page 307—was wrongly announced in an adjudication instead of a rule making. One judge dissented at length.

As the excerpt from *Bell Aerospace* quoted above shows, much of the debate on rule making *versus* adjudication concerned the adequacy of notice to those who would be governed by a new rule and their ability to be heard in the process. The Sixth Circuit adverts to those concerns, but they played no role in its decision. Instead, the court parsed the elements of an adjudication that allow it to be used to fashion a rule: it must be grounded in "the case-specific facts of the contemporaneous adjudication" and must be "create[d]. . .in furtherance of resolving the parties' dispute." Thus. the "unlawful turn" the Board had taken in *Cemex* is that, "[i]t created a new standard for issuing future bargaining orders that was neither derived from the case-specific facts *nor* in furtherance of fashioning a remedy that resolved the parties' dispute," the "new standard was based not on the case-specific facts, but on general observations from '[d]ecades of experience administering the. . .[prior] standard' in other adjudications" *and* was "not as a case-specific means to provide a remedy *to the parties*. . .but as a general rule it deemed necessary to carry out the provision" of the Labor Act "on a macro scale." A new standard announced for all future cases and not directed to solve the particular dispute before therefore must be reserved exclusively for a rule making.

If the Sixth Circuit's reasoning is followed, the Board could no longer bring its accumulated experience to bear in a case presented to it, make a sober assessment of the administrative quagmire its extant doctrine has created and to which adherence in the case before it will only add, and then decide to abandon it as it has long done. *E.g., Midland National Life Ins.* at page 176. According to the Sixth Circuit, after the unfair labor practices in *Brown-Forman* were litigated before the Administrative Law Judge and his decision appealed, the Board should have stayed the case and placed the union, the employer, and the aggrieved employees on hold while it engaged in a possibly protracted process of a rule making. As the courts grapple with *Brown-Forman*, a question presented is bound to echo what Justice Black suggested in his concurrence in *Wyman-Gordon*:

is there any "good reason to impose any such inflexible requirement. . . ."? 394 U.S. at 775 (Black, J. concurring).

2. ELECTION PROPAGANDA

(a) Threats of Reprisal

Page 167. Add after paragraph on *Dal-Tex Optical*:

What if, after a union drive free of unfair labor practice charges, and after voting but before the count, the Company announces to the workforce that: (1) it believes the union's election conduct and the Board's ballot eligibility determination have resulted in an unfair election; (2) if the union wins it will object to the election; and (3) if the union is certified nonetheless, it will refuse to bargain in order to secure a judicial determination of the matter? Is that statement an unfair labor practice? Blue School, 373 N.L.R.B. No. 120 (2024).

Page 174. Add at end of Problem 3:

The Fifth Circuit took up Musk's "stock options" tweet *en banc*. Tesla, Inc. v. NLRB, 120 F.4th 433 (5th Cir. 2024). The nine-member majority assumed the statement was a threat violative of § 8(a)(1), but held that the Board lacked the authority to order Musk to delete the tweet: his tweet was on a matter of public concern protected by the First Amendment. The eight dissenting members argued that because the tweet, which was on a matter of labor relations and within the ambit of the statutory prohibition on threats (as the NLRB found and as the majority conceded *arguendo*), was unlawful, it would not be constitutionally protected and was thus subject to an order of deletion. Which is correct?

(b) Factual Misrepresentations

Page 187. Add after the end of Problem 5:

6. In *Siren Retail Corp d/b/a Starbucks*, 373 N.L.R.B. No. 135 (2024). the Biden Board addressed what test should apply in determining whether the following statements by one of Siren's managers at a captive audience it had convened to address unionization:

> If you want a union to represent you—uh—you want to give your right to speak to leadership through a union, you're going to check off "yes" for the election. If you want to maintain a direct relationship with leadership, you'll check off "no."
>
> [And]
>
> [A] representation of a union is the rules of employment will then be grounded in a contract. And if it's not in that contract, it's not a conversation in my opinion that's going to happen with leadership. We'll be bound by the contract. So the union will be bound. And Starbucks will be bound. So I want to be clear on that. That a third party comes in and speaks for you. And everything will be

grounded, from my experience and my opinion through the lens of that contract.

The Board, overruling *Tri-Cast, Inc.,* 274 N.L.R.B. 377 (1985), provided a new test to evaluate whether such employer predictions about the impact of unionization on the relationship between individual employees and their employer are unlawful threats. *Tri-Cast* had deemed most employer statements about the impact of unionization on the relationship between individual employees and their employer to be categorically lawful. In *Siren Retail,* the Board held that, prospectively, it will analyze such statements under the same longstanding test it uses to evaluate other potentially threatening or coercive statements.

The Board majority highlighted that this approach, premised on the Supreme Court's decision in *NLRB v. Gissel Packing Co.,* 395 U.S. 575 (1969), mandates that employer predictions of negative impacts from unionization "must be carefully phrased on the basis of objective fact to convey an employer's belief as to demonstrably probable consequences beyond [its] control." If such a prediction is not grounded in objective fact, or predicts negative consequences that would result from the employer's own actions, it is no longer a reasonable prediction but a threat of retaliation based on misrepresentation and coercion. The Board reasoned that this approach not only is more consistent with its general approach to evaluating potentially threatening employer statements, but also better protects workers' right to make a free and fair choice about union representation while respecting an employer's prerogative to share their views in a non-coercive manner. The Board made this change prospective only to accommodate the reliance employers may have previously placed on *Tri-Cast*'s categorical rule.

Member Kaplan, concurring in part and dissenting in part, first argued that, for various reasons, it was inappropriate for the majority to overturn *Tri-Cast* and announce a new test in this case. Taking on the majority's reasoning, Member Kaplan argued that the "absence of threat" rationale set forth in *Tri-Cast* properly draws the line between an employer's unlawful threats and its lawful statements about changes brought on by unionization and exclusive representation, and that this line is consistent with the Act and Supreme Court precedent. He further argued that the majority's reasoning reveals a misunderstanding of the proviso to Section 9(a) addressing the right afforded to individual represented employees to have their grievances *adjusted* by their employer as long as such adjustment is not inconsistent with the CBA. Finally, he contested the majority's characterization of its test (and not *Tri-Cast*'s) as case-by-case approach: "[C]ontrary to their assertion, it appears that they want to put in place a categorial rule; specifically, that to be deemed lawful, employer predictions about the changing employer-employee relationship must recite almost verbatim even barely relevant and often misleading legal principles."

Under the *majority's* approach, are the statements in this case threats? Why or why not? How about statement (b) in Problem 3 on page 173?

3. OTHER FORMS OF INTERFERENCE, RESTRAINT OR COERCION

Page 196. Add to Problem 2:

Consider also Starbuck's Corp., 374 N.L.R.B. No. 9 (2024): a store manager asks an employee how he "felt about unionization" while both were "back of the house"—an area reserved for employment relations interactions. The manager did not know whether the employee supported the Union. The employee said in response to the manager that he believed a union would not be necessary if they were not overworked. Has the manager committed an unfair labor practice?

Page 197. Add to Problems for Discussion:

6. When the management of an enterprise learned of a union organizing drive, it hired a labor relations consultant to assist the company to "get ahead of the union talk." At his direction managers distributed "fact of the day" flyers to the workforce. They were instructed to record and report to the consultant on employee feedback; that is, whether employees showed interest or asked questions. Managers were instructed to report on the employees' body language and attitudes toward the flyers, including whether employees made eye contact, reacted in other ways, like crumpling the flyers, or spoke to anyone else after talking with a manager. The flyers included a bullet point guide to the NLRA pointing to what was termed the "risks" in the bargaining process, but they were entirely factual. Does the recording of and reporting on employee reaction violate § 8(a)(1)? Would it be significant if the workers were or were not aware that their reactions were being recorded and reported? NCRNC, LLC v. NLRB, 94 F.4th 67 (D.C. Cir. 2024).

Page 200. Add to Problem 3:

Assume Mako is a national company with offices in twenty-eight states and the unionizing drive is one location in one state. Assume that the April announcement was of an improved nationwide benefit. Did the announcement violate § 8(a)(1)? Amazon.com Services LLC, 374 N.L.R.B. No. 38 (2026).

C. DISCRIMINATION

Page 248. Add at the end of Problem 4:

Enf'd Quickway Transp., Inc. v. NLRB, 117 F.4th 789 (6th Cir. 2024) (applying *Darlington*). Judge Murphy concurred in the result, but disagreed that there was a duty to bargain over the partial closure under *First National Maintenance*.

D. REMEDIES FOR UNFAIR LABOR PRACTICES

Page 261. What follows replaces all the text after the incomplete paragraph at the top of the page.

Starbucks Corp. v. McKinney, Regional Director of Region 15

602 U.S. 339 (2024).

■ JUSTICE THOMAS delivered the opinion of the Court.

* * *

I

A

The National Labor Relations Act (NLRA) prohibits employers and unions from engaging in certain "unfair labor practice[s]." 49 Stat. 452, 29 U. S. C. §§ 158(a), (b). The National Labor Relations Board enforces that prohibition. § 160(a). The Board's "authority kicks in when a person files a charge with the agency alleging that" an employer or labor union has engaged in an unfair labor practice. *Glacier Northwest, Inc.* v. *Teamsters,* 598 U. S. 771, 775 (2023) (citing 29 CFR § 101.2 (2021)). A regional Director then investigates the charge. § 101.4 (2023). And, "[i]f the charge appears to have merit," the director institutes a formal action against the offending party by issuing an administrative complaint. § 101.8. This complaint triggers adjudicatory proceedings within the agency, first before an administrative law judge, and then before the Board itself. See 29 U. S. C. §§ 160(b), (c); 29 CFR §§ 101.10 to 101.12. A federal court of appeals may review the Board's final order, if an aggrieved party seeks judicial review or if the Board seeks enforcement of its order. 29 U. S. C. §§ 160(e)–(f). On review, the Board's findings of fact are "conclusive" "if supported by substantial evidence." *Ibid.*

Because the Board's administrative proceedings take years, Congress vested the Board with authority to seek a preliminary injunction in federal court while the proceedings unfold. Section 10(j) of the NLRA provides that, "upon issuance of a complaint," the Board may "petition any United States district court . . . for appropriate temporary relief." § 160(j). A district court considering a § 10(j) petition may "grant to the Board such temporary relief . . . as it deems just and proper." *Ibid.*

B

Starbucks is the world's largest coffeehouse chain, with over 34,000 locations. In 2022, six employees at a Memphis, Tennessee, location announced plans to unionize the store and formed an organizing committee. Several employees, including some members of the organizing committee, invited a news crew from a local television station to visit the store after hours to promote their unionizing effort. The news crew interviewed the employees about their reasons for organizing and what they hoped to achieve. The next day, store management learned about the media event and launched an investigation. Starbucks ultimately fired multiple employees involved with the media event for violating company policy. These included the members of the organizing committee who were in attendance. The union coordinating with the employees filed charges with the Board. The union alleged that Starbucks unlawfully interfered with the employees' right to unionize and discriminated against union supporters, in violation of 29 U.S.C. §§ 158(a)(1) and (3). After investigating the allegations, the Board issued a complaint against Starbucks. The regional Director then filed a § 10(j) petition in the United States District Court for the Western District of Tennessee, seeking a preliminary injunction that would, among other things, require Starbucks to reinstate the fired employees.

To assess whether the Board was entitled to a preliminary injunction under § 10(j), the District Court applied the two-part test established by Sixth Circuit precedent. That test asks whether "there is reasonable cause to believe that unfair labor practices have occurred," and whether injunctive relief is "just and proper." *McKinney* v. *Ozburn-Hessey Logistics, LLC*, 875 F. 3d 333, 339 (2017) (internal quotation marks omitted). The Board could establish reasonable cause by simply showing that its "legal theory [was] substantial and not frivolous." *Ibid.* (internal quotation marks omitted). And, relief would be just and proper if it were "necessary to return the parties to [the] status quo pending the Board's proceedings in order to protect the Board's remedial powers under the NLRA." *Ibid.* (internal quotation marks omitted). Applying this standard, the District Court granted an injunction to the Board. 2022 WL 5434206, *12 (WD Tenn., Aug. 18, 2022). And, applying Circuit precedent, the Sixth Circuit affirmed. 77 F. 4th 391, 400–401 (2023).

Not all courts evaluate petitions for § 10(j) injunctions under the standard applied by the Sixth Circuit. Some courts instead apply the four-part test for preliminary injunctions articulated in *Winter* v. *Natural Resources Defense Council, Inc.*, 555 U. S. 7. . . . That familiar standard requires a plaintiff to make a clear showing that "he is likely to succeed on the merits, that he is likely to suffer irreparable harm in the absence of preliminary relief, that the balance of equities tips in his favor, and that an injunction is in the public interest." *Winter*, 555 U. S., at 20, 22. We granted certiorari to resolve the Circuit split about what standard governs the Board's requests for preliminary injunctions under § 10(j), 601 U. S. ___ (2024), and now vacate and remand.

II

Section 10(j) authorizes a federal district court "to grant . . . such temporary relief . . . as it deems just and proper" during the pendency of the Board's administrative proceedings. § 160(j). When Congress empowers courts to grant equitable relief, there is a strong presumption that courts will exercise that authority in a manner consistent with traditional principles of equity. For preliminary injunctions, the four criteria identified in *Winter* encompass the relevant equitable principles. Nothing in § 10(j) displaces the presumption that those traditional principles govern. We therefore conclude that district courts must use the traditional four-part test when evaluating the Board's request for a preliminary injunction under § 10(j).

A

A preliminary injunction is an "extraordinary" equitable remedy that is "never awarded as of right." *Winter*, 555 U. S., at 24. Its purpose "is merely to preserve the relative positions of the parties until a trial on the merits can beheld." *University of Tex.* v. *Camenisch*, 451 U. S. 390, 395 (1981). The default rule is that a plaintiff seeking a preliminary injunction must make a clear showing that "he is likely to succeed on the merits, that he is likely to suffer irreparable harm in the absence of preliminary relief, that the balance of equities tips in his favor, and that an injunction is in the public interest." *Winter*, 555 U. S., at 20, 22. "These commonplace considerations applicable to cases in which injunctions are sought in the federal courts reflect a 'practice with a background of several hundred years of history.' " *Weinberger* v. *Romero-Barcelo*, 456 U. S. 305, 313 (1982) (quoting *Hecht Co.* v. *Bowles*, 321 U. S. 321, 329 (1944)). . . .

When interpreting a statute that authorizes federal courts to grant preliminary injunctions, "we do not lightly assume that Congress has intended to depart from established principles." *Romero-Barcelo*, 456 U. S., at 313; see also *Porter* v. *Warner Holding Co.*, 328 U. S. 395, 398 (1946). This Court has consistently employed this presumption when interpreting a wide variety of statutes that authorize preliminary and permanent injunctions. See, *e.g.*, *United States* v. *Oakland Cannabis Buyers' Cooperative*, 532 U. S. 483, 496 (2001) (Controlled Substances Act); *Romero-Barcelo*, 456 U. S., at 312–313 (Federal Water Pollution Control Act); *Amoco Production Co.* v. *Gambell*, 480 U. S. 531, 542–544 (1987) (Alaska National Interest Lands Conservation Act); *Hecht*, 321 U. S., at 329 (Emergency Price Control Act). Thus, absent a clear command from Congress, courts must adhere to the traditional four-factor test.

Nothing in § 10(j)'s text overcomes the presumption that the four traditional criteria govern a preliminary-injunction request by the Board. Section 10(j) authorizes a district court "to grant to the Board such temporary relief . . . as it deems just and proper." We do not understand the statutory directive to grant relief when the district court "deems" it "just and proper" to jettison the normal equitable rules. To the contrary, the phrase "just and proper" invokes the discretion that courts have traditionally exercised when faced with requests for equitable relief. As a matter of ordinary meaning, the word "just" means "fair" and "righteous." Funk & Wagnalls New Standard Dictionary 1334 (1942); see also Webster's New International Dictionary 1348 (2d ed. 1934) ("righteous" and "equitable"). And, the word "proper" means "appropriate," "suitable," or "correct." *Id.*, at 1983. Crafting "fair" and "appropriate" equitable relief necessitates the exercise of discretion—the hallmark of traditional equitable practice. See *Hecht*, 321 U. S., at 329 ("The essence of equity jurisdiction has been the power of the Chancellor to do equity and to mold each decree to the necessities of the particular case"); see also 77 F. 4th, at 403 (Readler, J., concurring); *Kinney* v. *Pioneer Press*, 881 F. 2d 485, 491 (CA7 1989) (Easterbrook, J.) ("Section 10(j) tells the district court to do what's 'just and proper', which we read as a statement that traditional rules govern").

This Court's precedent also counsels against reading§ 10(j) to supplant the traditional equitable principles governing injunctions. In *Hecht*, the Court interpreted the Emergency Price Control Act of 1942's instruction that an injunction "shall be granted" if the Office of Price Administration shows that a defendant "has engaged or is about to engage" in a prohibited act. 321 U. S., at 322 (quoting ch. 26, 56 Stat. 23, 50 U. S. C. App. § 925 (1940 ed., Supp. II)). This language is far more favorable to the agency than§ 10(j) because it seemingly suggests that courts *must* grant injunctive relief where the agency makes the required showing. Yet, the Court refused to read the Emergency Price Control Act to create such "a major departure from th[e] long tradition" of equity. 321 U. S., at 330. The Court reasoned that "if Congress desired to make such an abrupt departure from traditional equity practice . . ., it would have made its desire plain." *Ibid.* If the Emergency Price Control Act did not displace the presumption that traditional equitable principles apply, then § 10(j)'s discretion-inviting directive to grant injunctive relief as district courts "dee[m] just and proper" does not either.

Finally, § 10(j)'s text bears no resemblance to the language that Congress has employed when it has altered the normal equitable rules. Some statutes increase the burden for obtaining an injunction. Another provision in the NLRA itself, for example, makes it harder for the Government to obtain an injunction against union strikes and lockouts by requiring a showing that the strike or lockout "affects an entire industry or a substantial part thereof" and "imperil[s] the national health or safety." 29 U. S. C. § 178(a).And, courts evaluating preliminary-injunction requests under the Prison Litigation Reform Act must "give substantial weight to any adverse impact on public safety or the operation of a criminal justice system." 18 U. S. C. § 3626(a)(2). Other statutes expressly relieve the party moving for an injunction from showing that he can satisfy one of the traditional criteria. For instance, plaintiffs alleging trademark violations are entitled to "a rebuttable presumption of irreparable harm . . . upon a finding of likelihood of success on the merits." 132 Stat. 2208, 15 U. S. C. § 1116(a). Unlike these statutes, § 10(j) omits any specific instruction that suggests Congress altered the traditional equitable rules. It simply invites courts to grant equitable relief where they deem it "just and proper." And, in exercising this discretionary authority, courts must "be guided by sound [equitable] principles." *Nken* v. *Holder*, 556 U. S. 418, 434 (2009) (internal quotation marks omitted).

In sum, because nothing in § 10(j)'s text overcomes the presumption that traditional equitable principles govern, district courts considering the Board's request for a preliminary injunction must apply the *Winter* framework, which embodies those traditional principles.

B

Rather than contest that traditional equitable criteria govern, the Board recasts the dispute as one about how statutory context informs the application of those criteria. The Board highlights that Congress made the Board, not federal courts, responsible for adjudicating charges of unfair labor practices in the first instance and that courts of appeals must review the Board's final decisions deferentially. According to the Board, these contextual considerations require district courts evaluating § 10(j) petitions to apply the traditional criteria in a less exacting way, and the Sixth Circuit's reasonable-cause standard appropriately accounts for context. The partial dissent also asserts that "a district court's preliminary look at the merits" of a § 10(j) petition "should be far less searching than normal" for similar reasons. *Post*, at 14 (JACKSON, J., concurring in part, concurring in judgment, and dissenting in part). We disagree. The reasonable-cause standard goes far beyond simply fine tuning the traditional criteria to the § 10(j) context—it substantively lowers the bar for securing a preliminary injunction by requiring courts to yield to the Board's preliminary view of the facts, law, and equities. Nowhere is this more evident than with what the Board, as movant, must show about the merits of its claims. Under the traditional that it "is likely to succeed on the merits." *Winter*, 555 U. S., at 20. And, in assessing that likelihood, a district court must evaluate any factual conflicts or difficult questions of law. 11A C. Wright, A. Miller, & M. Kane, Federal Practice and Procedure § 2948.3 (3d ed. 2013). By contrast, the Board may obtain a § 10(j) injunction under the reasonable-cause standard by merely showing "reasonable cause to believe that unfair labor practices have occurred." *Ozburn-Hessey Logistics*, 875 F. 3d, at 339 (internal quotation marks omitted). The Board "need not convince the court of the validity of [its] theory of liability, as long as the theory is substantial and not frivolous." *Gottfried* v. *Frankel*, 818 F. 2d 485, 493 (CA6 1987). And, "[i]n reviewing the supporting facts, a district court may not resolve conflicting evidence or make credibility determinations." 77 F. 4th, at 397.

There is an obvious difference between having the Board show that it is "likely" to succeed on the merits and having it show only that its theory of the case is "substantial and not frivolous," without having to convince the court that its theory is likely meritorious. In fact, it is hard to imagine how the Board could lose under the reasonable-cause test if courts deferentially ask only whether the Board offered a minimally plausible legal theory, while ignoring conflicting law or facts. As Judge

Readler explained, if the reasonable-cause standard were "applied in the traditional civil litigation setting, any complaint that could withstand Rule12(b)(6) would automatically be deserving of injunctive relief as well, rendering the court more a spectator than a referee when it comes to matters of equity." *Id.*, at 408 (concurring opinion). Perhaps unsurprisingly, courts that apply the reasonable-cause standard freely acknowledge that the threshold merits showing is "significantly lower than a requirement to show . . . 'likelihood of success'" under the traditional standard. *Overstreet* v. *El Paso Disposal, L.P.*, 625 F. 3d 844, 851, n. 10 (CA5 2010); see also *Fleischut* v. *Nixon Detroit Diesel, Inc.*, 859 F. 2d 26, 29 (CA6 1988) (characterizing the Board's burden to show reasonable cause as "relatively insubstantial" (internal quotation marks omitted)).

Section 10(j)'s statutory context does not compel this watered-down approach to equity. The Board and the partial dissent are correct that § 10(j) proceedings are different from ordinary preliminary-injunction proceedings insofar as the Board, not the district court, will adjudicate the claims in the first instance. But, they do not explain why this difference should matter. The Board suggests that district courts risk supplanting its adjudicatory authority by conducting an independent assessment of the merits and equitable factors. But, no matter how searching the district court's merits inquiry or what evidence it considers or credits, the Board remains free to reach its own legal conclusions and develop its own record in its administrative proceedings. See *Camenisch*, 451 U. S., at 395. Also, since irreparable harm and the other equitable factors are not part of the unfair-labor-practice claim, the district court's assessment of those factors is completely irrelevant to the Board's adjudicatory authority.

The Board and the partial dissent also reason that district courts should apply a deferential standard because the Board's final decisions are reviewed deferentially by a court of appeals. But, none of the views advanced in a § 10(j) petition represent the Board's formal position—they are simply the preliminary legal and factual views of the Board's in-house attorneys who investigated and initiated the administrative complaint. And, deference to what is "nothing more than an agency's convenient litigating position" is "entirely inappropriate." *Bowen* v. *Georgetown Univ. Hospital*, 488 U. S. 204, 213 (1988). The Board's attempt to salvage the reasonable-cause standard using statutory context thus fails.

* * *

■ JUSTICE JACKSON, concurring in part, concurring in the judgment, and dissenting in part.

"When Congress entrusts to an equity court the enforcement of prohibitions contained in a regulatory enactment, it must be taken to have acted cognizant of the historic power of equity to provide complete relief in light of the statutory purposes." *Mitchell* v. *Robert DeMario Jewelry, Inc.*, 361 U. S. 288, 291–292 (1960). Accordingly, when interpreting a statute that authorizes equitable relief, like a preliminary injunction, this Court typically employs what amounts to a two-part inquiry focused on congressional intent. See *Hecht Co.* v. *Bowles*, 321 U. S. 321, 328–331 (1944). First, we determine whether Congress has stripped courts of their traditional equitable discretion by "a clear and valid legislative command." *Porter* v. *Warner Holding Co.*, 328 U. S. 395, 398 (1946). Second, if no such clear command is found, we look to the statutory context to assess how courts should exercise their equitable discretion " 'as conditioned by the necessities of the public interest which Congress has sought to protect.' " *Weinberger* v. *Romero-Barcelo*, 456 U. S. 305, 320 (1982) (quoting *Hecht*, 321 U. S., at 330).

Today, the Court correctly applies the first step, but ignores the second. I agree with the majority that nothing in the National Labor Relations Act (NLRA) clearly strips courts of their equitable discretion to determine whether to issue a so-called § 10(j) injunction. And I concur in the conclusion that we should vacate and remand for the Sixth Circuit to reevaluate this case under our traditional four-factor test for assessing requests for preliminary injunctions. But I cannot join the majority in ignoring the choices Congress has made in the NLRA about how courts should exercise their discretion in light of the National Labor Relations Board's authority over labor disputes. Because the majority chooses the simplicity of unfettered judicial discretion over the nuances of Congress's direction, I respectfully dissent in part.

I

The question in this case is how district courts should evaluate the Board's request for a preliminary injunction in light of Congress's intentions. See 29 U. S. C. § 160(j) (authorizing a district court to issue "such temporary relief or restraining order as it deems just and proper"). The majority suggests a sharp dichotomy: Either courts retain all of their equitable discretion, or the Board gets undue deference. See *ante*, at 8–10. But, "[w]hen Congress invokes the Chancellor's conscience to further transcendent legislative purposes, what is required is the principled application of standards consistent with those purposes," not unbridled equitable discretion, " 'which varies like the Chancellor's foot.' " *Albemarle Paper Co.* v. *Moody*, 422 U. S. 405, 417 (1975) (alteration omitted).

Our *Hecht* case is instructive, for it establishes the frame work we have long used to assess whether an injunction authorized by a statute should issue.[1] In *Hecht*, the Court was asked to determine whether the Emergency Price Control Act's direction that an injunction " 'shall be granted' " after a violation was found displaced a court's equitable

[1] As Judge Friendly explained, "Mr. Justice Douglas' classic opinion in *Hecht*" is "a decision of such widely recognized significance that it is not unreasonable to attribute knowledge of it to at least some of the framers of the Taft-Hartley Act of 1947 in which [§] 10(j) . . . originated." *Danielson* v. *Joint Bd. of Coat, Suit and Allied Garment Workers' Union*, 494 F. 2d 1230, 1240 (CA2 1974).

discretion. 321 U. S., at 322. As the majority acknowledges, after finding no clear indication that Congress intended to displace equitable discretion, the *Hecht* Court concluded that the answer was no. See *ante,* at 7.[2]

But *Hecht* did not end there. The Court emphasized that the mere fact that the Emergency Price Control Act lacked an "unequivocal statement" displacing courts' equitable discretion did not "imply that courts should administer [the Act] grudgingly." 321 U. S., at 329–330. Instead, the Court explained, courts should see themselves as partners of the agency that administered the Act. Congress "entrusted" each "with a share of . . . responsibility" for effectuating its goals. *Id.*, at 331. In other words, "[c]ourt and agency are the means adopted to attain the prescribed end, and so far as their duties are defined by the words of the statute, those words should be construed so as to attain that end through coordinated action." *Id.,* at 330. Therefore, a court's "discretion . . . must be exercised in light of the large objectives of the Act." *Id.*, at 331.

Hecht's two-step framework is still in use today. We only rarely find that a statute clearly displaces courts' equitable discretion. See, *e.g.*, *TVA* v. *Hill,* 437 U. S. 153, 193–195 (1978) (finding such displacement in the Endangered Species Act). So, in most cases in which equitable relief is authorized by statute, the movant must contend with the court's equitable authority. In statutes that involve preliminary injunctive relief, that means the party seeking relief "must establish [1] that he is likely to succeed on the merits, [2] that he is likely to suffer irreparable harm in the absence of preliminary relief, [3] that the balance of equities tips in his favor, and [4] that an injunction is in the public interest." *Winter* v. *Natural Resources Defense Council, Inc.*, 555 U. S. 7, 20 (2008).

Even so, under the *Hecht* framework, we have consistently held that courts' exercise of equitable discretion is informed by congressional intent. Put simply, "a court sitting in equity cannot 'ignore the judgment of Congress, deliberately expressed in legislation.' " *United States* v. *Oakland Cannabis Buyers' Cooperative,* 532 U. S. 483, 497 (2001) (quoting *Virginian R. Co.* v. *Railway Employees,* 300 U. S. 515, 551 (1937)). For each of the four factors, then, courts must look to the choices made by Congress for guidance. See *Oakland Cannabis*, 532 U. S., at 497 (" 'Once Congress, exercising its delegated powers, has decided the order of priorities in a given area, it is . . . for the courts to enforce them when enforcement is sought' " (quoting *Hill,* 437 U. S., at 194)).

---

[2] The majority correctly states this holding, but its analysis of *Hecht Co.* v. *Bowles,* 321 U.S. 321 (1944), misleadingly suggests a near-unobtainable standard for displacement. *Hecht* does not hold that the statutory phrase "shall be granted" is insufficiently clear to displace a court's equitable discretion. Contra, *ante,* at 6–7. Rather, the *Hecht* Court found that such language was "less mandatory than a literal reading might suggest" because of two other indicia of congressional intent. 321 U. S., at 328. First, the statute itself gave courts discretion to enter an injunction "or other order," as they deemed fit. *Ibid.* And, second, the legislative history suggested that courts should retain their equitable discretion to provide the relief " 'proper in the circumstances of each particular case.' " *Id.*, at 329 (quoting S. Rep. No. 931, 77th Cong., 2d Sess., 10 (1942)).

II

Here, the choices Congress has made regarding how labor disputes are to be resolved—including its decision to authorize preliminary injunctive relief in some circumstances—are clear and comprehensive. As briefly explained below, Congress has long sought to contain the unbounded exercise of judicial discretion to issue injunctions in the context of labor disputes, leaving the resolution of those particular conflicts primarily in the hands of the Board. See Brief for Service Employees International Union as *Amicus Curiae* 4–11.

That is for good reason. To put it bluntly, courts exercising their equitable discretion amidst labor disputes today do so against the backdrop of an ignominious history of abuse. See generally F. Frankfurter & N. Greene, The Labor Injunction (1930). "In the early part of [the 20th] century, the federal courts generally were regarded as allies of management in its attempt to prevent the organization and strengthening of labor unions." *Boys Markets, Inc.* v. *Retail Clerks,* 398 U. S. 235, 250 (1970). . . .

Congress reacted to this antidemocratic " 'government by injunction' " by seeking to cabin courts' power to intervene. *Milk Wagon Drivers* v. *Lake Valley Farm Products, Inc.,* 311 U. S. 91, 102 (1940). Its initial attempt, in the Clayton Act of 1914, was unsuccessful, due in large part to judicial frustration of congressional intent. See *BE&K Constr. Co.* v. *NLRB,* 536 U. S. 516, 543 (2002) (Breyer, J., concurring in part and concurring in judgment). Its next attempt, the Norris-LaGuardia Act of 1932, was impossible to ignore. There, Congress "deprive[d] the courts of jurisdiction to issue an injunction in any case involving or growing out of a labor dispute, except" under specified circumstances and with particular procedural checks. *New Negro Alliance* v. *Sanitary Grocery Co.,* 303 U. S. 552, 561–562 (1938); see also *Marine Cooks* v. *Panama S. S. Co.,* 362 U. S. 365, 369 (1960) ("The language [of the Norris-LaGuardia Act] is broad because Congress was intent upon taking the federal courts out of the labor injunction business except in very limited circumstances").

Three years later, in 1935, Congress passed the National Labor Relations Act, 29 U. S. C. § 151 *et seq.* The Act aimed to "eliminate the causes of certain substantial obstructions to the free flow of commerce" by protecting workers' rights.§ 151. To achieve this aim, the NLRA codified "[e]mployees['] . . . right to self-organization," to form and join unions, to collectively bargain, and to strike. § 157. It also made it unlawful for employers and unions to engage in particular unfair labor practices. See § 158. Employers, for example, cannot interfere with employees' efforts to organize a union or engage in collective bargaining. See §§ 157, 158(a). Similarly, unions cannot, *inter alia,* coerce employees to join a union or refuse to engage in collective bargaining. See § 158(b).

Notably, though, Congress did not leave it to courts to protect the rights established in the NLRA. See *Phelps Dodge Corp.* v. *NLRB,* 313 U.

S. 177, 193 (1941). Instead, Congress created an expert agency, the National Labor Relations Board, to investigate, adjudicate, and stop unfair labor practices. See 29 U. S. C. § 160(a). The agency is headed by a five-member board that is charged with resolving unfair labor practice cases, see § 153(a); the enforcement role is occupied by a General Counsel, see § 153(d). The General Counsel is charged with investigating and prosecuting unfair labor practice cases, as well as overseeing Regional Offices that carry out much of the day-to-day work of enforcing labor law and policy. See *ibid.*; see also *NLRB* v. *Food & Commercial Workers*, 484 U. S. 112, 117–118 (1987).

* * *

[JUSTICE JACKSON summarizes the Board's unfair labor practice procedure.]

B

Crucially for present purposes, Congress recognized that delay in vindicating labor rights "during the 'notoriously glacial' course of NLRB proceedings" can lead to their defeat. *Kinney* v. *Pioneer Press*, 881 F. 2d 485, 491 (CA7 1989). This case is illustrative of the problem. In February 2022, Starbucks fired five of six members of an organizing committee, along with two other union-aligned workers, just as a campaign for unionization was building momentum. The Board took up the workers' complaint soon after. Now, more than two years later, their case remains pending.

To respond to situations such as this one, Congress gave the Board specific power to seek preliminary injunctive relief. These injunctions are generally referred to as "§ 10(j)injunctions," named after the section of the Taft-Hartley Act of 1947 in which they were originally introduced. See 29 U. S. C. § 160(j). There is broad consensus about why Congress allowed the Board to seek § 10(j) injunctions. As summarized in the Senate Report on Taft-Hartley:

> "Time is usually of the essence in [labor disputes], and consequently the relatively slow procedure of Board hearing and order, followed many months later by an enforcing decree of the circuit court of appeals, falls short of achieving the desired objectives—the prompt elimination of the obstructions to the free flow of commerce and encouragement of the practice and procedure of free and private collective bargaining. Hence we have provided that the Board, acting in the public interest and not in vindication of purely private rights, may seek injunctive relief in the case of all types of unfair labor practices." S. Rep. No. 105, 80th Cong., 1st Sess., 8 (1947).

See also, *e.g.*, *Kinney*, 881 F. 2d, at 488 (Easterbrook, J.) (quoting this passage). . . .

In short, Congress designed § 10(j) " 'as a means of preserving or restoring the status quo as it existed before the onset of unfair labor practices' " so that the Board's ultimate ability to remedy an unfair labor practice would not be impeded. *NLRB* v. *Electro-Voice, Inc.*, 83 F. 3d 1559, 1575 (CA7 1996).

In addition to authorizing § 10(j) injunctions, Congress made two other pertinent choices in the statute. First, it granted *the Board* power to seek a § 10(j) injunction. See 29 U. S. C. § 160(j). No private party has authority to seek § 10(j) relief. See *Clothing Workers* v. *Richman Brothers Co.*, 348 U. S. 511, 517 (1955). And, by the statute's own terms, power is left to the Board itself, rather than the General Counsel or another member of the prosecutorial branch of the agency. That is unlike a closely related section of the statute, § 10(*l*), which authorizes the relevant "officer or regional attorney" to file for preliminary relief in cases involving certain unfair labor practices by unions. See 29 U. S. C. § 160(*l*). Second, Congress granted the Board *discretion* to determine whether or not to seek preliminary injunctive relief. See § 160(j). Thus, the Board need only seek § 10(j) relief when it deems doing so appropriate or necessary. Again, by contrast, requests for relief under § 10(*l*) are mandatory once an investigation yields "reasonable cause to believe" that an unfair labor practice has occurred. See § 160(*l*).

The NLRA does not specify how the Board should exercise its discretion to seek § 10(j) injunctions. But the agency has crafted an extensive, and strikingly deliberative, standard operating procedure. See Brief for Respondent 4 (citing Office of the General Counsel, NLRB, Section 10(j) Manual (Mar. 2020)). First, the Regional Director must submit a written memorandum to the General Counsel explaining why temporary relief is appropriate in a given case. Second, the General Counsel must review the memorandum and determine whether the request for relief is warranted. Third, if the General Counsel determines that a § 10(j) injunction should be sought, then she must present a recommendation to the Board. Fourth, and finally, the Board must either accept or reject the recommendation. It is only after the Board approves the filing of a request for a § 10(j) injunction in this fashion that the General Counsel or relevant Regional Director files that request in federal district court.

When the district court receives the Board's application for a § 10(j) injunction, the statutory scheme kicks back in. "Upon the filing of any such petition the court shall cause notice thereof to be served upon such person, and thereupon shall have jurisdiction to grant to the Board such temporary relief or restraining order as it deems just and proper." 29 U. S. C. § 160(j). If granted, a § 10(j) injunction returns workers, unions, and employers to the status quo as it existed before the alleged NLRA violation. See *Electro-Voice, Inc.*, 83 F. 3d, at 1575.

III

A

What standard should district courts use to decide whether granting the Board's § 10(j) request for interim relief is "just and proper"? That is the question this case presents, and as I previously explained, we use *Hecht's* framework to answer. So, first, we determine whether Congress has clearly displaced courts' equitable discretion. And, second, if no such clear statement exists, we evaluate how that discretion should be exercised in light of Congress's choices in the NLRA.

At step one, the parties here do not dispute that § 10(j)'s text, context, and legislative history lack the clear congressional intent required to preclude district courts from exercising equitable discretion. See Brief for Petitioner 15; Brief for Respondent 9. Also, no Circuit, not even the Sixth Circuit below, holds that § 10(j) deprives district courts of their equitable discretion. . . . I agree with the majority that courts faced with a Board petition for a § 10(j) injunction should evaluate that request using all four factors in our established *Winter* test. . . .

The remaining question—*Hecht's* second step—is the more challenging one. To the extent the majority addresses it at all, it has done an insufficient job of explaining *how* district courts' equitable discretion is channeled by Congress's choices within the NLRA.

The fact that this needs to be done is uncontroversial. "Obviously," Starbucks says, " 'statutory context is relevant to the consideration of equitable relief.' " Reply Brief 10(quoting Brief for Respondent 15). . . . And every relevant Circuit, including those that use the standard four-factor test, understands district courts' equitable discretion to issue a § 10(j) injunction has to be informed by the statutory context of the NLRA. . . .[Extensive list of authority omitted.] But the Court today provides little helpful guidance on this front.

B

Given our precedents and the statute's text, the interaction between Congress's choices in the NLRA and a district court's equitable assessment of a request for § 10(j) relief is straightforward for three of the four equitable factors. To show irreparable harm, the Board must establish that its ability to remedy a violation of labor rights will likely be precluded absent interim relief. See, *e.g.*, *Frankl* v. *HTH Corp.*, 650 F. 3d 1334, 1362 (CA9 2012) ("In the context of the NLRA, permitting an alleged unfair labor practice to reach fruition and thereby render meaningless the Board's remedial authority is irreparable harm" (alteration and internal quotation marks omitted)). When evaluating the balance of the equities, district courts may consider harms to an opposing party, but they are prohibited from crediting a party's desire to continue engaging in an alleged violation of the NLRA. See *Oakland Cannabis*, 532 U. S., at 498 ("[W]hen a court of equity exercises its discretion, it may not consider the advantages and disadvantages of nonenforcement of the statute"). When addressing the public interest, courts must defer to Congress's articulation of that interest in the NLRA itself. See 29 U. S. C. § 151 ("It is . . . the policy of the United States to . . . encourag[e] . . . collective bargaining and . . . protec[t] the exercise by workers of full freedom of association, self-organization, and designation of representatives of their own choosing"); see also *Virginian R. Co.*, 300 U. S., at 552 ("The fact that Congress has indicated its purpose . . . is in itself a declaration of public interest and policy which should be persuasive in inducing courts to give relief ").

The final factor—the likelihood of success on the merits—is more difficult to evaluate. That factor can be articulated in "a bewildering variety of formulations," but, at core, it asks courts to predict how likely it is that a party seeking preliminary relief will ultimately prevail on the merits of their claims. 11A C. Wright, A. Miller, & M. Kane, Federal Practice and Procedure § 2948.3, p. 197 (3d ed. 2013); see also *id.*, at 201 ("All courts agree that a plaintiff must present a prima facie case but need not show a certainty of winning" (footnote omitted)). In my view, three aspects of the NLRA's scheme should inform this evaluation.

First, as described above, the NLRA makes the Board, not district courts, the primary adjudicator of labor disputes and the central expositor of labor policy. See 29 U. S. C. § 160(a); see also *Beth Israel Hospital* v. *NLRB*, 437 U. S. 483, 500 (1978) ("It is the Board on which Congress conferred the authority to develop and apply fundamental national labor policy"); *Garner* v. *Teamsters*, 346 U. S. 485, 490 (1953) ("Congress . . . confide[d] primary interpretation and application of its rules to a specific and specially constituted tribunal," the Board). This means that, unlike in the typical preliminary injunction context, the district court is not making a predictive judgment about how it will rule on the merits itself. Instead, the court is predicting the future decision of the Board. See *Miller*, 19 F. 3d, at 460; *Bloedorn*, 276 F. 3d, at 288.

Second, as I previously explained, § 10(j) empowers the Board—acting in its adjudicatory capacity—to seek injunctive relief. 29 U. S. C. § 160(j); see also Brief for Respondent 28–29; Tr. of Oral Arg. 50, 63–64. When it does so, the Board is *not* acting as a party to the underlying dispute.[3] We also have evidence that the Board's screening process for determining when to seek a § 10(j) injunction is exceedingly rigorous: Of the roughly 20,000 unfair labor practice charges filed last year, the Board authorized the filing of a petition for § 10(j) relief *only 14 times*. See Brief for Respondent 39. This means that, by the time the district court gets a (rare) § 10(j) request, the Board has already deemed an unfair labor

[3] If it were, then, of course, the majority would be correct to observe that the Board should have to demonstrate the merits of its claims under the traditional test. See *ante*, at 8. What the majority fails to adequately address is the unique position of the Board when it seeks a § 10(j) injunction, per Congress's directives. Unlike other similar movants for interim relief, the Board *is the decider* of the merits of the underlying dispute. So all that the Board is requesting from the district court is a legally enforceable means of preserving the status quo until it can render its decision.

charge likely meritorious, and has determined that preservation of the status quo is needed to facilitate its own likely judgment.

Finally, the NLRA gives federal courts only a limited role in reviewing the Board's decisions. In the court of appeals, the Board's factual findings are "conclusive" if supported by substantial evidence. See §§ 160(e), (f). We have also long recognized that the Board's legal interpretations are to be accorded "considerable deference." *NLRB* v. *City Disposal Systems, Inc.*, 465 U. S. 822, 829 (1984); see also *Ford Motor Co. (Chicago Stamping Plant)* v. *NLRB*, 441 U. S. 488, 497 (1979) ("Of course, the judgment of the Board is subject to judicial review; but if its construction of the statute is reasonably defensible, it should not be rejected merely because the courts might prefer another view"); *NLRB* v. *United Ins. Co. of America*, 390 U. S. 254, 260 (1968) (same for "application of law to facts"). What is more, absent highly unusual circumstances, district courts play no role in the review process at all. See § 160(e) (allowing the Board to file enforcement orders in district courts only if "all the courts of appeals to which application may be made are in vacation").

These three features of the statutory scheme necessarily mean that a district court's preliminary look at the merits when considering the Board's petition for interim relief under § 10(j) should be far less searching than normal. A § 10(j) injunction request simply does not present the district court with an opportunity to wade into the midst of an ongoing labor dispute (over which it otherwise has no say) and offer its own take about how the merits should be decided. Instead, in deference to Congress's choices as codified in the NLRA, the district court's task is much simpler: to evaluate a petition for a § 10(j) injunction in a manner that accounts for the statutory scheme authorizing such relief and the district court's proper role within it. Thus, so long as the Board has presented "some evidence to support the unfair labor practice charge, together with an arguable legal theory," a district court should find this final factor satisfied. *Miller*, 19 F. 3d, at 460.

C

The majority's contrary conclusion on the likelihood-of-success factor is based on various misrepresentations about the Board's authority under the NLRA. For example, in addition to mistakenly consigning the Board to the status of a mere party movant, see n. 3, *supra,* the majority misstates the Board's role in seeking § 10(j) relief generally, see *ante,* at 10 ("[T]he views advanced in a § 10(j) petition . . . are simply the preliminary legal and factual views of the Board's in-house attorneys who investigated and initiated the administrative complaint"). Similarly, the majority misrepresents the Board's arguments in this case regarding how the statutory scheme informs district courts' analysis. Far from failing to explain the relevance of district courts' lack of jurisdiction over labor disputes, *ibid.*, the Board has offered a detailed argument, consistent with our precedent and the longstanding decisions of the lower courts, for why this structural feature of the NLRA is important and why it might well be dispositive of the likelihood of success analysis. See Brief for Respondent 26–29, 35–36; see also Tr. of Oral Arg. 35–36. The majority also completely misses the significance of the limited role that federal courts of appeal play in reviewing the Board's decisions. See *ante,* at 2, 10.

Unfortunately, today's decision appears to be another installment in a series of labor cases in which this Court has failed "to heed Congress's intent with respect to the Board's primary role in adjudicating labor disputes." *Glacier Northwest, Inc.* v. *Teamsters,* 598 U. S. 771, 814 (2023) (JACKSON, J., dissenting). And, like its earlier decisions, "[t]he Court's ruling is likely to cause considerable confusion among the lower courts," which have been for decades exercising their equitable discretion informed by the NLRA. *Ibid.* I recognize that, as a practical matter, the majority's decision here may make little difference, since requests for § 10(j) relief are rare. But that fact is more a function of the Board's gatekeeping role than anything else. Now that the Court has concluded the Board's authorization to seek § 10(j) interim relief is of no moment, the Board may find it unnecessary to play the gatekeeping role Congress designed for it in this context. As a result, today's decision might force not just courts, but also the Board, to disregard Congress's direction.

* * *

A petition for § 10(j) relief serves a straightforward, but significant purpose: "to preserve the NLRB's remedial power while the Board resolves an unfair labor practice charge." *Miller,* 19 F. 3d, at 452. Today, the majority casts a district court's decision regarding a § 10(j) request as one that invokes the full sweep of a court's traditional equitable discretion—without regard for the Board's authority or the statutory scheme that authorizes courts to issue such interim relief in the first place. In doing so, "the Court unnecessarily and casually substitutes the chancellor's clumsy foot for the rule of law." *Weinberger,* 456 U. S., at 335 (Stevens, J., dissenting). I am loath to bless this aggrandizement of judicial power where Congress has so plainly limited the discretion of the courts, and where it so clearly intends for the expert agency it has created to make the primary determinations about both merits and process.

QUESTIONS FOR DISCUSSION

1. The courts of appeals were divided over the standards to govern the issuance of a section 10(j) injunction. That was what occasioned the Supreme Court's resolution, which it did in Part IIA and in which Justice Jackson concurred. Does the Majority indicate there to be a similar division between the circuits that had adopted the four-part test on how that test should be applied? If not, what demonstrable need did Part IIB address?

2. Justice Thomas says there is

> an obvious difference between having the Board show that it is "likely" to succeed on the merits and having it show only that its theory of the case is "substantial and not frivolous," without having to convince the court that its theory is likely meritorious. In fact, it is hard to imagine how the Board could lose under the reasonable-cause test if courts deferentially ask only whether the Board offered a minimally plausible legal theory, while ignoring conflicting law or facts.

Were Justice Thomas' supposition sound, should there not be an obvious difference in the rate of 10(j) injunctions issued between the circuits that applied the four-part and those that applied the two-part test? The Board has compiled the statistics for the period 2012–2024. Here is the result:

Circuits	Average Success in Securing 10(j) Injunction
Apply Two-Part Test	67.7%
Apply Four-Part Test	73.5%

In other words, Justice Thomas presupposes the answer to an empirical question on which the raw facts are readily available. Why did the Court not look at them?

3. The Sixth Circuit gave its impress to the meaning of *Starbucks* in *Kerwin v. Trinity Grand Haven Hosp.*, 174 F.4th 942 (6th Cir. 2026), one judge dissenting vigorously. After a decertification election had been conducted, but before the votes were counted, a number of disaffected employees petitioned the Employer to withdraw Union recognition. It did. The votes were counted and the Union prevailed: 89 to 66. The Employer refused to bargain. A complaint of violation of § 8(a)(5) ensued in connection with which the Regional Director sought and received a § 10(j) injunction ordering the Employer to bargain. The Employer appealed. The Sixth Circuit denied enforcement. It zeroed in on two elements of the four part test: likelihood of success on the merits and irreparable harm.

Likelihood of success. The majority opined that the test is not of success before the Labor Board, but of success before the Sixth Circuit. The Board long held that electoral results control over any evidence of repudiation, but the court doubted that it would accept the Board's "categorical rule." It noted that nothing in the Act expressly so directs, nor did it find any statutory warrant for it. The majority acknowledged that *Brooks v. NLRB*, 348 U.S. 96 (1954) (found on page 317 of the text) was "analogous"; but, it saw the difference between a representative election, in *Brooks*, and the decertification election presented here to be dispositive, especially when the deference given the Board, the critical feature of *Brooks*, is no longer due as a result of *Loper Bright Enterprise v. Raimondo*, 603 U.S. 369 (2024) (discussed in this Supplement at page 116). The majority concluded that the Board's reasoning rested "at best [on] shaky legal grounding." But, when the facts surrounding the withdrawal petition are examined there was no basis to dispute that the petition was not reliable.

Irreparable harm. The Regional Director grounded her finding of irreparable harm on the impact on the employees and the Union of the evisceration of the Union's capacity to bargain for the period of time, potentially considerable, while the process of hearing the unfair labor practice went forward. The court found the legal basis to rest only on a decision of the Ninth Circuit that did not bind the Sixth. The majority then rejected such "inherent" harm as "speculative": an independent factual basis must be provided, and it was not. The evidence offered for the Union's experience post-withdrawal—off declining attendance at meetings, testimony of "frustration and fear" among employees—failed to prove "irreparably declining union support," or make a "clear showing" of irreparable harm. What the Employer did or could do unilaterally on wages, hours, and working conditions in the absence of an injunction could be addressed in later bargaining if the Union prevailed. Nor need such unilateral action be adverse to the employees; the Employer might well improve wages and "perks." The court further stated that to accept the Board's view of irreparable harm would militate toward an injunction in every refusal to bargain case. Finally, the delay between the issuance of the complaint and the § 10(j) petition—four months—negated the claim of irreparable harm, it "undercuts the 'sense of urgency' " a § 10(j) petition implies.

Judge Boggs dissented. He found the fact of irreparable harm to be sufficient for a case of this nature:

> The Board's remedial powers are fragile. Its core remedy for an unlawful withdrawal of union recognition is an order directing the employer to engage in good-faith collective bargaining with the union. . . .But the effectiveness of that final remedy depends on the resilience of union support and the original bargaining positions of the union and employer. . . .If a union is "weakened in the interim" between the inception of an alleged unfair-labor practice and the resolution of unfair-labor-practice claims, "it will be difficult to recreate the original status quo with the same relative position of the bargaining parties.". . .And the bargaining process may fail altogether if the employer suppresses union support to the point that the workforce is no longer "inclined to unionize." So, when the [Regional] Director demonstrates a likelihood that an employer's unlawful conduct will diminish union support below a critical level, preliminary injunctive relief is appropriate "to preserve the relative positions of the parties" during litigation. *Starbucks*, 602 U.S. at 346 (quoting *Univ. of Tex. v. Camenisch*, 451 U.S. 390, 395 (1981)).

174 F.4th at 961–62 (Boggs, J. dissenting) (references omitted).

The majority and dissenting opinions in Kerwin raise a number of questions:

(a) Inasmuch as the likelihood of success was satisfied on the facts, why did the court detour into the relationship of the decertification vote to the withdrawal of recognition? Apropos of that, you should reread *Brooks*, at page 317 of the text. The Sixth Circuit discounts that decision, though "analogous," as an anachronistic deferral to the Board, a deference no longer due in consequence of *Loper Bright*. *Loper Bright*, not a Labor Act case, repudiated the *Chevron* doctrine governing the deference due to an agency interpretation of its organic statute. It was decided in 1984. *Brooks* was decided in 1954. As this Supplement observes, in *Loper Bright*, the Board has not relied on *Chevron*:

> In fact, the *Loper Bright* majority relies on two of the Court's labor law decisions—NLRB v. Hearst Pub., Inc., 322 U.S. 111 (1944), and Allentown Mack Sales & Services, Inc. v. NLRB, 522 U.S. 359 (1998)—as capturing the judiciary's independent, non-*Chevron* role even as these decisions defer to the NLRB's judgment.

Supplement at p. 116–117.

Study Justice Frankfurter's opinion in *Brooks* at the bottom of page 318 and the top of 319 of the text. Does he accept the Board's reading because of its role as statute-reader or does he arrive at the result by an independent reading of the Act's policy? In light of what Frankfurter says, do you see any difference between a certification election and decertification election? If so, what is it?

(b) To Judge Boggs, the harm lies in the loss of representation and the consequent weakening of the union for a possibly protracted period of time during which the Employer is free to act unilaterally. To the majority there is no harm because if the Union ultimately prevails it can bargain to catch up. Is there a difference in bargaining about an employer proposal—*e.g.*, to institute a system of algorithmic employee supervision and control—and bargaining to abolish it after the company has let a multi-million dollar contract for installation and operation?

(c) The majority scoffs at there being any urgency in the need for the 10(j) injunction, an element it saw as inherent in the provision, because the Regional Director took four months to seek it. How long does the process take? That is a matter of public record. If delay is of legal relevance, why did the court not consider that question?

In FY 2022, the last year in which statistics are available, the average time from the filing of an unfair labor practice charge to the Regions' "disposition" of it—dismissal, settlement, complaint—was 84.4 days. GC Memorandum GC 23-06 (April 13, 2023), at p. 2. Once a complaint issues, in order to seek a 10(j) injunction the Regional Director must proceed through the Board's Injunction Litigation Branch. In that year, the average time from complaint to 10(j) petition was 211.5 days, about seven months. *Id.* In other words, Regional Director went to court in considerably less time than the process usually takes. If four months is inordinate would not a fatal lack of requisite urgency be present in most 10(j) petitions?

II. SELECTION OF THE REPRESENTATIVE FOR THE PURPOSES OF COLLECTIVE BARGAINING

A. GROUNDS FOR NOT PROCEEDING TO AN INVESTIGATION AND CERTIFICATION

Page 264. Add to the end of the last paragraph:

On August 1, 2024, the Biden Board adopted the Final Rule, rescinding the Trump Board's 2020 rule and returning to prior law on these three matters, largely consistent with language of the Proposed Rule. *See* 89 Fed. Reg. 62952. With regard to blocking charges specifically, the Board returned to the approach reflected in the 2014 (Obama Board) rule. *See* 89 Fed. Reg. at 62987 (codified at 29 C.F.R. § 103.20). Member Kaplan dissented.

B. APPROPRIATE BARGAINING UNIT

4. MULTIEMPLOYER AND COORDINATED BARGAINING

Page 291. Add to Problem for Discussion:

A multi-employer bargaining agreement provides that it will continue from year to year unless a party gives written notice at least sixty (60) days prior to the end of the contract year—April 1—of its intent to terminate the agreement. On February 19, the Employer Association notified the union that it wished to resume negotiations for a successor agreement upon termination of the contract term. On April 11, the Employee Association proposed dates for "discussion to begin." On May 2, the Union wrote to the Association that it was withdrawing from bargaining with the Association. The Association insisted the withdrawal was untimely and that the Union bargain with it. The Union has refused and has charged a violation of § 8(a)(5). Is the Association's insistence on multi-employer bargaining in violation of the Act? Rieth-Riley Construction, Inc., 374 N.L.R.B. No. 13 (2024) *enf'd* 172 F.4th 492(6th Cir. 2026). The Association believes the Union withdrawal was untimely and locks out the unionized workers until, it said, the union "agrees to come to the table." Has it committed an unfair labor practice? *See id.*

Page 294. Add before Questions for Discussion:

In March 2024, a District Court judge in the Eastern District of Texas vacated the Board's new joint employer rule, concluding that the rule is invalid because it unlawfully sweeps beyond common-law limits on employer status imposed by law. Chamber of Commerce of the United States v. NLRB, 723 F. Supp. 3d 498 (E.D. Tex. March 18, 2024). After initially appealing this decision, the Board later voluntarily withdrew the appeal. On February 25, 2026, the Board repudiated the rule, readopting the 2020 rule, Member Prouty disagreeing with it. *See* 91 Fed. Reg. 9707. This new rule appears in 29 CFR Pt. 103:

§ 103.40 Joint employers.

(a) An employer, as defined by section 2(2) of the National Labor Relations Act (the Act), may be considered a joint employer of a separate employer's employees only if the two employers share or codetermine the employees' essential terms and conditions of employment. To establish that an entity shares or codetermines the essential terms and conditions of another employer's employees, the entity must possess and exercise such substantial direct and immediate control over one or more essential terms or conditions of their employment as would warrant finding that the entity meaningfully affects matters relating to the employment relationship with those employees. Evidence of the entity's indirect control over essential terms and conditions of employment of another employer's employees, the entity's contractually reserved but never exercised authority over the essential terms and conditions of employment of another employer's employees, or the entity's control over mandatory subjects of bargaining other than the essential terms and conditions of employment is probative of joint-employer status but only to the extent it supplements and reinforces evidence of the entity's possession or exercise of direct and immediate control over a particular essential term and condition of employment. Joint-employer status must be determined on the totality of the relevant facts in each particular employment setting. The party asserting that an entity is a joint employer has the burden of proof.

(b) *Essential terms and conditions of employment* means wages, benefits, hours of work, hiring, discharge, discipline, supervision, and direction.

(c) *Direct and immediate control* means each respective essential employment term or condition in paragraphs (c)(1) through (8) of this section:

(1) *Wages.* An entity exercises direct and immediate control over wages if it actually determines the wage rates, salary or other rate of pay that is paid to another employer's individual employees or job classifications. An entity does not exercise direct and immediate control over wages by entering into a cost-plus contract (with or without a maximum reimbursable wage rate).

(2) *Benefits.* An entity exercises direct and immediate control over benefits if it actually determines the fringe benefits

to be provided or offered to another employer's employees. This would include selecting the benefit plans (such as health insurance plans and pension plans) and/or level of benefits provided to another employer's employees. An entity does not exercise direct and immediate control over benefits by permitting another employer, under an arm's-length contract, to participate in its benefit plans.

(3) *Hours of work.* An entity exercises direct and immediate control over hours of work if it actually determines work schedules or the work hours, including overtime, of another employer's employees. An entity does not exercise direct and immediate control over hours of work by establishing an enterprise's operating hours or when it needs the services provided by another employer.

(4) *Hiring.* An entity exercises direct and immediate control over hiring if it actually determines which particular employees will be hired and which employees will not. An entity does not exercise direct and immediate control over hiring by requesting changes in staffing levels to accomplish tasks or by setting minimal standards such as those required by government regulation.

(5) *Discharge.* An entity exercises direct and immediate control over discharge if it actually decides to terminate the employment of another employer's employee. An entity does not exercise direct and immediate control over discharge by bringing misconduct or poor performance to the attention of another employer that makes the actual discharge decision, by expressing a negative opinion of another employer's employee, by refusing to allow another employer's employee to continue performing work under a contract, or by setting minimal standards of performance or conduct, such as those required by government regulation.

(6) *Discipline.* An entity exercises direct and immediate control over discipline if it actually decides to suspend or otherwise discipline another employer's employee. An entity does not exercise direct and immediate control over discipline by bringing misconduct or poor performance to the attention of another employer that makes the actual disciplinary decision, by expressing a negative opinion of another employer's employee, or by refusing to allow another employer's employee to access its premises or perform work under a contract.

(7) *Supervision.* An entity exercises direct and immediate control over supervision by actually instructing another employer's employees how to perform their work or by actually issuing employee performance appraisals. An entity does not exercise direct and immediate control over supervision when its

instructions are limited and routine and consist primarily of telling another employer's employees what work to perform, or where and when to perform the work, but not how to perform it.

(8) *Direction.* An entity exercises direct and immediate control over direction by assigning particular employees their individual work schedules, positions, and tasks. An entity does not exercise direct and immediate control over direction by setting schedules for completion of a project or by describing the work to be accomplished on a project.

(d) *Substantial direct and immediate control* means direct and immediate control that has a regular or continuous consequential effect on an essential term or condition of employment of another employer's employees. Such control is not "substantial" if only exercised on a sporadic, isolated, or de minimis basis.

(e) *Indirect control* means indirect control over essential terms and conditions of employment of another employer's employees but not control or influence over setting the objectives, basic ground rules, or expectations for another entity's performance under a contract.

(f) *Contractually reserved authority over essential terms and conditions of employment* means the authority that an entity reserves to itself, under the terms of a contract with another employer, over the essential terms and conditions of employment of that other employer's employees, but that has never been exercised.

On how finely the line is drawn between direct and indirect control, see South Sound Inpatient Physicians, PLLC, 374 N.L.R.B. No. 101 (2026).

It is worth noting that, during this entire period and reflecting the Board's back-and-forth on the applicable test, the *Browning-Ferris* litigation continued. After further proceedings before the Board, and another appeal and remand, the Board ultimately concluded again that Browning-Ferris is a joint employer and ordered it to bargain with the union. 374 N.L.R.B. No. 46 (February 23, 2026). The Board limited its holding to the case, in part because the D.C. Circuit had stated in its remand that it should adhere retroactively to the (now abandoned) 2015 standard.

C. REVIEW OF REPRESENTATION PROCEEDINGS

Page 302. At the bottom of the page, replace "Leedon" with "Leedom."

III. SECURING BARGAINING RIGHTS THROUGH OTHER METHODS

Page 315. Add before the last paragraph:

On February 14, 2025, Acting General Counsel William B. Cowen issued a memo to all field offices rescinding this and a number of other memos issued by former General Counsel Abruzzo. *See* GC Memorandum 25-05.

Page 315. Add at the end of the discussion on *Cemex*:

The Sixth Circuit's treatment of the *Cemex* rule in *Brown-Forman v. NLRB, supra,* as having been improperly fashioned in an adjudication, is treated in connection with that matter at page 164 of this Supplement. The Board's Deputy Associate General Counsel wrote to the Ninth Circuit on April 9, 2026, urging it to disregard the Sixth Circuit's holding in *Brown-Forman* that *Cemex* was wrongly issued as the produce of an adjudication. The Ninth Circuit enforced the *Cemex* bargaining order as in conformity with *Gissel* but declined to reach the new standard. Int'l Bro. of Teamsters v. NLRB, No. 23–2081, 2026 WL 1079297 (April 21, 2026).

QUESTION FOR DISCUSSION

The Sixth Circuit remanded *Brown-Forman* to the Board for consideration in light of its holding that the *Cemex* rule was unlawfully made. On remand, what rule should the Board apply? *Gissel*? But was not *Gissel* the wrongful product of an adjudication? Would the "good faith doubt" rule apply? It was the product of adjudication in the terms the Sixth Circuit set out, but both *Gissel* and *Cemex* repudiated it.

Page 316. Add to the end of Problem 1:

See generally Matthew Finkin and Robert Gorman, *The Gissel Tzimmes*, 57 SETON HALL L. REV. ___ (2026) (in press).

Page 316. Add to the end of Problem 2:

Can an employer's election petition (RM) filed more than 30 days after a union recognition demand be entertained by the Board? St. John's College, 374 N.L.R.B. No. 72 (2026).

Page 317. Add at the end of Problem 5:

The NLRB reported that, as of July 2024, it had encountered a 2,000% increase in employer-filed union representation election petitions over the previous year, which it attributed to the *Cemex* decision. Union filed petitions were up by 13%; decertification petitions were up by 12%. Unions won 79% of union-filed elections and 70% of employer-filed ones.

Page 317. Add to Problems for Discussion:

6. NP Red Rock LLC, 373 N.L.R.B. No. 67 (2024), is the first decision to apply *Cemex*. It sets out an exacting remedial schedule. The *Cemex* decision itself is currently on appeal before the Ninth Circuit Court of Appeals.

Page 321. Add to text before the second full paragraph:

The District of Columbia Circuit affirmed the lawfulness of the Board doctrine of longstanding that it may extend the certification year for the period of employer failure to bargain in good faith. J.G. Kern Enterprises, Inc. v. NLRB, 94 F.4th 18 (D.C. Cir. 2024).

Page 323. Add at the end of the section before Problems for Discussion:

In a final rule adopted on August 1, 2024, the Biden Board rescinded the Trump Board's rule and codified the traditional voluntary-recognition bar, as refined in *Lamons Gasket*, to define the reasonable period for collective bargaining that sets the duration of the bar. *See* 89 Fed. Reg. 62952, 62989 (codified at 29 C.F.R. § 103.21). Member Kaplan dissented.

Page 334. Add to Problems for Discussion:

4. During a two-year hiatus following the expiration of the collective bargaining agreement between the Service Staff Union and the Happy Living Center, the Union made no offers for a new agreement. After negotiations began a group of employees signed a decertification petition. Management responded by informing employees that they could revoke their authorization for dues deductions and that that will have no effect on their employment; 90% of the employees did so. After negotiations with the Union started, the Company invited employees to resume dues deductions, but none did. Happy Living then announced that it would poll the workforce on the degree of support of the Union. Happy Living notified the Union that it was conducting the poll because it had a "good faith doubt" of the Union's majority status pointing to: (1) the fact that nearly every employee had elected to stop paying dues; (2) that no employees opted to resume dues deduction after they were invited to do so; and (3) that it believed that about 50% of unit employees had backed the decertification petition.

The poll mimicked the process used in an NLRB election: it was conducted by secret ballot subject to oversight by a retired judge. The Union lost 61 to 9. Happy Living withdrew its recognition. Has it committed any unfair labor practices? New Concepts for Living, Inc. v. NLRB, 94 F.4th 272 (3d Cir. 2024).

PART THREE

NEGOTIATION OF THE COLLECTIVE BARGAINING AGREEMENT

II. THE DUTY TO BARGAIN IN GOOD FAITH

Page 362. Add to Problems for Discussion:

5. A newly certified union presents the Company with a detailed set of terms for the collective agreement, some are economic—wages, hours, health and retirement benefits; some are non-economic—duration of the agreement, union recognition, non-discrimination. The Company has insisted on bargaining about the latter first, *i.e.*, that it would not consider the economic demands until the non-economic matters were resolved. Has the Company committed a violation of § 8(a)(5)? Troutbrook Co. LLC, 107 F.4th 994 (D.C. Cir. 2024).

Page 385. Add at end of Problem 5:

See also Century Tel. of Montana, Inc., 373 N.L.R.B. No. 128 (2024) (demand for detailed information about independent contractors working in the area of coverage of a collective bargaining agreement resisted by the company because the workers were not bargaining unit members).

III. SUBJECTS OF COLLECTIVE BARGAINING

Page 412. Add to Problems for Discussion:

4. The Picayune Intelligencer Gazette (PIG), a daily newspaper with several editorial offices located in the Greater Siloplex area, has been suffering a steady loss of circulation and income. The staff is unionized. Bargaining for a collective agreement commenced in February 2023. A major bone of contention had been what would happen if the management resorted to lay-offs. In the summer of 2023, the parties reached impasse and the Company implemented its Last Best Final Offer (LBFO) which included the following:

> Whenever conditions are considered by the Company such as to warrant layoffs, part-timing, reclassifications or a combination thereof, the Company agrees to give the Union thirty (30) calendar days' notice of its intended plan, together with a description of work locations, job titles (levels within channels) and work groups so affected as determined by the Company.

The LBFO went on: (1) temporary employees in the selected locations or work group will be laid off first; (2) transfers, if possible, will be offered in order of seniority to employees subject to the Company's determination of qualifications and of those positions are available to be filled: (3) offers of severance pay will be made, the number of employees and the amount of severance to be determined by the Company; and (4) disputes related to separation are not subject to the arbitration provision of this Agreement.

On September 12, 2023, the Union expressed an interest in reopening negotiation. The Company agreed; a bargaining session was to be scheduled. On September 15, the Company gave written notice of its intent to layoff over twenty percent of the editorial unit at specified work locations thirty days hence. The Union replied that no layoff could be effected without bargaining with the Union first. The Company replied that, as it was acting pursuant to the extant LBFO, there was nothing to bargain about. The Union has filed a charge of violation of § 8(a)(5). You are the NLRB Regional Director. Will you issue a complaint? What arguments would you expect? How persuasive are they? Thryv, Inc. v. NLRB, 102 F.4th 727 (5th Cir. 2024).

Page 422. Add at the End of Problem 2:

The staff of the Annie Hall Assisted Living Facility is unionized. The COVID pandemic has suddenly ravaged nursing homes in the state. The Company has issued the following memo to all employees: "to ensure the safety and recognize the commitment and hard work of our dedicated healthcare workers on the front lines fighting this pandemic," the Company will issue "a special COVID19 hourly rate bonus" to all staff. The bonuses will be "equal to 25% of each employee's current hourly rate," "effective Thursday, April 2nd and thru at least April 30th," and would apply "to all worked hours (excluding any paid-time-off pay)." On April 7 the Company published a second memo increasing the bonuses" for all nursing staff to "100% of their current hourly rate."

The Union learned of the notice—it had not been notified by the Company—and wrote that it "agreed to the proposed wage increase, but demanded to bargain about any future change." The Company did not respond. When the pandemic's urgency ceased the Company reduced the 100% "bonus" of the nursing staff to 25% for all hours worked and for all others the 25% was reduced to 10%. The Union, which, again, had not been informed, protested the reduction in "wages." Again, the Company did not reply. A month later the Company informed all employees that the "bonus" was terminated. Has the Company committed an unfair labor practice? Alaris Health at Blvd. East v. NLRB, 123 F. 4th 107 (3rd Cir. 2024).

Page 446. Add at end of discussion of *Dorsey Trailers*:

In Quickway Transp., Inc. v. NLRB, 117 F.4th 789 (6th Cir. 2024), the Court of Appeals enforced the Board's remedy for extensive unfair labor practices that culminated in the partial closure of the Employer's operations. The Board had ordered the Employer to "reopen and restore its business operations" at the closed facility.

V. BARGAINING REMEDIES

Page 475. Add after the end of *Ex-Cell-O Corp.*:

In Longmont United Hospital, 374 N.L.R.B. No. 52 (2026), a two member majority declined to overrule *Ex-Cell-O*. It explained in part:

> The only way that an employer can obtain judicial review of a Board certification is by refusing to bargain. This is because the courts do not have jurisdiction to directly review a certification and because an employer waives its right to challenge a union's certification in court if it recognizes and bargains with the union. Requiring a certification-testing employer to pay compensatory damages for refusing to bargain in order to challenge a Board-issued certification would "present a realistic threat of interference" with this "regulatory scheme." It would also impermissibly burden the exercise of the right to seek judicial review. And "any attempt by a court," or by the Board, "at preventing an appeal is unwarranted and cannot be tolerated."

Id., slip op. at 1 (footnotes omitted). Member Prouty dissented.

Page 477. Add at the end of the paragraph following the bullet points:

For further discussion on the more extensive Board remedies, see Spike Enterprise, Inc., 373 N.L.R.B. No. 41(2024).

In *Thryv, Inc. v. NLRB*, 102 F.4th 727 (5th Cir. 2024), the Fifth Circuit vacated the Board's order, concluding that substantial evidence did not support the Board's finding that the employer violated the Act when it laid off employees pursuant to the terms of a last best final offer while the parties were bargaining for a successor contract. However, the court declined to rule on whether the Board has authority to award the remedies outlined in its decision. Later, the Ninth Circuit affirmed the Board's power to award employees compensation "for any other direct or foreseeable pecuniary harms incurred as the result of [an] unlawful lockout, including reasonable search-for-work and interim employment expenses." IUOE v. NLRB, 127 F.4th 58 (9th Cir. 2024) (one judge dissenting) (distinguishing Starbucks v. NLRB, 125 F.4th 78 (3rd Cir. 2024)). The Ninth Circuit further held that, as Thryv remedies were equitable in nature, no right to a jury trial was involved. NLRB v. North Mountain Foothills Apts. , 9th Cir. No. 24–2223 (Oct. 28, 2025). Shortly thereafter, the Sixth Circuit held the Board without power to award Thryv remedies, one judge dissenting, creating a circuit split. NLRB v. Starbucks Corp., 159 F.4th 455 (6th Cir. 2025).

On February 14, 2025, Acting General Counsel William B. Cowen issued a memo to all field offices rescinding a number of memos issued by former General Counsel Abruzzo, including those urging Regional Directors to include specific remedies or types of remedies in settlement agreements and complaints. *See* GC Mem. 25-05. On May 16, 2025, the AGC issued another memorandum, calling into question the *Thryv* majority's approach to damages. *See* GC Mem. 25-06. After noting that the majority itself acknowledged that the Board does not have the authority to award consequential damages akin to those in tort, the AGC stated as follows:

> So the question is—What is a "*direct or foreseeable pecuniary harm*" that falls short of "consequential damages" or "tort damages"? The majority opinion in *Thryv* does not provide a discernable standard for answering this question. The dissent, however, does provide a standard:
>
>> In our view, employees should also be made whole for losses indirectly caused by an unfair labor practice *where the causal link between the loss and the unfair labor practice is sufficiently clear*.
>
> 372 NLRB No. 22 at 16 (emphasis added). The majority did not address the dissent's formulation, but it seems clear that the majority would include all harms encompassed by the dissent's standard. What is not clear is what additional harms the majority would include that would not be included by the dissent.
>
> In sum, both the majority and dissent in *Thryv* agree that foreseeable "harms" or "losses" should be remedied if they "result from" the unfair labor practices or where the "causal link" between the loss and the unfair labor practice is "sufficiently clear." Thus, at least for purposes of Settlements, Regions should focus on addressing foreseeable harms that are clearly caused by the unfair labor practice. While this admittedly is the standard advocated by the dissent, it is the only standard reasonably capable of application.

Concerns about employer delay tactics in first-contract bargaining—and the lack of corresponding, adequate bargaining remedies—recently have gotten some attention in Congress. In March 2025, Senators Hawley and Booker co-sponsored the Fast Labor Contracts Act, which would, among other things, 1) amend the NLRA to require that after workers have voted to form a union, employers must begin negotiating with the new union within ten days; 2) provide that if no agreement is reached within ninety days, the dispute will be referred to mediation; and 3) mandate that if mediation fails within thirty days, or additional periods agreed upon by the parties, the dispute will be referred to binding arbitration to secure an initial contract. The bill, which has been referred to committee but made no further progress, can be found here: https://www.congress.gov/bill/119th-congress/senate-bill/844.

In Atlantic American Fire Protection Co., 374 N.L.R.B. No. 114 (2026), the two-member Board majority adhered to its declination to overrule Ex-Cell-O in *Longmont* (see above), again over the dissent of Member Prouty. The Board also declined, without a three-member majority, to take up challenges to *Thryv* as it ordered "extraordinary" remedies in this case. The Board largely affirmed the ALJ's findings regarding the employer's numerous unfair labor practices during the course of the union's organizing campaign. It then ordered, as amended, broad notice-reading and cease and desist remedies, as well as reinstatement of and make-whole compensation for certain terminated employees. The Board also ordered the employer to bargain with the union for a minimum of 24 hours a month for at least six hours per session until agreement is reached or there is a lawful impasse. Finally, the Board further ordered that the employer submit bargaining progress reports every 15 days.

PART FOUR

PROTESTS AND PICKETING, STRIKES AND BOYCOTTS

I. RIGHTS OF EMPLOYEE PROTESTERS UNDER THE NLRA

A. PROTECTED AND UNPROTECTED CONCERTED ACTIVITY

Page 493. Add to the citation at the end of Problem 4:

, *vacated,* Home Depot U.S.A., Inc. v. NLRB, 158 F.4th 910 (8th Cir. 2025) (holding that there were special circumstances—safety concerns—justifying a prohibition on wearing such messages in a customer-facing job during this period of time, which was months after the murder of George Floyd only seven miles away and the resulting unrest that had had an effect on this particular store).

Page 496. Add after the first (carryover) paragraph:

The Third Circuit upheld the Board's approach to concerted activity in *Miller Plastic* while remanding the matter to the Board to address an evidentiary issue. Miller Plastic Prods., Inc. v. NLRB, 141 F.4th 492 (3rd Cir. 2025).

Page 512. Add to Problems for Discussion:

5. Adam Archer and Arthur Chan worked at the Cedars Hotel in Silo City. After an incident of a fatal shooting of a black suspect by a white Silo City police officer a protest rally was called by the local chapter of Black Lives Matter. Archer and Chan attended. Marvin Van Dyke, Cedars' manager, witnessed a heated conversation between the two and several other employees in the lunchroom, the latter arguing that as the suspect was armed the use of deadly force was justified. Van Dyke told the two they should not have attended the rally and advised them not to do it again. Has Cedars violated the Labor Act? SFR, Inc., 373 N.L.R.B. No. 84 (2024).

Page 518. Add after the first full paragraph:

In Pfizer, Inc., 374 N.L.R.B. No. 55 (2026), the three Member Board, two Republicans and one Democrat, applied *California Commerce Club.* Member Prouty, the Democrat, concurred that the Board was bound by the absence of a three-member majority needed to overrule it.

Page 533. Add at the end of Problem 7:

, *on remand* Oncor Electric Delivery Co., LLC, 373 N.L.R.B. No. 80 (2024), *enf't denied* Oncor Electric Delivery Co. LLC v. NLRB, 174 F.4th 161 (D.C. Cir. 2026) (on the ground that the testimony was not tied to nor did the employee attempt to tie it to a labor dispute).

Page 540. Add at the end of *Lion Elastomers*:

Lion Elastomers originally was decided under *Atlantic Steel*. While on appeal to the Fifth Circuit, the Board decided *General Motors* and moved the court to remand. The court remanded for the Board to determine "whether *General Motors* affects the Board's analysis in this case." On remand, the (Biden) Board overruled *General Motors*. The case then went back to the Fifth Circuit, which now has held that that action was not within the scope of its remand: namely, to apply the new standard of *General Motors*, not to reconsider it. Lion Elastomers, LLC v. NLRB, 108 F.4th 252 (5th Cir. July 9, 2024). The court also held it a violation of due process for the Board to have disallowed the Company an opportunity to be heard on the change in Board law. The court remanded to the Board to apply *General Motors*.

Page 541. Add at the end of Question 1:

In a case involving an altercation between a manager and a union officer in the manager's office—in the course of which the union officer refused to leave—the ALJ found no violation under *General Motors*, before *Lion Elastomers* was decided. The Board decided the dispute afresh under *Atlantic Steel* and found an unfair labor practice. The case provides insight into how the two standards differ. Intertype Polymer Corp., 373 N.L.R.B. No. 65 (2024).

B. EMPLOYER RESPONSES TO CONCERTED ACTIVITIES

Page 564. Add to Problems for Discussion:

3. Wimbles, Inc. has given the HVAC Workers Union its "best and last offer" to expire on November 14. The Union has rejected the offer and workers have gone on strike. Wimbles had written the Union on November 10 reminding it that no offer from it would be on the table after November 14. On November 16 the Union made an unconditional offer to return to work. Later that day Wimbles informed the Union that it would not return the employees to work until there was a collective bargaining agreement. Has Wimbles violated section 8(a)(5)? IUOE v. NLRB, 127 F.4th 58 (9th Cir. 2024).

III. THE NATIONAL LABOR RELATIONS ACT

B. SECONDARY PRESSURE

1. UNDER THE TAFT-HARTLEY ACT

Page 662. Add to citation at the end of *Moore Dry Dock*:

, *on remand* Preferred Bldg. Servs., Inc., 374 N.L.R.B. No. 11 (2024).

PART FIVE

ADMINISTRATION OF THE COLLECTIVE AGREEMENT

III. JUDICIAL ENFORCEMENT OF COLLECTIVE AGREEMENTS

Page 733. Add following *Lincoln Mills*:

PROBLEM FOR DISCUSSION

A collective agreement provided for the arbitration of the terms of a successor agreement should the parties fail to agree. The Employer has refused to arbitrate those future terms that it insists are permissive bargaining subjects. The Tenth Circuit approached that determination thusly: first, collective bargaining agreements are to be interpreted "according to ordinary, principles of contract law," citing M&G Polymers USA, LLC v. Tackett, 574 U.S. 427, 435 (2015); and, second, because the parties are based in Oklahoma and because the work was to be performed there, the prior precept directs the court to Oklahoma contract law. Is either correct? Reread *Lincoln Mills* and also consider the discussion of *M&G Polymers* at casebook page 853.

Page 757. Add to the end of Problem 3:

In the 2019 *Valley Hospital* decision, the Trump Labor Board overruled Board precedent to hold that an employer's obligation to check off union dues under a collective agreement expires with the agreement's expiration. The case was remanded by the Ninth Circuit. On remand the Biden Board reversed the decision and returned to the prior rule. Valley Hospital Medical Center, Inc., 371 N.L.R.B. No. 160 (2022). The Ninth Circuit affirmed the Board. Valley Hospital Med. Ctr., Inc. v. NLRB, 100 F.4th 994 (9th Cir. 2024). Judge O'Scannlain wrote separately to express dismay on the Board's "seesawing back and forth between statutory interpretation depending on its political composition leaving workers, employers, and unions in the lurch."

Page 765. Add to Problems for Discussion:

5. The collective bargaining agreement between ABC Liefer, Inc., a logistics company, and the Warehouse Workers Union provides that the top 80% of the seniority list are guaranteed 40 hours of work per week "or its equipment in pay" except "in the event of an act of God". In the wake of the COVID epidemic ABC's clients cancelled all shipments. ABC shut down for the duration. The Union demanded that the workers on the top 80% by seniority be paid for 40 hours per week for the period of the shutdown. The Company rejected the demand invoking the Act of God clause. The dispute was arbitrated. The Arbitrator sustained the Grievance. She opined that the term "Act of God" is ordinarily "understood to mean a natural hazard outside of human control, something for which no human may be held responsible." The downturn in business in response to which ABC shut down was due to the government's failure adequately to respond to the pandemic; that is, it was an act of "human control." How should the court rule? Quality Custom Distribution v. Teamsters, Local 110, 722 F. Supp. 3d 817 (N.D. Ill. 2024).

IV. THE ROLE OF THE NATIONAL LABOR RELATIONS BOARD AND THE ARBITRATOR DURING THE TERM OF A COLLECTIVE AGREEMENT

A. CONDUCT WHICH ALLEGEDLY VIOLATES BOTH THE CONTRACT AND THE LABOR ACT

Page 819. Add to Problems for Discussion:

5. If the Union refuses to pursue the civil rights claim to arbitration for reasons not violative of its duty of fair representation, what recourse, if any, would the employee have? Garcia v. 35 W. 9th Owners Co-Op., 808 F. Supp. 3d 668 (S.D.N.Y. 2025).

B. THE DUTY TO BARGAIN DURING THE TERM OF AN EXISTING AGREEMENT

Page 843. Substitute for *MV Transportation*:

Endurance Environmental Solutions, LLC

373 N.L.R.B. No. 141 (2024).

* * * In this case, we reconsider the standard to be applied in unfair labor practice cases arising under Section 8(a)(5) and (1) of the National Labor Relations Act (the Act or NLRA) to evaluate an employer's affirmative defense that employees, through their union representative, contractually surrendered the fundamental statutory right "to bargain collectively" with respect to wages, hours, or other terms and conditions of employment. The specific issue presented here is whether the Respondent violated Section 8(a)(5) and (1) of the Act by failing to provide the Union notice and an opportunity to bargain over the Respondent's decision to install cameras to monitor unit employees and by refusing the Union's requests to bargain over the decision. Applying the "contract coverage" test adopted by a divided Board in *MV Transportation, Inc.*, 368 NLRB No. 66 (2019), the judge found that the decision came "within the compass or scope" of contract language granting the Respondent the right to "implement changes in equipment." The judge therefore found that the Respondent was not required to bargain further with the Union, either as to the decision to install the cameras or as to the effects of the decision on unit employees.

[W]e find that the contract coverage test adopted in *MV Transportation* undermines the Act's central policy of promoting industrial stability by encouraging the practice and procedure of collective bargaining. We therefore overrule *MV Transportation* and restore the rule consistently followed by the Board for more than 70 years and endorsed by the Supreme Court. . . . Under that standard, the Board will not lightly infer a contractual waiver of the statutory right to bargain and will instead require such a waiver to be "clear and unmistakable." We respectfully disagree with the minority of federal courts of appeals that have rejected the waiver standard in favor of the "contract coverage" standard . . . . In undertaking the Board's assigned task today, we have carefully considered the views of those courts adhering to the contract coverage standard and have explained why we return to the traditional waiver standard.

. . .

[A]bsent a valid defense, an employer violates Section 8(a)(5) and (1) of the Act either by making a change to a mandatory subject of bargaining without first providing the union that represents its employees with notice and an opportunity to bargain, or by failing and refusing to bargain over a mandatory subject on request by the union. An employer can defend an allegation that a unilateral change or refusal to bargain violates Section 8(a)(5) of the Act on the basis that the union contractually surrendered the right to bargain.

The Board's clear and unmistakable waiver standard is of longstanding vintage, as explained in [*Provena St. Joseph Medical Center*, 350 NLRB 808, 812 (2007).] In *Provena*, the Board reaffirmed its adherence to "one of the oldest and most familiar of Board doctrines": the clear and unmistakable waiver standard for determining whether a union has contractually surrendered the fundamental statutory right to bargain. Drawing on decades of Supreme Court and Board precedent, the Board explained that the waiver standard "requires bargaining partners to unequivocally and specifically express their mutual intention to permit unilateral employer action with respect to a particular employment term, notwithstanding the statutory duty to bargain that would otherwise apply." The Board further explained that the waiver standard "reflects the Board's policy choice, grounded in the Act, in favor of collective bargaining concerning changes in working conditions that might precipitate labor disputes."

The *Provena* Board expressly rejected the less exacting contract coverage standard endorsed by the dissent in that case. . . .

Twelve years later, in *MV Transportation*, a divided Board overruled *Provena* and rejected the clear and unmistakable waiver standard in favor of a version of the contract coverage test. As described by the *MV Transportation* majority, under the Board's contract coverage test, the Board applies "ordinary principles of contract interpretation" to determine whether a disputed change was "within the compass or scope" of any contractual provision authorizing unilateral action by the employer. If so, the Board will find that the contract "authorized the employer to make the disputed change unilaterally, and the employer will not have violated Section 8(a)(5)." The majority emphasized that an employer's unilateral action may be "covered" by a contract even if the contract does not "specifically mention, refer to or address the employer decision at issue." "On the other hand," the *MV Transportation* majority explained, "if it is determined that the disputed act does *not* come within the compass or scope of a contract provision that grants the employer the right to act unilaterally, the analysis is one of waiver."

[Because the Board's decision in *MV Transportation* undermines the Act's fundamental policies, the decision is overruled.]

II. Background

A. Facts

The Respondent hauls trash and other materials to landfills. The Union represents a bargaining unit of drivers, mechanics, and loaders at the Respondent's Florence, Kentucky facility. The Respondent and the Union were parties to a collective-bargaining agreement which was effective from September 24, 2018, through September 26, 2021. The following management-rights language was included in Article III of the agreement:

> The management of the plant and direction of the working force is vested exclusively in the Company, and in furtherance and not in limitation of such authority, shall include the right to assign, to suspend or to terminate employees for just cause, to transfer and relieve employees from duty because of lack of work and for other legitimate reasons, to subcontract bargaining unit work, to make shop rules and regulations, to create new jobs, develop new processes, and implement changes in equipment, changes in the content of jobs or improvements brought about by the Company in the interest of improved methods and product, PROVIDED, that this exercise of management's rights will not violate or supersede any other provisions of this Agreement. The parties acknowledge that, as part of its right to make shop rules and regulations, the Company has the right to issue an employee handbook. The Union acknowledges that the Company provided it with a copy of its most recent draft employee handbook for consideration and bargaining during the collective bargaining negotiations.

In August 2020, the Respondent decided to purchase and install cameras in its entire fleet of 400 trucks, including the 5 or 6 trucks housed at its Florence facility, which are driven by unit employees. The Lytx camera system purchased by the Respondent is mounted on the inside front windshield and consists of two cameras, one directed inward toward the driver, and another directed outward toward the road. The system continuously records video, as well as audio footage, but it only permanently retains the 10 seconds before and the 5 seconds after a triggering event. Triggering events include collisions, hard braking, hard acceleration, sudden lane changes, speeding, and failure to maintain a safe following distance. After such a triggering event, a third party views the captured footage, looks for driver behaviors such as texting or falling asleep, assigns a score to the event, and alerts the Respondent. The Respondent then reviews the footage and decides whether coaching or discipline is warranted.

[The Respondent decided to install the Lytx camera system in its entire fleet of company-owned vehicles, purchased the camera system, and announced to unit employees that it had begun the process of installing the cameras, without providing the Union with prior notice or opportunity to bargain over the decision or its effects. The Respondent's Safety Manager Kevin Blackwell announced on August 11, 2020, the "the pending installation" of the Lytx camera system to the Respondent's regional managers. However, installation was delayed during COVID due to supply chain disruption.

In early January 2021, a regional manager visited the subject facility, the union steward and unit employee then contacted the Union to report that the Respondent was planning to install cameras in trucks driven by unit employees. The Union protested the Respondent's failure to provide the Union with notice and the opportunity to bargain over its decision to install the cameras prior to announcing the decision to unit employees, and demanded that the Respondent bargain over the installation. Blackwell refused and Respondent began the installation process.

The Union again protested the Respondent's failure to provide notice or opportunity to bargain prior to announcing its decision to unit employees. The Union also advised the Respondent that the use of cameras and other forms of employee surveillance devices is a mandatory subject of bargaining under well-established Board precedent, and it again demanded that the Respondent bargain over the decision and its effects, rescind any steps it had taken toward implementation, and provide the Union with relevant information. The union once again protested.

By letter dated March 1, Blackwell contested the Union's assertion that the installation of the cameras was a mandatory subject of bargaining, and he stated that the Board precedent the Union had cited for that proposition did not apply. As in his previous letter, Blackwell did not specifically respond to the Union's request to bargain or to its demand that the Respondent rescind the decision and cease any steps it had taken toward implementation. And, while Blackwell stated in the closing paragraph of his letter that he "welcomed discussion" and invited the Union to contact him for that purpose, the invitation was preceded by the following sentence, which had a red line through it but was still legible:

"In closing, bargaining at the expense of safety cannot be a starting point."]

The Union filed a charge alleging that the Respondent violated Section 8(a)(5) and (1) of the Act by unilaterally implementing a program of installing cameras and other employee surveillance devices in trucks driven by unit employees; rejecting the Union's demands to bargain over the matter; and failing to respond fully to the Union's January 12, 2021 request for information. [After initially dismissing the portions of the charges relating to the unilateral implementation and refusal-to-bargain allegation, the Regional Director for Region 8 issued a complaint on the refusal-to-provide information allegation. the Acting General Counsel ordered the Regional Director to issue a complaint on the dismissed portions of the charge.] . . . .

The judge found that the Respondent's decision to install cameras that monitor unit employees while they work was a mandatory subject of bargaining. The judge further found that the Respondent violated Section 8(a)(5) and (1) of the Act by failing to furnish, or inform the Union that it did not possess, information regarding the decision that was requested by the Union in its January 12, 2021, letter. The judge additionally found that the Respondent failed to provide the Union with a timely and meaningful opportunity to bargain over the decision. . . . However, the judge concluded that *MV Transportation* compelled dismissal of the complaint allegations. Specifically, the judge found that the Respondent's action was "covered" by the management-rights language in Article III of the parties' collective-bargaining agreement granting the Respondent the right to "implement changes in equipment." Thus, the judge found that the Respondent's trucks are "equipment" and that the installation of cameras in the trucks falls within the compass of the contractual language granting the Respondent the right to "implement changes in equipment."

The judge also found that by agreeing to the management-rights language in Article III, the Union relinquished the right to bargain over the effects of the Respondent's decision to install the cameras. . . .

III. Discussion

* * *

It is well settled than an employer violates Section 8(a)(5) if it changes terms and conditions of employment that are mandatory subjects of bargaining without providing the union representing its employees with prior notice and the opportunity to bargain. . . .

Where a specific term and condition of employment is incorporated in a collective-bargaining agreement, the Act creates a different, but related set of rules that also govern an employer's statutory duty to bargain. Under Section 8(d), neither party to a contract shall be required "to discuss or agree to any modification of the terms and conditions contained in" a currently effective contract. A party seeking to modify the terms of an existing contract must obtain the other party's consent, and either party may refuse to negotiate over midterm changes to any terms and conditions "contained in" a contract. Where, however, a specific term and condition is *not* "contained in" a contract, the employer's statutory duty to bargain still applies. Thus, the employer remains obligated "to bargain collectively with the representatives of his employees" regarding any term and condition that is not "contained in" an agreement, and the employer can only change such a term and condition after it has bargained in good faith to impasse with the union. Accordingly, the Board distinguishes between (1) unfair labor practice allegations that an employer has made an unlawful mid-term modification of the collective-bargaining agreement and (2) as in the instant case, allegations that an employer has failed and refused to bargain on request or made a unilateral change.

B. Development of the Clear and Unmistakable Waiver Standard

The Board developed the waiver standard to address employers' contractual defenses to unilateral-change and refusal-to-bargain allegations. The standard was first articulated shortly after the enactment of the Taft-Hartley amendments, in *Tide Water Associated Oil Co.*, 85 NLRB 1096 (1949). . . .

The Supreme Court approved the Board's clear and unmistakable waiver standard in *NLRB v. C & C Plywood Corp.*, 385 U.S. 421 (1967). . . .

The Court reaffirmed its approval of the Board's waiver analysis in *Metropolitan Edison Co. v. NLRB*, 460 U.S. 693 (1983). There, the Court held that a union could waive in a collective-bargaining agreement its officers' statutory right under Section 8(a)(3) of the Act to be free from antiunion discrimination. However, the Court stated, "we will not infer from a general contractual provision that the parties intended to waive a statutorily protected right unless the undertaking is 'explicitly stated.' More succinctly, the waiver must be clear and unmistakable." . . . .

Since *Metropolitan Edison*, the Supreme Court has repeatedly affirmed, in a variety of contexts, the principle that a contractual waiver of a statutorily protected right must be "explicitly stated" and "clear and unmistakable." . . . .

C. Subsequent Judicial Decisions

Following the Supreme Court's lead, the majority of Courts of Appeals—the Third, Fourth, Sixth, Eighth, Ninth, and Tenth Circuits—have consistently deferred to the Board's clear and unmistakable waiver standard as a rational and permissible interpretation of the Act. . . .

Despite widespread judicial approval of the Board's clear and unmistakable waiver standard and the standard's grounding in Supreme Court precedent, several Courts of Appeals have criticized the Board's approach. . . .

None of these circuit decisions, however, addressed the Supreme Court's approval of the clear and unmistakable waiver standard in *C & C Plywood* or explained how their rejection of that standard is consistent with the Court's holding. Nor have these courts grappled with the Court's admonition that the Board's choice of standard was entitled to considerable deference.

D. The Board's Decision in MV Transportation

As described above, in *MV Transportation, . . .* the Board adopted a version of the contract coverage standard for the first time. Under that standard, the Board announced that it would "examine the plain language of the collective-bargaining agreement to determine whether action taken by an employer was within the compass or scope of contractual language granting the employer the right to act unilaterally." If "the agreement does not cover the employer's disputed act, and that act has materially, substantially, and significantly changed a term or condition of employment constituting a mandatory subject of bargaining, the employer will have violated Section 8(a)(5) and (1) unless it demonstrates that the union clearly and unmistakably waived its right to bargain over the change or that its unilateral action was privileged for some other reason."

Echoing the criticism of [one circuit court], a Board majority in *MV Transportation* claimed that the waiver standard alters the parties' bargain and undermines contractual stability and repose by directing heightened scrutiny exclusively to those parts of the collective-bargaining agreement that allegedly authorize unilateral employer action, leads to conflicting contract interpretations by the Board and the courts, undermines grievance arbitration, and is indefensible and unenforceable.

. . . The *MV Transportation* Board's decision to overrule *Provena* and adopt the contract coverage standard was based on a series of erroneous assumptions. Accordingly, we find merit in the General Counsel's argument, on exception, that the Board should overrule *MV Transportation* and return to its traditional clear and unmistakable waiver standard.

* * *

B. MV Transportation Rests on Mistaken Premises

1.

The heart of the Board majority's rationale in *MV Transportation* (rearticulated by our dissenting colleague) is that the waiver standard interferes with the parties' bargained-for exchange. First, the Board majority explained, "[t]he terms of the agreement represent the parties' bargained-for deal, arrived at through the give-and-take of negotiations, and the parties are entitled to the benefit of their bargain based on the language they agreed to include in their contract." And quoting the

Supreme Court's decision in *NLRB v. American National Insurance Co.*, 343 U.S. at 404, the Board majority stated that it " 'may not, either directly or indirectly, compel concessions or otherwise sit in judgment upon the substantive terms of collective bargaining agreements.' " The Board majority reasoned that under the clear and unmistakable waiver standard, "the Board will refuse to give effect to contract provisions granting rights of unilateral action to the employer unless those provisions meet the exacting standards imposed by the Board," thereby "effectively writ[ing] out of the contract language the parties agreed to put into it."

In *C & C Plywood*, however, the Supreme Court rejected these arguments. The Court explained that the Board had "not construed a labor agreement to determine the extent of the contractual rights which were given the union by the employer. It has not imposed its own view of what the terms and conditions of the labor agreement should be. It has done no more than merely enforce a statutory right which Congress considered necessary." 385 U.S. at 428. The Court therefore rejected the notion that general freedom-of-contract principles foreclose the Board's authority to evaluate contract language raised as a defense to an alleged statutory bargaining obligation. In addition, the Court recognized that the Board had the authority to interpret the terms of a collective-bargaining agreement in the course of determining whether an unfair labor practice has been committed, rejecting the argument that "since the contract contained a provision which *might* have allowed" the employer to act unilaterally, the Board was "powerless to determine whether that provision *did* authorize the [employer's] action, because the question was one for a state or federal court under § 301 of the Act." Id. at 425–426 (emphasis in original).

Indeed, this characterization of the clear and unmistakable waiver standard reveals the *MV Transportation* majority's (and our dissenting colleague's) fundamental misconception of the task before the Board when it addresses the interpretation of contractual provisions that implicate the statutory right to bargain. Under the traditional waiver standard, the Board evaluated whether an employer successfully carried its burden of proving, as an affirmative defense, that "a contract provision authorized its unilateral change in working conditions." *Provena*, 350 NLRB at 812. Like the *Provena* Board, we find it appropriate to hold an employer seeking to establish, as an affirmative defense to an allegation of unlawful unilateral action or refusal to bargain, that a union waived its statutory right to bargain, to the same standard as we hold a party seeking to establish any other affirmative defense to an alleged unfair labor practice.

In addition, as discussed above, the waiver standard was settled Board law for 70 years and was approved by the Supreme Court and a majority of appellate courts. It is therefore reasonable to assume that collective-bargaining agreements negotiated during that period were reached with the waiver standard in mind, and any attempt to give effect to the intentions of the parties or respect contractual repose therefore would entail continuing to analyze those agreements under the waiver standard. The immediate imposition of the contract coverage standard, in contrast, unquestionably upset the settled expectations of unions who previously thought they were assured of the right to bargain collectively over matters that were not explicitly waived.

2.

Relatedly, the *MV Transportation* Board argued that the waiver standard unfairly "tilts [the] decision in the union's favor" by directing extra scrutiny exclusively to the provisions in a collective-bargaining agreement in which the union allegedly relinquished its statutory right to bargain. As discussed above, however, the Supreme Court has repeatedly affirmed that contractual waivers of statutory rights must be explicitly stated and clear and unmistakable, and courts (including those that apply the contract coverage standard) routinely apply the clear and unmistakable waiver standard when interpreting collectively bargained language that is alleged to waive or surrender rights arising under other statutes. Neither the *MV Transportation* Board nor courts that have adopted the contract coverage test have ever adequately explained why contract language that allegedly waives or surrenders the fundamental statutory right to bargain should be subject to a lower level of scrutiny than alleged contractual waivers of other statutory rights. Similarly, neither the *MV Transportation* Board nor the courts that have criticized the waiver standard have set forth a convincing argument as to why the Board should evaluate an employer's contractual defense to conduct that would otherwise violate the Act less rigorously than other defenses to alleged violations of the Act or defenses asserting waiver of other statutory rights.

In this respect, we emphasize that the Board, with court approval, has consistently recognized that contract proposals granting an employer discretionary control over terms and conditions of employment, while generally lawful, can be evidence of bad-faith bargaining when evaluating whether an employer has bargained in good faith *before* an agreement is reached. . . . Likewise, an employer is normally entitled to unilaterally implement its final offer after reaching lawful impasse, but proposals granting an employer discretionary control over terms and conditions of employment are treated differently from other proposals for this purpose as well. . . . And provisions granting an employer discretionary control over terms and conditions of employment are also treated differently from other contract terms *after* the agreement has expired. . . . The *MV Transportation* Board's assumption that contract provisions granting an employer discretionary control over terms and conditions of employment should be treated the same as other contract provisions *during* the term of a collective-bargaining agreement cannot be reconciled with these settled principles. Finally, the waiver standard creates no unfair tilt in favor of unions insofar as it makes unilateral employer action more difficult. The standard instead effectuates the Act's fundamental policy of encouraging the practice and procedure of collective bargaining to reduce industrial strife. . . .

3.

In this regard, we also reject the *MV Transportation* Board's claim that the waiver standard should be abandoned on the grounds that it "is, in practice, all but impossible to meet." The Board's experience applying the clear and unmistakable waiver standard for more than 70 years proves the contrary, as the Board has often found that the standard was satisfied. As the Board's cases demonstrate, negotiators—who must be presumed to be aware of the Act—know how to draft language that clearly and unmistakably waives the statutory right to bargain over particular employment terms.

4.

An additional reason advanced by the *MV Transportation* Board for abandoning the clear and unmistakable waiver standard is that the standard undermines grievance arbitration. . . . As the Board explained in *Provena*, this concern is misplaced. The Act makes clear that the Board is not prevented from returning to the traditional waiver standard because it might conflict with the practice of arbitrators or undermine grievance arbitration. In Section 10(a) and (c) of the Act, Congress committed to the Board the exclusive power to decide whether unfair labor practices have been committed and Section 10(a) explicitly provides that the Board's power in this regard "shall not be affected by any other means of adjustment or prevention that has been or may be established by agreement, law or otherwise." 29 U.S.C. § 160(a). Thus, there is no question that the authority of the Board to decide unfair labor practice charges is not displaced by the presence of an arbitration provision within the parties' agreement. Moreover, the Board will decide cases involving contract interpretation—including unilateral change cases—only where there is no basis for deferral to the parties' grievance-arbitration process. And if other standards for deferral are met, the Board will defer to an arbitration award even if the arbitrator does not apply the clear and unmistakable waiver standard.

5.

The *MV Transportation* Board also defended its adoption of the contract coverage standard on the basis that the clear and unmistakable waiver standard had become indefensible and unenforceable. However, as an administrative agency charged by Congress with the uniform and effective administration of a national labor policy, the Board is not bound to acquiesce in the views of the circuit courts that conflict with those of the Board, even in cases arising in those circuits (which could be reviewed elsewhere). . . .

6.

Finally, we disagree with the view expressed by the *MV Transportation* Board and several appellate courts that the Board's evaluation of an employer's contractual defense to conduct that would otherwise violate the Act is not entitled to deference because the issue is strictly one of contract interpretation. Likewise, we reject as misplaced the contention that the Supreme Court has held that the Federal courts—which have jurisdiction over labor-contract disputes under Section 301 of the Labor-Management Relations Act, 29 U.S.C. § 185—owe the Board no deference in contract interpretation when the interpretation of a contract is inextricably intertwined with a statutory issue, i.e., whether the employer's unilateral change in terms and conditions of employment violates the duty to bargain. Section 301(a) authorizes federal courts to fashion a body of federal law for the enforcement of collective-bargaining agreements. *Textile Workers of America v. Lincoln Mills,* 353 U.S. 448 (1957). However, as discussed previously, "Congress assigned to the Board the primary task of construing [Sections 8(a)(5) and 8(d) of the Act] in the course of adjudicating charges of unfair refusals to bargain." [*Ford Motor Co. v. NLRB,* 441 U.S. 488, 495 (1979).] Because the Board has "the primary responsibility of marking out the scope of the statutory language and of the statutory duty to bargain," its construction of these provisions is "entitled to considerable deference." Id. at 495–496. And this, of course, is what the Supreme Court held in *C & C Plywood,* as already explained.

We have determined that the policies underlying the Act in general, and Section 8(a)(5) and 8(d) in particular, strongly support the application of the clear and unmistakable waiver standard in cases where an employer asserts a contractual defense to a charge of unlawful unilateral action. . . .

C. The Provena Standard

In summary, none of the *MV Transportation* Board's reasons for abandoning the waiver standard withstands scrutiny. In our view, moreover, the waiver standard better promotes the purposes and policies of the Act. The waiver standard simplifies the bargaining process by encouraging the parties to focus on matters of immediate importance. It also reduces litigation by assuring that the parties know the scope of their respective rights and obligations. As the Board explained in *Provena,*

> The waiver standard . . . effectively requires the parties to focus on particular subjects over which the employer seeks the right to act unilaterally. Such a narrow focus has two clear benefits. First, it encourages the parties to bargain only over subjects of importance at the time and to leave other subjects to future bargaining. Second, if a waiver is won—in clear and unmistakable language—the employer's right to take future unilateral action should be apparent to all concerned.

350 NLRB at 813. Additionally, the clear and unmistakable waiver standard properly balances the Act's competing goals of encouraging collective bargaining and providing stability to collective-bargaining relationships by providing consistency and a respite from change to *both* parties. It protects employers, during the term of a collective-bargaining agreement, from the disruption of continuous bargaining over terms and conditions "contained in" the agreement, while also protecting employees' fundamental statutory right to bargain over mandatory subjects as to which no mutual understanding was reached.

In contrast, as described by then-Member McFerran in her *MV Transportation* dissent, the contract coverage standard

> makes it easier for employers to unilaterally change employees' terms and conditions of employment—wages, hours, benefits, job duties, safety practices, disciplinary rules, and more—in a manner that will frustrate the bargaining process, inject uncertainty into labor-management relationships, and ultimately increase the prospect for labor unrest . . . .

Stated more succinctly, the contract coverage standard creates an escape hatch for employers to avoid their bargaining obligations during the term of a collective-bargaining agreement without actually securing contract language that make it plain—including plain to the union and the employees it represents—that the employer has the authority to act unilaterally with respect to a particular term and condition of employment. The contract coverage standard also exacerbates the difficulties associated with negotiating collective-bargaining agreements by encouraging employers to insist on the broadest possible language, while unions necessarily feel constrained to insist on exacting specificity lest they be held to have bargained away their statutory rights. By encouraging employers to seek broad and ambiguous language, instead of bargaining over unforeseen and unanticipated events as they arise and as their importance becomes apparent, a needless impediment is placed in the way of successful collective bargaining. It is inevitable, moreover, that disputes as to the meaning of ambiguous and broadly worded management-rights language will proliferate.

Finally, permitting employers to make discretionary unilateral changes, without a clear manifestation of the union's agreement, destabilizes relations not only between labor and management, but also between a union and the employees it represents. . . .

[The majority then explained why retroactive application is appropriate and therefore found, under the traditional clear and unmistakable waiver standard, that the Respondent violated Section 8(a)(5) and (1) of the Act by failing to provide the Union notice and an opportunity to bargain over the decision to install cameras to monitor unit employees and by refusing the Union's request for bargaining over the decision and its effects. The majority went on to offer further responses to the dissent, including the dissent's differing views on the facts and, correspondingly, what had transpired in this case (including that there had been no unilateral change and no refusal to bargain). Thus, the majority rejected the dissent's claim that the clear and unmistakable standard should not have been an issue in this case. It also pushed back against the assertion that courts—not the Board—have primary jurisdiction over this type of dispute.

In his dissent, Member Kaplan spent considerable time explaining his differing view on what had occurred in this case and whether addressing the appropriate standard for waiver was even necessary. As for the standard, he offered the various arguments to which the majority responded above, arguing that the contract coverage standard adopted in *MV Transportation* best effectuates the policies of the Act. Of particular note is Member Kaplan's emphasis on the fact that the contract coverage standard—which applies ordinary principles of contract interpretation—properly recognizes that management-rights provisions are standard industrial practice, as recognized by the Supreme Court, and, as such, serve the interests of employers, employees, and unions alike. In his view, the contract coverage standard properly balances the statutory policy of "encouraging the practice and procedure of collective bargaining" with the intent of Congress to stabilize collective bargaining agreements during their term. Congress intended collective bargaining to be "a process that looked to the ordering of the parties' industrial relationship through the formation of a contract."

Indeed, in part because he views the clear and unmistakable waiver standard as establishing an irrebuttable presumption that the contract provision does not authorize unilateral action without exacting specificity, he contests the majority's view that the clear and unmistakable waiver standard respects the statutory policy favoring collective bargaining. He concludes that, even if the standard were genuinely at issue in this case, "the contract coverage standard best effectuates the policies of the Act, best conforms to current Supreme Court precedent, is the most reasonable standard to use in determining both the rights and the obligations of employers under a collective-bargaining agreement," and, in the instant case, would support Endurance's claim that it was entitled to install the cameras based on the parties agreement.]

Page 855. Add to Problems for Discussion:

5. Paragon Paramedical Services, Inc., operates ambulance and medical transportation service in the Four Cities area. It employs emergency medical technicians and paramedics who are dispatched out of six terminals, the largest in Silo City. They are represented by the Paramedical Workers Union. Section 23.03 of their collective bargaining agreement, captioned "Disasters," provides:

> The parties agree that the Employer shall be relieved of any and all obligations hereunder relating to scheduled paid time off, job posting, shift changes and transfers, in the events of and during the

term of a disaster or catastrophe such as fire, flood, explosion, power failure, earthquake, or other act outside the control of the Employer and causing disruption to the Employer's normal operations.

In the wake of the COVID-19 pandemic, Paragon invoked § 23.03 to reduce shifts, increase "on-call" hours on shifts, and shifted Silo City work to another division just outside the Four Cities that was not unionized. The Union has demanded that Paragon provide it with the following information: (1) a list of Union members removed from the schedule; (2) Silo City call volume data; (3) data on outside crews responding in the Silo City coverage area; (4) Silo City response times; and (5) a list of Union members affected by shift cuts.

Paragon has refused on the ground that as § 23.03 waives the union's right to bargain or grieve over these decisions Paragon's duty to disclose that information has also been contractually waived. The Union has filed a charge of violation of § 8(a)(5). You are the Regional Director. Will you issue a complaint? If so, how do you respond to Paragon's argument? American National Response of Connecticut, Inc. v. NLRB, 93 F.4th 491 (D.C. Cir. 2024).

PART SEVEN

LABOR AND THE ANTITRUST LAWS

Page 897. Add to Problem for Discussion:

Cosgrove Harris is a producer of successful musicals, some award winning. He is also a notoriously difficult person to work with. The union of theatrical performers called a one day strike to protest his abusive behavior, failure timely to pay wages, and unsafe working conditions. The union membership met thereafter and, dissatisfied with this lack of Harris' responsiveness, voted to place him on its "Do Not Work List" which discourages its members from working with him. It has asked the members of other unions—musicians, stage hands, performers in television, film, and concerts—to join in the boycott. The listing continues indefinitely. Harris has sued the union for a violation of federal antitrust law. The Union has moved to dismiss. How should the court rule? Drabensky v. Actors' Equity Ass'n, 106 F.4th 206 (2d Cir. 2024).

Page 920. Add to the Problems for Discussion:

3. City Market and Green Glen Stores are grocery stores located in the greater Chambana area. They are owned by Vermillion Investments, but are operated as separate enterprises. The Meat and Markets Workers Union, Local 8, has separate collective bargaining agreements with each; both expired on the same date. After the contracts expired, the Union secured a collective agreement at City Market but was unable to reach agreement at Green Glen and went on strike there. The Director of Labor Relations at Green Glen has told his counterpart at City Market that he had learned that the Union planned to encourage its members at Green Glen to apply for jobs at City Market and inquired of what City Market would do. The Director of Labor Relations at City Market informed her counterpart that City Market would not accept any applications from Green Glen employees. Have the two engaged in a combination in restraint of trade violative of antitrust law? Morgan v. Kroger Co., 2026 WL 685408 (D. Colo. Feb. 6, 2026).

PART EIGHT

FEDERALISM AND LABOR RELATIONS

I. PREEMPTION OF STATE LABOR LAW: AN OVERVIEW

Page 954. Add at the end of Problem 7:

In Amazon.com Services LLC, 373 N.L.R.B. No. 136 (2024), the Board held the conduct of mandatory captive audience speeches for the presentation of employer views on unionization violated section 8(a)(1). As a result, these state laws, insofar as they address speech on unionization and insofar as they apply to statutory employees under the Labor Act, are now preempted under *Garmon*. However, it is a certainty that the Trump Labor Board will overrule that decision, its reasoning possibly presaged in Member Kaplan's dissent. In that event, the preemption question would be resurrected; and in that event, Member Kaplan's dissent would seem to set the stage for analysis of both the threshold step of the likely challenge—not to unconstitutionality as a matter of federal supremacy, but of unconstitutionality under the first amendment—and for the question of preemption.

The *Amazon.com Services* majority and Member Kaplan agree that the prohibition is content, not viewpoint restrictive. Labor speech as a category of speech is proscribed for captive audition irrespective of whether the employer would favor or disfavor unionization. A proscription on the latter ground would be a viewpoint restriction; it could not survive a First Amendment challenge. But of content restriction, Member Kaplan rightly opines that these are "presumptively unconstitutional"; *i.e.*, they can survive attack on a showing of a sufficiently compelling state interest. As a future contest over these laws is likely, and as the burden of proof would rest on the states to defend their laws, it would be a useful instructional exercise to lay out for student evaluation what the state's likely line of argument would be. The line of argument is set out below. How persuasive do you find it?

Content restriction. The Board majority rests its analysis in part on the employee's having a right to be "let alone," a right to "privacy and autonomy". Member Kaplan speaks only of being "let alone", which he prefers to call an "interest", not a right. Even so, he does not seem to doubt that such an interest could sustain a content restriction albeit not by the Labor Board for want of statutory grounding. There would seem to be little doubt that the individual's interest in maintaining the privacy of her thoughts and beliefs and in the freedom from having that intruded upon could support a prohibition on captive audition. Federal and cognate employment discrimination state law, for example, prohibit secular employers from subjecting employees to mandatory religious indoctrination. *E.g.* Salemi v. Gloria's Tribeca, Inc., 982 N.Y.S.2d 458 (App. Div. 2014); Garcimonde-Fisher v. Area 203 Mktg., LLC, 105 F. Supp. 3d 825, 838 (E.D. Tenn. 2015). And for some, the role unions play in their lives occupies a place that religion does in others.

However, the freedom from religious indoctrination is but a part of a more comprehensive interest than the Board majority references. As Charles Black put it almost seventy-five years ago:

> Few shafts could strike with more on-target insult at the very manhood of humanity than its degradation into a collectivized *object* of speech, powerless to escape and powerless to answer. . . .What is perfectly clear is that the claim to freedom from unwanted speech rests on grounds of high policy and on convictions of human dignity closely similar to if not identical with those classically brought forward in support of freedom of speech in the usual sense. . . .

Charles L. Black, Jr., *He Cannot But Hear: The Plight of the Captive Auditor*, 53 Colum. L. Rev. 960, 967 (1953) (emphasis in original). He argued that since antiquity to be made silently to endure the speech of another has been a badge of servility. He supplied no examples, but these abound. Of the hubbub (*thorobos*) the Athenians created in the Assembly, it has been noted that in

> Greek ideology and practice, the obligation to sit quietly without speaking, to listen silently to whatever someone said, was a hated characteristic of monarchy, tyranny, and oligarchy.

Robert Wallace, *The Power to Speak—And Not to Listen—in Ancient Athens* in FREE SPEECH IN CLASSICAL ANTIQUITY 221, 226 (Ineke Sluter & Ralph Rosen ed. 2004).

In Rome, slaves could be and were ordered to strict silent obedience on pain of corporal or even capital punishment by their masters. Matthew Finkin, *The Mathematical Management of People: Insight From the Ancient World*, ___ INDUS. L.J. ___ [U.K.] (in press) (reviewing the history).

In 1280, Edward I of England "issued instructions to Jews to attend Dominican sermons. They were required to listen 'without tumult, contention, or blasphemy'." Anthony Julius, TRIALS OF THE DIASPORA 139 (2010). In modern usage, those subject to captive audition are made to hear and "shut up." Electrolux Home Pdts., 368 N.L.R.B. No. 34, slip. op. at 4, ns. 13–14. (then Member Kaplan on the panel).

A pre-Civil War manual for slaveholders on giving religious instruction to their slaves advised:

> The *strictest order* should be preserved at all the religious meetings of the Negroes, especially those held on the Sabbath day. . . No *audible* expression of feeling in the way of groanings, cries, or noises of any kind, should be allowed. . . .
>
> . . . Disturbers of the public peace should be noted down; the cases investigated and summary punishment inflicted by the proper authorities on the guilty.

Charles C. Jones, THE RELIGIOUS INSTRUCTION OF THE NEGROES IN THE UNITED STATES 262 (1842) (italics in original). It is relevant that many democracies prohibit captive audition for political (and religious) propaganda including on unionization. *See Symposium: The Captive Audience*, 29 Comp. Lab. L. & Pol'y J. No. 2 (2008).

Member Kaplan opined that even as the employee's interest in privacy and autonomy could be a ground of statutory prohibition, nothing of that nature could expressly be found in the Labor Act. *Per contra*: can anything in the Labor Act expressly be found to grant employers a right of captive audition?

Section 8(c). Employers use captive audition as a tool of union avoidance because of its psychological power. Even as employers can access their employees in all manner of ways, captive audition allows the employer to deploy a wide range of social influence tactics—to create a false social consensus, set the issue agenda, control information flow and, perhaps most importantly, inoculate and counter any pro-union message to create an environment where there is considerable social pressure to accept the Employer's view. *See* Anthony R. Pratkanis, *Social Influence Analysis: An Index of Tactics*, *in* THE SCIENCE OF SOCIAL INFLUENCE: ADVANCES AND FUTURE PROGRESS 17 (Anthony R. Pratkanis ed., 2007).

Does the reason for employer use of captive audition bear on how section 8(c) should be read? Return to the Court's address to union organizers' ability to speak to workers in *Lechmere*, casebook page 124. The Court disallowed it where access by the union to the workers was otherwise available, when the workforce was in the stream of ordinary communication: "*Access* to employees, not *success* in winning them over is the critical [statutory] issue." 502 U.S. 540 (emphases in original). Is *Lechmere* relevant to the 8(c) argument?

Preemption. If the Trump Board overrules *Amazon.com Services LLC*, *Garmon* would be inapplicable, would it not? Perhaps before inquiring into what the preemption analysis would then be consider what the Court said in 1947:

> In the National Labor Relations Act, Congress has sought to reach some aspects of the employer-employee relation . . . It has dealt with the subject or relationship but partially, and has left outside of the scope of its delegation other closely related matters. Where it leaves the employer-employee relation free of regulation in some aspects, it implies that in such matters federal policy is indifferent, and since it is indifferent to what the individual of his own volition may do we can only assume it to be equally indifferent to what he may do under the compulsion of the state . . . However, the power of the state may not so deal with matters left to its control as to stand "as an obstacle to the accomplishment and execution of the full purposes and objectives of Congress."

Bethlehem Steel Co. v. N.Y. State Labor Relations Board, 330 U.S. 767, 773 (1947) (the concluding caution was reiterated in Brown v. Hotel & Restaurant Employees Union, 468 U.S. 491, 501 (1984)).

In what way is a state prohibition of captive audition, enacted to protect employee privacy and autonomy, an obstacle to the "accomplishment and execution of the full purpose and objectives" of the National Labor Relations Act?

Page 980. Add to Problems for Discussion:

9. Minnesota has enacted a law to protect the employees of nursing homes. Minn. Stat. §§ 181.211–218. In pertinent part it, designates fourteen specific dates as statutory "holidays." Workers who work on those dates are to be paid a minimum of time-and-one-half their hourly wage for the hours worked. But it provides a partial carve-out:

> A nursing home employer may substitute up to four holidays for an alternate day in the same calendar year if the substitution is agreed upon by a majority of affected nursing home workers or the exclusive representation of the affected nursing home workers if one exists.

Is this law preempted under *Garmon* because it would cause a violation of section 8(a)(2)? Or *Machinists* for its exacting specificity in holiday designations—*see* 520 South Michigan Ave. Associates, Ltd. v. Shannon, 549 F.3d 1119 (7th Cir. 2008)? As inducing nursing home employers to foster unionization in order to secure holiday carve-outs—see Chamber of Commerce v. Brown text at p. 971? LeadingAge Minnesota v. Blissenbach, 791 F. Supp. 3d 913 (D. Minn. 2025).

II. SPECIFIC APPLICATIONS: REPRESENTATION, BARGAINING AND CONCERTED ACTIVITIES

A. SELECTION OF BARGAINING REPRESENTATIVE

Page 982. Add to Problems for Discussion:

4. Several foreign automobile manufacturers have located facilities in the South, encouraged in part by generous economic development grants from these states. The United Auto Workers Union (UAW) has for more than a decade pursued a plan to unionize the southern transplants. It lost an election at VW in Chattanooga in 2014 in the face of strong opposition to the Union, not by VW but by the state's Republican political leadership. The Union persevered. In May 2024, the UAW received a 73% majority at VW Chattanooga. The Union campaign moved on to Mercedes in Alabama. A public statement of opposition to the Union was released by the Governors of Alabama, Georgia, Mississippi, South Carolina, and Tennessee. The Union lost by 56%.

The legislatures of Alabama and Georgia have enacted nearly identical laws. The Alabama law is set out below:

> (b) No employer shall be eligible to receive an economic development incentive for a project if the employer does any of the following:
>
> (1) Voluntarily grants recognition rights for the employer's employees solely and exclusively on the basis of signed labor organization authorization cards if the selection of

a bargaining representative may be conducted through a secret ballot election.

(2) Voluntarily discloses an employee's personal contact information to a labor organization or third party acting on behalf of a labor organization without the employee's prior written consent, unless otherwise required by state or federal law.

(3) Requires a subcontractor to engage in activities prohibited by subdivision (1) or (2).

(c) An employer that engages in any activity prohibited by subsection (b) which has received an economic development incentive for any project shall be required to repay all economic development incentives received over the life of the project.

Alabama Act No. 2024–340 (signed May 13, 2024).

(a) Why would these states not desire a greater number of better paid workers and taxpayers? The public justification was the potential loss of new businesses locating in the state, discouraged by the prospect by Union growth. If so, where would would-be investors place their facilities instead? As funds would be denied for the expansion of existing plants in the state, does the claim hold up?

(b) Return to Question 2 at page 188, *supra*, and to the section preceding it on the application of the "laboratory conditions" test of *General Shoe* to campaign speech by third parties. Will it be possible for the Labor Board to conduct a fair election in any company that receives economic development funds in Alabama or Georgia? *See* UAW, *Objections to Conduct Affection Election*, Volkswagen Group of America, Inc., Case 10–RM–121704 (Feb. 21, 2014).

(c) Consider *Cemex Construction Materials Pacific, LLC*, at page 307, *supra*. Are these laws in Alabama and Georgia preempted by the Labor Act under *Garmon*? Under *Machinists*? Under *Chamber of Commerce* v. *Brown*?

5. Workers exempt from statutory coverage for being independent contractors at common law can be considered employees under state law and accorded a right to collective representation. Platform workers in transportation, notably drivers for Uber and Lyft, have been legislated for in California and Massachusetts, for example; there is no question of the state's capacity to act. In view of periods where the NLRB was unable to function for the lack of quorum, notably where the President has declined to nominate candidates to fill vacancies, three states enacted laws to render state collective bargaining laws applicable: CAL. LAB. CODE § 923.1(b)(1); N.Y. LAB. LAW § 715; WASH. REV. CODE § 49.32.020. The Labor Board has sued to enjoin the California law on preemption grounds as has Amazon in New York. Does the fact that the Board now has a quorum render these cases moot? There is an exception to the mootness doctrine where the matter complained of is likely to recur. Are these laws preempted nevertheless? In thinking about that the student might well return to Guss v. Utah Labor Relations Board, 353 U.S. 1 (1957).

B. COLLECTIVE BARGAINING

Page 1008. Add to Problems for Discussion:

7. Illinois' Day and Temporary Labor Services Act provides in pertinent part:

> No day and temporary labor service agency may send a day or temporary laborer to a place where a strike, a lockout, or other labor trouble exists without providing, at or before the time of dispatch, a statement, in writing and in a language that the day and temporary laborer understands, informing the day or temporary laborer of the labor dispute and the day or temporary laborer's right to refuse the assignment without prejudice to receiving another assignment.

820 ILCS/175/11(a). Is this law preempted under *Garmon*? *Machinists*? Staffing Services Ass'n v. Flanagan, 720 F. Supp. 3d 627 (N.D. Ill. 2024).

PART NINE

THE INDIVIDUAL AND THE UNION

III. UNION SECURITY AND THE ENCOURAGEMENT OF UNION ACTIVITY

A. UNION SECURITY AND THE USE OF UNION DUES

Page 1096. Add at the end of Problem 5:

Wycliffe University is a nationally prominent private research university. Its paid graduate student assistants have elected One Big Union (OBU), an organization with deep roots in community activism, as their collective bargaining representative. Because OBU has long vehemently campaigned for the boycott of Israel, a group of graduate students sympathetic to Israel have opted out of membership; they pay the agency fee. OBU has now called for the recognition of a unitary state. "From the [Jordan] River to the [Mediterranean] Sea," which entails the eradication of the State of Israel. A pro-Israel graduate student group has answered that they refuse to be represented by a group they find morally repugnant, with which very association they claim stigmatizes them in their relationship to undergraduate students and compromises their freedom of academic and political speech. They have sued to enjoin payment of the agency fee, arguing that payment violates the first amendment. How should the court rule? Graduate Students for Academic Freedom, Inc. v. United Electoral Workers, No. 1:24–cv–06143 (N.D. Ill. July 22, 2024); *cf.* Buckley v. AFTRA, 496 F.2d 305 (2d Cir. 1974).

PART TEN

THE LABOR ACT TODAY

IV. LABOR LAW REFORM

Page 1145. Add at the end of text:

The 119th Congress, 1st session, saw a flurry of proposals to amend the Labor Act, several sponsored by the Chairman of the Senate Committee on Health, Education, Labor and Pensions, Bill Cassidy (R, La.). These include the following:

1. S.3115 (the "NLRB Stability Act") would require the NLRB to follow court of appeals precedent in the circuit where the unfair labor practice is alleged to have occurred.
2. S.3116 (the "Fairness in Filing Act") would impose a $5,000 fine on any person who files a charge of unfair labor practice in bad faith or engages in a pattern or practice of filing frivolous charges or who does not satisfy the extensive documentation of charges the Act would also require.
3. S.3117 (the "Worker Results Act"—for Reforming Elections for Speedy and Unimpeded Labor Talks) would require a secret ballot election for recognition as well as certification, a House proposal for the Taft-Hartley Act which the Senate rejected; would allow a decertification petition in the period after an election and during the period of bargaining for a first collective agreement if the Board finds the union not to be bargaining in good faith; would expand the decertification "window" from 30 to 90 days once every two years; would regulate the use of a "blocking charge"; would prohibit any delay in an election petition in the case of a successor employer; and would forbid unions to agree with other unions not to compete with them for representation of employee groups.

On the other hand, S.844, a bill with bipartisan support, would provide for the arbitration of first collective bargaining agreements after a 90-day period for bargaining and a 30-day period for mediation. As this goes to press the measure was passed by the House.

In the second session Rep. Cassidy introduced S.5213 (the "Union Members Right to Know Act"). Apart from requiring unions to give notice to their members of specified legal rights it would require written consent by members and agency-fee payers to the use of dues or fees "for any purpose not directly related to the labor organization's collective bargaining or contract administration functions on behalf of the represented unit employees."

ADDENDUM

On June 29, 2026, the United States Supreme Court handed down *Trump v. Slaughter*, testing the statutory restriction on the removal of a Commissioner of the Federal Trade Commission against the developing law of separation of powers. That restriction had been upheld in *Humphrey's Estate v. United States*, 279 U.S. 602 (1935). The student will recall that earlier in the Supplement the NLRB was placed in that context by the removal of Board Member Wilcox; in fact, the removal provision in the Labor Act echoed the provision in the Federal Trade Commission Act verbatim.

The Supreme Court overruled *Humphrey's Estate* in a six-to-three decision; the Chief Justice writing for the majority, Justice Sotomayor writing for herself and Justices Kagan and Jackson. Both opinions on the reading of Art. II of the Constitution are lengthy and densely argued; but there is no doubt that the decision applies to the Labor Board, that all Board members serve at the pleasure of the President.

The most obvious consequence is that a President may displace any or all incumbents *instanter* and put a new slate in, that is, it gives the President the power more rapidly to select a Board compatible with the President's labor law policy. But it remains to be seen whether more is involved. The implications are explored in Part One, "A Note on Board Makeup and Status in the Trump II Administration," pp. 117–120, *supra*, but it is well to rehearse that afresh in light of *Slaughter*.

On February 18, 2025, Trump issued Executive Order 14215, which provides in pertinent part:

> The President. . .shall provide authoritative interpretations of law for the executive branch [including the "so-called" independent regulatory agencies]. The President['s] opinions on questions of law are controlling on all employees in the conduct of their official duties. No employee of the executive branch acting in their official capacity may advance an interpretation of the law as the position of the United States that contravenes the President['s] opinion on a matter of law, including but not limited to the issuance of regulations, guidance, and positions advanced in litigation.

Given the heavy stress the *Slaughter* Court repeatedly placed on the need for officers in the executive branch to be accountable to the President, that there are no executive agencies independent of the President, a question has been posed of whether the President may direct the Board to decide a case a certain way; *i.e.*, to direct the abandonment or adoption of specific labor law doctrine, Branden Campbell, *New Questions for NLRB After Justices Upend Firing Limits*, Law 360 (June 29, 2026), for example, to abandon the right of an employee to wear a union button while at work. The short answer is that final decisions of the Board are subject to judicial review. A presidential directive dictating a rule of labor law does not insulate the Board's decision executing that directive from attack as being arbitrary, capricious, an abuse of discretion or otherwise not in accordance with the Act, the provenance of the Board's decision notwithstanding.

However, there may be more. Whatever doubt there may have been heretofore that the Board's General Counsel serves at the President's pleasure has now been definitively dispelled. Under the theory of the "unitary executive" embraced by the *Slaughter* Court, could the President direct the General Counsel to issue no complaint resting on a Presidentially-disfavored doctrine—for example, in cases charging discipline or discharge for wearing a union button? The Court has said repeatedly that the General Counsel's exercise of discretion in the issuance of complaints is "unreviewable." Were the President so to direct and were the General Counsel to obey, in practical effect abrogating a longstanding bedrock principle of labor law, would the charging party have any recourse? If so, on what legal ground?